Constitutions and political theory

This book is dedicated to Gordon Smith of the London School of Economics, for his great generosity during all the years of support and guidance in Academia.

Constitutions and political theory

Jan-Erik Lane

Manchester University Press
Manchester and New York

distributed exclusively in the USA and Canada by St. Martin's Press

Copyright © Manchester University Press 1996.

Published by Manchester University Press
Oxford Road, Manchester M13 9NR, UK
and Room 400, 175 Fifth Avenue,
New York, NY 10010, USA.

Distributed exclusively in the USA and Canada
by St. Martin's Press, Inc., 175 Fifth Avenue, New York,
NY 10010, USA

British Library Cataloguing-in-Publication Data
A catalogue record for this book is available from the British
Library.

Library of Congress Cataloging-in-Publication Data
Lane, Jan-Erik.
  Constitutions and political theory / Jan-Erik Lane.
    p.   cm.
    ISBN 0–7190–4647–5 (alk. paper). — ISBN 0–7190–4648–3 (pbk. alk. paper)
    1. Comparative government.   2. Constitutional history. I. Title.
  JF51.L355 1996
  320.3—cc20   95–4963
                                                                              CIP

ISBN 0 7190 4647 5 *hardback*
     0 7190 4648 3 *paperback*

First published in 1996
00 99 98 97 96   10 9 8 7 6 5 4 3 2 1

Typeset in Great Britain
by Northern Phototypesetting Co Ltd, Bolton
Printed in Great Britain
by Bell & Bain Ltd, Glasgow

Contents

List of tables and figures

Tables

Figures

Preface

Politics all over the world in the 1990s has a sharp constitutional ring. Why is there so much emphasis on constitutions? What consequences do constitutions actually have on the State and what role could, or ought, they play? The purpose of this book is to explore what political theory can do for the understanding of crucial constitutional questions that have become highly relevant in the political developments of the 1990s.

Modern political theory has expanded into a huge set of theoretical approaches, conceptual frameworks and mathematical models. The distance between formal modelling, like game theory, and postmodernist frameworks is vast. Yet, since we live in a constitutional age, new constitutions being introduced in Eastern Europe, South Africa and many other States in the Third World, how can we find concepts and models that help us understand the place of this special set of institutions, constitutions, in the State?

Since political theory is now so rich, we should be able to draw upon it when penetrating constitutional problems. After all, much of political thought focused upon constitutional matters in the well-known doctrine of constitutionalism. We consult both the literature on historical political thought as well as modern political theory when addressing a few key problems concerning constitutions and the State.

Yet our book deals only with constitutional theory, or what modern political theory entails for key questions concerning the existence, origins and consequences of constitutions. Thus, we will discuss problems such as: What is a constitution? Why are there constitutions? Where did constitutionalism originate? Do constitutional institutions matter? How is the constitutional State related to democracy and justice? What is distinctive about this volume is not only the attempt to embrace a number of different threads – theoretical, empirical, moral – concerning constitutions, but also our ambition to use public choice theory and neo-institutional ideas.

The 1990s being a constitutional decade, many ask whether some constitutional frame is more suitable to address critical questions than others. Do constitutions matter? Will a democratic constitution bring about economic and social development? A few scholars have recommended that the new democracies spreading around the world in this recent major democratization wave adopt a parliamentary regime and not a presidential one. It has been claimed that alternative democratic regimes result in different social and economic outcomes. Looking at data about the consequences of various constitiutional set-ups on a number of performance measures, can we substantiate these hypotheses that emphasize one set of democratic institutions ahead of another set such as consensus democracy or corporatist democracy?

The structure of the book reflects the attempt to penetrate a few basic ideas about the *is* and the *ought* in constitutional theory, looking at various aspects of constitutions and their role in the modern State as well as bringing forward a few ideas about the normative relevance of constitutionalism. The classical doctrine of constitutionalism is in a modernized form today a vital element of any democratic regime, because democracies must be constitutional States. The implications for the State of the tremendous growth in the relevance of international law are yet to be drawn, in particular for the constitutional recognition of human rights.

It is hoped that the presentation is so elementary that the book can be used in undergraduate teaching. Actually, the stimulus to write the book stemmed from the fact that when asked to teach a course on constitutions and constitutionalism at the University of Oslo it was difficult to identify a concise text about modern constitutional theory in all the literature that is relevant for the topic. The final version was completed when I was teaching in the University of Cape Town in Rondebosch, South Africa. Svante Ersson drew up the structure of Chapter 9 and read all the chapters suggesting numerous and vital improvements.

Cape Town, October 1995

Part I

Introduction

1

The two meanings of 'constitution'

Introduction

Perhaps it is questionable to speak about 'constitutional theory'. Certainly, there exists nothing like a compact theory about constitutions. What there is is a set of ideas, concepts and models drawn from various disciplines that refer to constitutions, either the constitutions of the many countries in the world or to some ideal constitution or other. Even though constitutional theory hardly possesses a core of established notions, principles or facts, it is an interesting field, because new ideas are launched, sometimes almost immediately.

Constitutional theory can draw upon pieces of knowledge in jurisprudence (constitutional law), political science (comparative politics) and economics (constitutional political economy). It has close ties with political theory and legal theory. And it has a history that dates back to Aristotle – the doctrine of constitutionalism or the importance of limited government playing a major role in political thought time and time again.

The purpose of this introduction is to identify some of the chief concerns of constitutional theory. Perhaps they have not been given the attention that they deserve given the usual focus on constitutional problems in practical politics all over the world. Or maybe one could say that valuable pieces of knowledge about constitutions have been dealt with in isolation from each other. What would be the chief questions to be addressed in modern constitutional theory?

Some key questions in constitutional theory

Perhaps it is premature to speak of constitutional theory. As things now stand, there is only a loose set of concepts and models whose theoretical relevance is up in the air and whose empirical validity is debatable. Can we define 'constitution' in a satisfactory way? Do we know whether constitutions matter? Can we evaluate constitutions and recommend one constitution as better than another?

Modern constitutional theory would encompass both the IS and the OUGHT. It will describe and analyse the constitutions of the world as well as discuss what a good or just constitution amounts to. Although it may not establish a specific body of knowledge, it can integrate a couple of ideas that underline the importance of constitutions for politics and civil society. Modern constitutionalism covers a set of theories about what a constitution is, which impact it has and what a good constitution amounts to. These theories are in no way always coherent with each other nor do they cover each and every aspect of constitutions. Typical of constitutional theory is a variety of contending arguments both about the *is* and the *ought*.

With the collapse of the so-called Second World, i.e. the Communist countries, constitutional issues had to surface in a conspicuous manner in politics. Searching for democracy and a market economy the former Communist States need constitutional models that outline new institutions that hopefully work better than the Leninist ones. The difficult question is not only to find attractive new institutions but also to implement them in such a way that they can live up to their promise of enhancing a better life.

Yet, constitutional problems have also become highly relevant in the so-called First and Third Worlds. In many Thirld World countries there is institutional reform on a major scale in order to improve the performance of the State in a search for a stable democratic regime. In the OECD countries there is a debate about the pros and cons of various basic institutions, as the welfare state is assessed in a climate where market values are given more and more attention.

Not only have many new States been founded since 1989 when the breakdown of the Second World began. Also, a number of States have changed their constitutions in order to introduce new institutions, as the democratization wave is still strong. In addition there is the search for new economic institutions as many countries have transformed their economic institutions in a basic way, with constitutional implications replacing the command economy or various state dirigisme systems with the institutions of the market economy.

The constitutional drive present in so many ways raises a number of critical questions about the nature of constitutions and the role they play or should play in political life. Here, we approach these numerous problems by making a distinction between three kinds of questions that one could ask about constitutions:

(Q1) What is a constitution? How can we define the concept of a constitution? And what kinds of constitutions are there?

(Q2) What impact does a constitution have? Does it matter if a country institutionalizes one set of fundamental political institutions rather than another?

(Q3) Which constitution is the best one? Is it possible to lay down criteria which a just constitution fulfils?

(Q1) concerns the nature of a constitution whereas (Q2) refers to the causal impact of constitutions. The first chapters in the book attempt to elucidate (Q1) whereas the latter chapters probe (Q2). The normative question about what a good constitution looks like, (Q3), will be brought up in the final chapter.

When one speaks about constitutions and how they vary from one State to another, as well as claims that constitutions are of crucial importance not only for political matters but also in a broader way for social and economic outcomes, then it is vital to notice that the word 'constitution' is ambiguous. It has two senses which are most often mixed up: 'constitution' meaning either a compact written document, comprising paragraphs with rules for the governance of the State, or 'constitution' standing for the regime, i.e. the real institutions in terms of which the State is actually operated. 'Constitution' as a 'set of rules' is an expression with double meanings: (1) constitutional articles in a written document or (2) constitutional institutions as they are actually practised in ongoing state activities.

Ambiguity of 'constitution'

First and foremost, a constitution is a compact document that comprises a number of articles about the State, laying down rules which State activities are supposed to follow. Whether these rules are obeyed or implemented is another question. The bare document is typically called the 'constitution of country' X and it has been enacted on or issued at a day Y some year Z. A constitution in this sense of a written document exists simply as a written set of instructions. Whether it also applies is another question.

Most countries have a constitution is this sense – see *Constitutions of the Countries of the World* (1972–) edited by A. Blaustein and G.

Flanz. Since the great revolutions of the eighteenth century – the American revolution of 1776 and the French revolution of 1789, it has become praxis that States enact constitutions. Actually, only a few countries such as, for example, the United Kingdom, New Zealand up until the Constitution Act 1986, Israel and Saudi Arabia lack a constitution, because most States have a special document that they designate as their 'constitution', dating it back to a date of enactment or year of emission. However, it is not always the case that such a document called 'the constitution' is really legally valid, i.e. is implemented by the State. In several countries the formally enacted constitution has been suspended, particularly in dictatorships.

Countries that lack a constitution in this sense of a single formally enacted constitutional document tend to have other kinds of written documents that have constitutional status. This means that in these States there is no one single document called 'the constitution', but instead there is a set of documents designated as of constitutional import. What creates some confusion is that in countries with a single formally enacted constitutional document there exist, in addition, other documents that are of constitutional importance. This means that it is difficult to make a sharp distinction between those States that have one single constitutional document and those countries that have several constitutionally relevant documents.

Take the example of the United Kingdom, of which it is always stated that it lacks a constitution. However, the British State has a large number of constitutional documents, ranging from the Magna Charta from 1215 to acts of Parliaments such as the Habeas Corpus Act of 1679, the Bill of Rights of 1689 and the 1832 reform of the House of Commons and the 1911 reform of the House of Lords, including in addition customary law, conventions and most recently European Community law. It is true that the so-called Common Law tradition and the conventions about the fundamental role of Parliament and its powers in relation to the Monarch and the judiciary have never been codified in a single constitutional document, but there can be no doubt about how strongly institutionalized a large number of constitutional principles are, deriving from many sources in the British State and society – see Stanley De Smith's and Rodney Brazier's *Constitutional and Administrative Law* (1990).

In Great Britain there has only existed one constitution in the meaning of that word as a compact single document, viz. Oliver

Cromwell's *Instrument of Government* from 1653. It was in force up until 1660. However, a large set of constitutional documents are today considered applicable (Brazier, 1990) and they are almost as rigid as any constitution that it is very difficult to change, like for example the American constitution. In Israel there are similarly important constitutional documents, called 'fundamental laws', whereas Saudi Arabia regards Shariah Law as the source of constitutional practice.

A constitution as a single written document is regarded as a legal document, because it usually makes up the bulk of the constitutional law in a country. However, a State's constitutional law comprises more than the written constitution. Besides the written constitution, often considered as a higher form of statute law (Lex Superior), constitutional law includes: (a) constitutional customs; (b) constitutional conventions; (c) constitutional precedents where the courts interpret the constitution, and (d) ordinary statute laws with constitutional implications. What is decisive for constitutional practice – the formally enacted constitution, customs, precedents or conventions – is an open question, the answer to which depends upon the country studied.

Even in countries that have a compact constitution comprising a neatly delimited number of articles do customary law and conventions play a large role. For instance, in the United States precedents or judge-made law, in the form of a number of key decisions by the Supreme Courts concerning the interpretation of the constitution, have played a very major political role for determining constitutional practice. A key ingredient in the constitutional law in any country is customary law or precedents, even in countries where the effort to produce constitutional codification has been strong.

One often talks about the distinction between public and private law as well as the distinction between statute law and customary law. These distinctions have been much discussed in legal theory (Kelsen, 1961; Hart, 1970; Harris, 1979; Simmonds, 1986). Constitutional law enters public law, the bulk of which is made up of administrative law, which is 'concerned with the composition, procedures, powers, duties, rights, and liabilities of the various organs of government which are engaged in administering public policies' (Bradley and Ewing, 1993: 603). Private law includes contract law, the law of torts and family law for instance.

Statute law is a rule enacted by Parliament whereas customary law consists of custom, i.e. long established practice considered as unwritten law. Customary law includes precedents laid down by various courts. One sometimes talks about a country's legal order as either predominantly based upon statute law or predominantly based upon judge-made law or what is called case law. Thus, law in the continental European countries as well as in Scandinavia tends to be orientated towards statute law – the Roman–Germanic approach – whereas the Anglo-Saxon tradition is based upon the common law approach. Typical of Scandinavian, French and German law is the effort at major codification such as for instance Code Napoleon from 1807. Typical of English and American law is case law or the use of customary law and precedents in accordance with the tradition writers such as Edward Coke, who collected parts and pieces of the common law in the *Institutes of the Laws of England* (1628–44), and William Blackstone, whose *Commentaries on the Laws of England* (1765–69) were very influential in spreading the common law tradition.

Some countries attempt to make a sharp separation between constitutional law and ordinary law by treating the constitutional document in a special way – the Lex Superior approach. Constitutional rules may have to be changed in a special fashion that is different from the way ordinary law is made. Alternatively constitutional rules may be interpreted by means of a special court with only this task, a so-called constitutional court. However much the special place of the constitution within the legal order is underlined, it remains a fact that constitutional practice will always include customary law, precedents or conventions overriding to some extent or complementing the formally enacted constitution.

Thus, when one speaks about the constitution as a written document, the codified constitution, then one has to remember two things. First, a State does not have to have such a constitution, as States may operate on the basis of constitutional practice made up of customary law and conventions. Secondly, the existence of a codified constitution does in no way guarantee that the country in question is ruled in accordance with this document. The question of how the constitutional document reads must be kept separate from the question of whether the rules in this document also apply, i.e. whether the institutions by which that country is run are matched by the written articles of the formal constitution. The stronger the role of customary law, precedents and conventions, the lesser is the relevance of the formally enacted constitution.

It is impossible to cover everything in a country's constitutional law in one single document. The formally enacted constitution, however much it is worshipped, comprises only a section of that country's constitution. Each and every constitution is attended by customs, precedents and conventions, which not only complements the constitution but also amends it to some extent. Thus, although no one would question the validity of the 1814 Norwegian constitution, it remains a fact that the parliamentary principle which replaces Norway's rules about monarchical rule has not been codified. Since the same applied to the 1809 Swedish constitution, it was decided to replace it with a new one in 1974 in which the parliamentary system was formally acknowledged. However, it is impossible to codify each and every aspect of constitutional practice in one single document.

Constitutional practice may distance itself more or less from the formally enacted constitution. In some countries, the formally enacted constitution may be almost irrelevant to the actual way in which the country is governed, the constitution having been suspended or simply neglected. In other countries, key rules in the constitution may be considered old-fashioned or obsolete, at the same time as the rules actually employed in governing the country have not been codified or even laid down in any document. However, few would argue that such countries lack a real constitution, i.e. a regime in accordance with which the State is operating.

Here, we have the second meaning of 'constitution', standing for the actual principles or maxims in terms of which the country is ruled. Except for States which suffer from anarchy or civil war or which are about to be dissolved or have just recently been founded, each state has a constitutional practice. This practice need not be in accordance with the formally enacted constitution nor must there be a single constitutional document giving guidance. 'Constitution' here refers not to a written document, but to the actual manner in which a country is ruled, the regime or the set of fundamental state institutions.

The distance between the written constitution and the real regime may be very large, as when dictatorships employ a written facade or camouflage constitution. When such regimes employ the declaration of martial law or use emergency powers, then the gulf between constitutional *formalia* and constitutional *realia* is openly acknowledged. However, some authoritarian regimes have enacted written constitutions that legitimate dictatorial rule. One could question whether such documents are really to be called 'constitutions', as implicit in the concept of a constitution is the notion of restraints on State power.

Two constitutional contexts

'Constitution' is a word that is systematically ambiguous, because it is not always easy to tell when it stands for a written document and when it refers to the regime. Much argument in constitutional theory focuses upon the document and its interpretation, but a part of constitutional theory is also heavily concerned with how countries are actually ruled.

We will call these two meanings of 'constitution' the two constitutional contexts: context 1 and context 2, as it were. Constitutional context 1 is orientated towards the analysis of constitutional law, i.e. the interpretation of legal documents and the understanding of the relationships between statutes, precedents and conventions – the hermeneutic side.

Constitutional context 2 focuses on the study of the regime of a country, looking at how the country is actually run, pinning down the key principles of politics and administration of that country. Thus, we classify States as democracies or dictatorships, although their constitutional documents do not employ these terms nor do the formally written constitutions employ a language that correctly represent the actual way in which the country is governed. Similarly, we state that some countries have a welfare state regime whereas other countries adhere to a welfare society regime, a distinction which cannot be located in constitutional law.

When there is talk about the real constitution of a country, then we are in the second constitutional context. Political science and public administration seek to unravel the actual way in which the public sector is structured and operated. Constitutional law is only one among many sources of information about the regime of a country – the behavioural side.

One could state that constitutional context 1 refers to formal matters whereas constitutional context 2 deals with substantive matters. Both formal and substantive constitutional matters are worth studying, but they each require a different methodology. Constitutional law draws heavily upon the techniques of jurisprudence whereas the analysis of the regime requires the empirical tools of political science. In order to understand the formal side of the constitution it may be necessary to use information about the substantive side, and vice versa. But the two contexts of 'constitution' should be kept separate from an analytical point of view.

When one sets out to classify state constitutions in the world today, then one would wish to employ the distinction between a democratic and a dictatorial constitution. Such a separation may involve two different things, the written constitution or the real constitution. Among the countries with a real democratic constitution, it is only the United Kingdom that lacks a written democratic constitution. Among the countries with a real dictatorial constitution, some have a written democratic constitution which is either a facade constitution or which has been suspended, whereas others have a written authoritarian constitution.

Written constittions and regimes

What creates much confusion in constitutional theory is that the two constitutional contexts are connected in various ways. In an ideal world the formal constitution may be in agreement with the substantive constitution. This would mean that the rules of the formal constitution are fully implemented in the State and that the basic way in which the State operates is covered by the explicit rules of the formal constitution. In reality there is always more or less mismatch between the formal and the substantive constitution.

In *Modern Constitutions* Kenneth Wheare defines 'constitution' as 'the rules which establish and regulate or govern the government' (Wheare, 1966: 1). Applying our distinction between the two constitutional contexts, we ask whether these rules are the formally laid down rules (constitutional articles) or those rules that are actually applied in the governance of the State (institutions). They could be the very same rules, but that is an open question. One may picture this crucial distinction between constitutional *formalia* and constitutional *realia* by means of a simple picture (Table 1.1).

On the one hand we have the constitution as a formal document comprising a number of articles, or written rules. On the other hand we have the constitution as a regime, a set of fundamental institutions for the state, or real rules. The degree of correspondence between the paragraphs and the institutions measures the extent to which the formal constitution is put into force or implemented in real life institutions, as well as the extent to which actually-employed institutions have been codified into statute law by formulating explicit rules by means of articles in a so-called basic law.

Table 1.1
The Two Constitutional Contexts: articles versus institutions

Formal level:	A1	A2	A3	A4	A5	A6	An
Degree of correspondence	↕	↕	↕	↕	↕	↕	↕
Substantive level	I1	I2	I3	I4	I5	I6	In

Note: A = articles; I = institution.

In an ideal world there would be a one-to-one correspondence between the paragraphs of the written constitution and the actually-employed institutions of the real constitution. In reality, many paragraphs do not apply and several institutions that actually are employed remain implicit or at least lack constitutional recognition. We use the word 'rule' to speak about both the articles in constitutional law and the real life institutions in the State.

To the constitutional lawyer, the formal level with its set of articles is of primary interest. A number of interesting things may be looked at in relation to a formal constitution: its wording, its degree of comprehensiveness, its coherence or possible lack of clarity, its rules of amendment – all questions of textual interpretation or so-called matters of validity. However, in constitutional law there is also the problem of efficacy, or the degree to which the paragraphs of the constitution match the institutions in terms of which the country is governed. To judge efficacy the constitutional lawyer needs information about the substantive level.

To the political scientist, the formal level is of secondary interest, because he/she is first and foremost interested in describing the real constitution, or how the country is actually ruled. This may often involve searching for patterns of behaviour that work contrary to what the formal constitution requires. Constitutional *formalia* or paragraphs may in some cases guide the political scientist to the identification of the basic state institutions, but information about various aspects of the formal level is only one piece in the constitutional puzzle of pinpointing how a country is ruled behind a constitutional set of documents.

Both the constitutional lawyer and the political scientist look at the formal and the substantive aspects of a country's constitution – constitutional context 1 and constitutional context 2. However, their purposes are different as constitutional law is more orientated towards the formal side, the system of legal articles, whereas the political scientist is more focused on the substantive side, the institutions which actually govern behaviour.

There are a variety of relationships between the two constitutional contexts, the formal constitution and the substantive constitution. One way to change the political institutions of a country is to try the constitutional method, i.e. introduce a new formal constitution with new written rules for the political game. Whether it succeeds or not depends upon many factors. And one way to safeguard an already existing set of political institutions is to have them recognized formally in a constitutional document by codification.

A constitutional document may play a major role in political life due to the fact that it may take on a charismatic aura or because its interpretation may be essentially contested. In some countries politics is to an extraordinary degree constitutional politics. Political conflict involves to a considerable extent constitutional conflict. Changes in the formal constitution are considered important, but they may be very difficult to achieve. Constitutional politics may be fought on different agendas: the parliamentary scene or in the courts.

In other countries there is constitutional policy-making (Hesse and Johnson, 1995). Here the formal constitution is looked upon from an instrumental point of view. It is used as a tool to change the actual way the country is run and should changes be deemed necessary, then they can be introduced relatively easy. Constitutional policy-making is considered a tool for institutional change and innovation, for example in major system transformations when established institutions in the polity or the economy are done away with, or in minor institutional reform when practices are reformed.

Constitutional formalism and pragmatism

In constitutional theory the two constitutional contexts have been differently evaluated. To some scholars the written constitution is of utmost importance. The constitution of a country should be stated explicitly in a set of written rules that are clearly and coherently formulated and that are implemented as closely as possible to the intent of those who framed the constitution – constitutional formalism.

The opposite standpoint emphasizes constitutional practice. The living constitution of a country can never be fully codified. Constitutional institutions change all the time, adapting to new circumstances in a way that can make constitutional statutes outdated by the time they are enacted. And always crucial in constitutional practice is the actual interpretation of the constitutional statutes, whether by the courts or by the participants in politics. It is more important to get the institutions right than to enact a comprehensive formal constitution – this is the argument of constitutional pragmatism.

Constitutional debate in continental Europe has always had a preference for constitutional formalism, as expressed for example in Hans Kelsen's legal theory, whereas constitutional theory in the United Kingdom has been greatly dominated by constitutional pragmatism – see e.g. Geoffrey Marshall's *Constitutional Theory* (1971). The continental States lean towards codification and the use of statute law whereas British constitutionalism rejects codification and underlines the force of customary law and conventions. American constitutionalism is a blend of both constitutional formalism and constitutional pragmatism, in so far as constitutional practice in the United States is heavily centred upon upholding the oldest formally valid constitution in the world while, at the same time, interpretation and legal review play a major role in changing the content of the constitution without amending its written rules.

The distinction between constitutional articles and institutions has far-reaching implications for constitutional theory. Thus, it makes a large difference whether the three key problems listed above – (Q1)–(Q3) – are interpreted as questions about constitutional paragraphs or constitutional institutions.

(Q1) deals with the nature of a constitution. Interpreted formally this is a question about the typical wording of a constitutional document. Interpreted substantially the question refers to how one separates the basic State institutions from all other types of institutions. (Q2) asks questions about the impact of constitutions, either the formal one or the real life one. The answers will differ profoundly depending on whether it is a matter of the consequences of the formally written constitution or the real constitution. (Q3) refers to normative problems in devising a just constitution, which again may be interpreted as either a formal or a substantial problem, or both.

We will deal with both the formal constitution and the real constitution. In some countries the first is a proper guide to the second, but in many countries there is a clear gulf between constitutional *formalia* and constitutional *realia*, not only in those countries which lack a formal constitution or which have suspended it or which directly neglect the formal constitution. In no State with a few years of existence does constitutional formalia cover all essential elements of constitutional practice.

Interest in constitutional theory has risen sharply following the major efforts at State reform and institutional reorientation in many countries. However, constitutional theory is not a well articulated set of neatly structured concepts and models. Constitutional theory is a mixture of conceptions and hypotheses from various academic corners: political theory, jurisprudence and economics.

When dealing with problems in constitutional theory one has to keep in mind the distinction between 'constitution' meaning the written fundamental law(s) and 'constitution' as the basic State institutions. When we discuss constitutional variety in the world today, then the focus is the first meaning of 'constitution' (context 1), whereas when we probe into the actual consequences – political, social and economic – of constitutions, then it is more a matter of the second meaning of 'constitution' (context 2).

Conclusion

Constitutional theory, when identified today as a distinct body of knowledge, would have three major concerns: the nature of a constitution, the impact of constitutions and the search for a good or just constitution. It encompasses both the **is** and the **ought**, attempting to understand the role constitutions play in the State as well as drawing up an outline for how state constitutions should be made or changed. This book is based upon the belief that there is now enough materials about these three aspects to be assembled in one volume.

In the history of political thought the normative elements of constitutional theory have been much discussed in the form of the doctrine of constitutionalism. It must be emphasized that constitutionalism has a wider application than the state concept. Although it is impossible to discuss the nature of the State without referring to constitutional law, one may speak of constitutions without any reference to the State. The State as a distinct unit appears during the Renaissance in the city-states in Northern Italy. It becomes the basic form for political organization in the emerging nation-states in western and northern Europe, spreading to other parts of the world as worldhistory has evolved though the French and American revolutions into the twentieth century.

However, constitutionalism as a doctrine and as a practice predated the development of the modern State and its scope is larger than the State. When there was systematic reflection about political life, whether in the form of a state or not, constitutionalist thought emerged, as was the case in the city-states and the Roman Empire in the Ancient period as well as during the Middle Ages, which saw constitutionalist practices emerge in spiritual and earthly matters. With the advances of legal thought, as described in Harold J. Berman's *Law and Revolution. The Formation of the Western Legal Tradition* (1983), the new legal conceptions spread from canon law to royal and feudal law meaning that constitutional ideas about proper political authority became more and more distinct and well reasoned. Constitutionalism became the philosophy of constitutional law, but since the sixteenth century constitutionalism has also covered the international scene, viz. the relationship between States as formulated in ideas about international regimes in the Suarez-Grotius' tradition (see Chapter 2, Section 3 International law).

Let us begin our examination of themes in constitutional theory by making an overview of the history of constitutionalism in Chapter 2 – a doctrine which is still relevant today. After that we will take up a few questions about the development of constitutions and constitutional thought in Chapters 3 and 4. Chapters 5, 6 and 7 describe some painstaking features in constitutions as they exist and operate today. Then in Chapters 8 and 9 questions about the rationale and impact of constitutions are examined, first looking at written constitutions and then the impact of real constitutions. Finally, normative concerns in constitutional theory are discussed, first in relation to moral theory in Chapter 10 and then in relation to democracy in Chapter 11. Politics in the 1990s is to a considerable extent constitutional politics (Greenberg *et al.*, 1993). How and why?

Part II

Origins

2

History of constitutionalism

Introduction

Constitutionalism is the political doctrine that claims that political authority should be bound by institutions that restrict the exercise of power. Such institutions offer rules that bind both the persons in authority as well as the organs or bodies that exercise political power. Human rights are one central component of constitutionalism; another essential element is the separation of powers in government. Thirdly, there are the restrictions that derive from international law and its obligations on the State. Human rights are also bolstered by international regimes such as the United Nations and the Council of Europe.

Where and how did such constitutionalist ideas originate? The puzzling thing is that they have a strong Western tone, because they emerged in occidental political thought. Why is there so little of constitutionalism in other cultures, such as in Islam, Indian culture, Chinese history, or in the ancient cultures of Africa and America? Why such a strong constitutionalist current in Western Europe? The purpose of this Chapters is to map the history of constitutionalism in Europe and offer a few explanatory ideas of the connection between constitutionalism and occidental political thought.

Origins of constitutionalism

Speaking generally, constitutionalism or the doctrine that political rule has to be bound by restrictions of various kinds developed out of three main sources: (1) Germanic law and feudalism; (2) Roman law, or more specifically its notion of natural law; (3) Aristotelianism. Constitutionalism emerges as a compact set of principles during the Renaissance, to be applied in the new political struggle when

Medieval institutions were no longer respected (Wormuth, 1949; McIlwain, 1958; Wheeler, 1975). Yet, at the same time constitutionalism has deep roots in medieval thought (Ullmann, 1988).

(1) Germanic law and feudalism

The notion of the rule of law, or that political power is restricted by an established system of institutions, originates in the special interpretation of law that is connected with various kinds of Germanic tribes populating Northern Europe in the early Middle Ages. It is a quite distinct conception of law from that encountered in the Roman law tradition (Brunner, 1965; Schulze, 1990–92).

The prevailing concept of law in the Medieval Ages was that law is custom; it exists and cannot be made. It is basically unwritten, and it stands above each and everyone, yeoman as well as king and noblemen. Fritz Kern states in *Law and Constitution in the Middle Ages*: (1952):

> The Medieval Ages did not recognize the doctrine of the sovereignty of the people. The ruler is not subordinate to any human being. But he is subordinate to the law. The fact that this sovereign law, which the ruler is subordinate to, is no written law is, given this line of thought, self-evident (Kern, 1952: 65).

The legal order is not something specific, codified in certain documents that may be changed by making statute law. The legal order constituted a natural order of things that was considered just and unalterable. Kern goes on:

> The ruler is subordinate not to a specific constitutional document, but to the law in a most general sense restricting and binding him (Kern, 1952: 65).

Kern points out that this was the legal theory prevailing in the country which relied upon customary law, but that actual practice did not always involve rulers behaving according to the spirit of this law. Often specific constitutional mechanisms were resorted to in order to maintain checks and balances upon the ruler (Kern, 1939; Ullmann, 1980). One such device was the king's oath in which he, often on coronation day, promised to uphold the law. Another device was to codify the law, inserting certain basic principles corresponding to the king's oath into the codification. A third mechanism was to set up a court or a parliament which the king would have to consult or even ask for permission before he went ahead with major projects, such as collecting a new tax or engaging in warfare – see J.C. Holt's *Magna Carta* (1992).

The emergence of the feudal society in continental Europe strengthened constitutionalist trends, deriving from the customary law tradition. Feudal institutions also ensured that the ruler had limited power and was bound by mutual obligations and reciprocities. The king, the lords and their vassals were bound in a hierarchical fashion on the basis of the fief institution which meant that a person could hold land by doing services. In some countries feudal relationships became highly complicated as the vassals in their turn were lords for still other vassals and because the Church also figured prominently in such relationships. In other countries the centrifugal forces of feudalism were counteracted by the emergence of representative institutions placed around the king or the emperor – the so-called 'Ständerstaat'. The lords would then be part of a Parliament (Butt, 1989), where other estates of the realm could also be represented, as described by Heinrich Mitteis in *The State in the Middle Ages* (1975).

Notions of the ancient law as well as feudal law concepts were intermingled and provided the bedrock for constitutionalist ideas about limits upon royal power and central authority (Ullmann, 1975). Such notions were systematized by medieval jurists in England delivering the doctrine of the king's two bodies, the individual man or King ('status coronae') and the office or Crown ('status regni'). For the Crown and its resources, the fiscus, there were rules or laws that the King had to obey, as the Crown was not considered a fictitious person or legal corporation above the King. As Ernest H. Kantorowicz states:

> The Crown, as the embodiment of all sovereign rights – within the realm and without – of the whole body politic, was superior to all its individual members, including the king, though not separated from them (Kantorowicz, 1981: 381).

English constitutionalism was expressed in the Common Law tradition, which built upon the medieval approach to law as 'the law of the land' as well as upon feudal conceptions, as shown by J.G.A. Pocock in *The Ancient Constitution and the Feudal Law* (1987). The peculiar feudal distinction between the King and the Crown was stated clearly in the famous so-called Calvin's case in 1608 argued by

Edward Coke. Another equally famous law case – Doctor Bonham's case, ruled by Coke in 1610, where an act of Parliament was declared void – has been looked upon as the initiation of judicial review or the right of a court to rule on the constitutionality of legislation (Stoner, 1992). The identification of the concept of the state required a somewhat different legal approach, separating 'status' out and making it into a separate legal person, as in the concept of *stato* in the early Renaissance.

(2) Roman law

The relationship between Roman law and its tradition and European constitutionalism has always been a contradictory one, as Roman law included different elements with opposite effects (Kelley, 1991). Some of the ingredients in Roman law, and visible in its strong revival in medieval times in Southern Europe, were actually conducive to absolutism. But there was one element that was to enrich constitutionalism, viz. the natural law conception of inalienable human rights.

It may be pointed out that the word 'constitution' has a source in the Roman law term 'constitutiones', which denoted the statutes promulgated by the Emperor. In the Roman law tradition there existed different types of law: (i) *jus civile*; (ii) *jus gentium*; (iii) *jus naturale*. While the first category included Roman law proper, the middle category covered the law of the other people in the Roman Empire, and the final category identified the law of Reason or God. Roman law includes the codification made by Emperor Justinian around 520AD – *Corpus Juris Civilis* as well as cases and comments from great Roman lawyers, collected in the *Digest* or the *Pandects* (Kunkel, 1990; Nicholas, 1975).

The fact that the emperor could make law indicates an absolutist trend in Roman law. Its conception of authority (*Imperium, majestas*) attracted the attention of absolutist legal scholars when Roman law began to be studied again in the twelfth century. Thus, the *Corpus Juris Civilis* and the *Digest* declare:

> The imperial majesty should be armed with laws as well as glorified with arms, that there may be good government in times both of war and of peace.

Although legislation in Rome included various bodies, the Senate as well as the People's Assembly, some phrases in Roman law underline the absolute power of the emperor: *Quod principi placuit legis habet vigorem* as well as the principle: *Rex legibus solutus est*. At the same time the *Lex Regia* notion that the authority of rulers originated with those ruled was combined with an emphasis upon the purpose of law and political rule, viz. the common good, or: *Salus populi Suprema Lex*.

However, Roman law is fundamentally civil law, or the codification of institutions for handling matters relating to persons, things and actions. It does not comprise constitutional law or administrative law in their modern sense. It was adapted to Church matters in the form of Canon Law, which had a strong top-down orientation underlining the claims of the Pope. However, when Roman law was rediscovered around 1100 and started to be taught at Bologna a process of legal rationalization was initiated that was to change all kinds of law: church, royal, feudal, manorial and mercantile. The glossators from Gratian and onwords used Justinian's texts to derive corporate legal concepts as the foundation for the institutions of the Papacy: the chancery, the Apostolic chamber, the consistory and the penitentiary (Berman, 1983).

The natural law component is the ingredient in Roman law that had the greatest constitutional implications. It originated in Stoicist philosophy (Seneca, Cicero) and pinpointed the connection between law and natural principles of reason concerning justice and equity. It made possible the harmonization of various customary law (*consuetudo*) among different peoples as they were conquered and entered into the empire into a body of *jus gentium*, or a kind of law of nations. Natural law conceptions underlined the equality of men before the law and the protection of private property. It entered, by means of a combination with the new Christian thought, into a synthesis with divine law from which it was not disentangled until natural law was secularized in the sixteenth century (Finnis, 1980).

(3) Aristotelianism

Since Aristotle offered the main framework for philosophical speculation about man/woman and nature in medieval times as expressed in the integration of Aristotle into scholasticism by Thomas Aquinas, his influence on political thought in general can hardly be overemphasized. Here, however we deal more specifically with his impact upon constitutionalism. What comes readily to mind is his idea of a good constitution, launched in *Politics*, as one that combines elements from an oligarchy and a democracy, balancing these against each other; although a monarchy could be the perfect constitution given the proper circumstances. Aristotle cited Sparta as an example of all three forms being compounded into one regime. In the constitutionalist debate in the sixteenth and seventeenth centuries similar notions were incorporated into the doctrine of a mixed monarchy.

The interpretation by Polybius in his *Histories* from the first century BC of Rome's ascendancy to power filled the conception of mixed government with more substance. The strength and vitality of the classical Roman state derived from the balance between a monarchical component (the two consuls), an aristocratic element (the Senate) and a democractic component (the People's Assembly) (Bleicken, 1993)

Yet Cicero made a classical argument in favour of a mixed government in his *The Republic*. Following an interpretation of history along lines already drawn up by Livius and Polybius, Cicero points out that each of the three forms of government tend to degenerate – see Aristotle's scheme below. A fourth type may be devised that combines all three, a mixed government which embodies the *caritas* of the monarchy, the *consilium* of the aristocracy and the *libertas* of the democracy. Similar ideas about the virtues of a mixed government were expressed in the constitutionalist ideas of the sixteenth and seventeenth centuries, both in the form of a mixed monarchy and also in arguments favouring a republic.

In order to make these notions about the rule of law and the value of separation of powers politically relevant, another idea had to be added, the notion of accountability. This concept implied that the ruler could be called upon to answer questions about his/her rule. Ultimately, accountability implied that those ruled could dispose of the ruler if the law and historically given rights and obligations were not respected. When the constitutionalist ideas of resistance theory, consent or contract theory as well as representation theory are added, then we come to the first major constitutionalist frameworks in the history of political thought, i.e. we enter the period of secularization of constitutionalism during Renaissance and Reformation times.

However, the foundation for this secularization had been laid in medieval constitutionalism by a very unique blend of the Germanic law conceptions and feudalist notions, both implying severe restraints on government and the power of monarchs. While Germanic law tied the king to the law as a means of keeping the peace, feudalism tied the monarch into reciprocities first with the nobility and later to the estates.

Feudalism involved the combination of the vassalage and the fief (Ganshof, 1966). Vassalage regulated the mutual promises between the lord and the vassal, involving the hommage, the fealty and the felony, the *auxilium* and the *consilium* on the part of the vassal. The fief was the lord's compensation for these services. The *consilium* involved the vassal giving advice to the suzerain. With regard to the king, this involved the setting up of a *curia* or a court which met regularly to discuss major matters of the realm.

Outside of the feudal society in northern Europe the Germanic kingship developed along similar constitutionalist lines, involving the codification of traditional limitations on governmental power, as in, for instance, the Swedish county laws (Lagerroth, 1947). A court was also set up to give the king advice, whether he wanted it or not. Feudal institutions merged with Germanic law institutions in the so-called estate state of the high Medieval Ages, whose charateristic feature was the development of representative institutions for the estates of the realm: the nobility, the clergymen, the merchants and artisans and in some cases the free holders (Ullmann, 1966). These representative institutions were later to play a major role in bringing about the constitutional monarchy or republic involving a parliament with established competencies for legislation and financial matters.

The emergence of modern constitutionalism *circa* 1600

Two ideas are basic to constitutionalism: (a) the limitation of the State versus society in the form of respect for a set of human rights covering not only civic rights but also political and economic rights; and (b) the implementation of separation of powers within the state. While the first principle is an external one, confining State powers in relation to civil society, the second principle is an internal one, making sure that no State body, organ or person can prevail within the State.

The combination of these two ideas form the core of constitutionalism. Its relevance can be seen to be increasing in the world when one looks ahead to the twenty-first century. It is a distinctly occidental theory about politics, which emerges fully blown when the Renaissance and the Reformation calls for a separation between the worldly and the spiritual swords.

We have already seen that constitutionalism derived the idea of the rule of law from medieval practices, which stipulated that political power should be wielded only under the given customs which safeguarded the good of the community. The king was bound by these institutions, because: *rex major singulis minor universis*. Early constitutionalism also involved a strong dose of natural law, which in medieval thought was combined with notions about divine law which the ruler must respect. Finally, there was the ideal of a mixed government, which somehow in either its Aristotelian-Ciceronian version or in its feudal version implied reciprocity between the king and other actors, be these the nobility, the Church or the estates of the realm.

A synthesis of these notions was made by St Thomas Aquinas in his *Summae Theologiae* (1276–73). He included under law the following four types: (a) eternal law; (b) divine law; (c) natural law, and (d) human positive law. The eternal law is God's most basic law as governor of mankind and the cosmos whereas divine law is the rules laid down in Scripture, God's revealed rules. Natural law includes the dictates that follow from reason, stemming from the fact that human beings are conscious, social and moral creatures, while human positive law involves the enactment of rules.

There is, thus, scope for an autonomous, rationally derived and positively enacted human law. Its purpose is, according to Aristotelian notions, the common well-being of all mankind, or the welfare of the political community. In the end, however, human law and natural law must be in agreement with divine law and eternal law. Similarly, Aquinas endorses the doctrine of the two swords, the spiritual and the worldly swords, giving to each its proper domain, or *ecclesia* versus *res publica* (Aquinas, 1960: xxxv).

The worldly domain was best governed by a mixed monarchy where the kings ruled together with the nobility and other estates. Yet, again in the end the spiritual sword prevails over the wordly sword. He states:

> In order that spiritual matters might be kept separate from temporal ones, the ministry of this kingdom was entrusted not to earthly kings, but to priests and especially to the highest of them, the successor of St. Peter, vicar of Christ, the Roman Pontiff to whom all kings must be subject just as they are subject to out Lord Jesus (Aquinas, 1960: xxxiii).

The synthesis created by Aquinas started to break up almost immediately that it had been formulated. The decline of the Papacy provoked the conciliatory movement calling for more influence within *ecclesia* (Tierney, 1979). In addition the centralization of power to the emerging national kingdoms in western Europe had the consequence not only that the dream of universal empire, *res publica*, led by one earthly sword had to be relinquished, but also that the internal power structure of *ecclesia* was questioned by men such as Ockham around 1330 and Gerson and Nicholaus of Cusa around 1400. Marsilius of Padua in *The Defender of Peace* (1324) argued that all worldly powers were derived from the people, and also those of the spiritual sword (Gewith, 1951–56). What definitely broke up the Medieval world view was the Reformation, which did away with the unsteady balance between the spiritual and the worldly.

Resistance theory

Constitutionalism emphasizes the role of institutions in political life. Yet, if such a constitution is to function effectively, i.e. restrict the exercise of political power, it needs institutions that will safeguard against neglecting the constitution. How could such institutions be devised? Constitutionalist thought in the modern period is much focused upon the derivation of a set of impersonal mechanisms through which constitutions can be upheld. One major idea is that the people have the right to resist a ruler who disobeys the constitution in the sense stated in a text from 1564: 'the whole of the laws and institutions handed down by tradition' (Lloyd, 1991: 255).

The political theory of popular resistance towards the Monarch had a strong affiliation with the developments within Christian thought. Resistance theory implied somehow that political power was wielded conditionally. If certain conditions were not met by the ruler, then the ruled had a right to uproar. But where did these conditions come from? Who had laid them down and where and when? It used to be stated that custom was the source of the conditions for political rule, but with the evolution of State legislative powers, such a construction was considerably weakened. If law could be made, how could custom deliver the basic political conditions that had to be respected by each and everyone, including the monarch? The rationalization of life required another construction, which only contract theory could deliver.

Resistance theory as a vital part of modern constitutionalism had several sources in medieval constitutionalism, as described by Kern in *Kingship and Law in the Middle Ages* (1939). The concept of rule of law, so strongly entrenched in both Germanic law and feudalism, implied that a king who did not respect old custom and agreement could be forced to step down. Actually, the famous king's oath made on coronation day involved an explicit promise to respect the peace, as the law was called. Medieval *Sachsenspiegel* stated: 'A man may resist his king and judge when he acts contrary to the law and may even help make war on him. Thereby, he does not violate the duty of fealty.'

The new conception of religion as a direct relationship between man/woman and God, proposed by Martin Luther and Jean Calvin, had formidable consequences for politics and political thought. If spiritual matters concerned the private relation between man/woman and God, if churches were simply congregations of men/women, if there were no other superior authority than Scripture, and if religion referred to matters after death, then what actually was the role of the church and the priests? Who was to make decisions, in so far as religious matters required al least a minimum of worldly concern?

The principle of *Cuius regio eius religio* suited the expansionary tendencies of kings at the time, allowing them to confiscate the possessions of *ecclesia* and rebuke papism. But, did the monarch really have the right to suppress religious beliefs? And what was to be done if the monarch began to persecute people belonging to the 'wrong' creed? While neither Luther nor Calvin reached any radical conclusions about the rights of the people versus the prince – each of them fearing the anarchy of anabaptism – other puritans drew specific constitutionalist conclusions from the doctrine that human beings were equal in the face of God. J. W. Allen states in *A History of Political Thought in the Sixteenth Century* (1964):

> they all assert vigorously that there exists no absolute sovereignty save that of God ... There can be no such thing as unlimited human authority. God recognizes Kings as his agents and has, indeed, created them (Allen, 1964: 316).

The relation of God to the king being one of trust, the king had to govern the country bound by law, divine and customary, and to the common good of his people.

Within early Calvinist religion there developed a school of thought that claimed the right to resistance if the king/queen did not respect religious creed, this group being the so-called monarchomachs. They, like François Hotman in *Francogallia* from 1573 claimed, referring to 'ancient law', that kings who paid no attention to custom should be resisted, especially by the so-called higher and lower magistrates, i.e. representative bodies at the national, regional or local level.

Ancient law comprised so-called fundamental laws or 'constitutions' (in the words of calvinist Theodore Beza) which restricted the power of kings. If these rules were not respected, then there existed a right to overrule the monarch, in the last resort by means of violence. 'Ancient law' or customary law was interpreted as reciprocity between the rulers and those ruled, involving respect for mutual rights and obligations. The expansion of the new conception of law as statute law, however, called for another construction, as it could not be claimed that ancient law always gave guidance. The notion of a contract of some kind replaced customary law as the starting-point for constitutionalist thought.

Consent theory

The conception of a contract as the basis of political authority followed from the puritan idea that rulers wield power as a trust. George Buchanan in 1578 reached the radical conclusions of Reformation thought, which crushed any claims about royal or papal absolutism:

> Political authority can be rationally conceived only as derived from the people and held conditionally. The people is the lawgiver and the King must rule in its interests and be bound by law or be justly deposed (Allen, 1964: 340).

The most systematic consent theory was launched by another Calvinist scholar, Johannes Althusius in his *Systematic Analysis of Politics* from 1603. Althusius conceived the principle of *consociatio* according to which individuals and groups associated to generate larger organizations. Such processes were explicitly founded upon a *pactum*, starting from the most simple units, the household and the corporation, and moving to the most general form, the State as a combination of local and regional organizations. The maxim of *quod omnes tangit* applied right through Althusius corporatist framework, meaning that all those concerned, at various levels of government had to be consulted.

Althusius' system was basically oligarchic, as the representatives at the highest level were to be recruited from the governments at lower levels – cities, provinces, regions, estates, corporations. His scheme

has been interpreted as federalism. Be that as it may, the constitutionalist implication is strong, as authority may only be exercised in
accordance with the rules of an agreement or *consociatio*. What were
the rules that could figure in such a consociational approach?

International law

The doctrine of medieval constitutionalism had relied strongly on the
traditional conception of law as custom. The new concept of the
State introduced in the aftermath of the Renaissance and the Reformation implied, however, that law could be created as if it were a
command of the State, overruling ancient practices. The absolutist
ideas that prevalied in the sixteenth, seventeenth and eighteenth centuries claimed that the monarch was not unconditionally bound by
ancient practice. What, then, could modern constitutionalism argue
did bind the monarch? Natural law.

The first natural law doctrine freed from the synthesis of Aquinas,
mixing Chritianity, Aristotelianism and Stoicism, was launched by
Hugo Grotius. Influenced by natural rights scholar Francesco Suarez,
Grotius, in his *On Law in War and Peace* (1625) launched a theory
about the rules that bind States in their interaction on the basis of
an axiomatic natural law approach, starting from a few key assumptions about human nature and deriving moral implications about
society and international politics. 'Natural law is so immutable that
it cannot be changed by God himself', stated Grotius.

Grotius founded his natural law system on the principle of self-
interest, which he considered to be universally true, irrespective of
culture and history. Given rational egoism as 'the first principle of
the whole natural order' Grotius derived two moral principles, the
right to defend oneself and the right to property, ideas that were both
to be developed by natural right theorists (Tuck, 1993a). However,
in Grotius the natural rights approach was not employed to draw
radical political conclusions. Actually, the same applies to several
scholars within this tradition such as Spinoza, Leibniz and Pufendorf.
It was not until Locke stated a quite different interpretation of natural rights that the doctrine could be used to back revolutionary or
democratic claims (Finnis, 1980; George, 1994).

Grotius' contribution to constitutionalism is more specifically the
system of rules that he suggested States should obey in their conduct
of international affairs. He suggested a number of principles, such as
for example *pacta sunt servanda*, or rules governing *bellum iustum*,

or the freedom of the sea. Several of these rules, derived from the necessity that States survive, have played a major role in the identification of international law. The growing relevance of international regimes has meant that the principles of international law have crept back into state constitutions in the twentieth century.

Republicanism
Constitutionalist ideas were not only propagated against monarchs with absolutist ambitions (claiming what they called the 'divine rights of kings') as with Robert Filmer acting in the great English revolution or invoking the principles in Roman law about majestas, imperium and dominium (Kelley, 1991). A strong current in the constitutionalist traditions is republican thought, or the set of ideas that a good polity need not be a monarchy. Actually, republicanism dates back to the Greek and Roman city-states and its political thought tended strongly towards a preference for a mixed government.

The few examples of republican government at that time made a deep impression on many scholars, who referred with admiration to Venice, Switzerland and the United Provinces or the Netherlands. Often they draw upon Machiavelli, in particular his analysis in *The Discourses* (1513) which, in contradistinction to *The Prince* (1513) is distinctly constitutionalist in character, making use of the standard sources on the republics in the ancient period such as Polybius, Livius, Plutarch, Cicero and Tacitus.

Republicanism flourished among Italian Renaissance humanists and Dutch political theorists, but perhaps the English legacy left the strongest impact upon constitutionalism, where republican theory was stimulated by the huge political upheavals during the English civil war and Cromwell's ascent to power – see the volume *Machiavelli and Republicanism* (Bock et al., 1993). The major work, *Oceana* by Harrington was published in 1656, advocating a radical redistribution of land as the basis for a republic run by two elected assemblies somehow dominated by the gentry.

The republicans were strong believers in institutionalism, or the idea that institutions matter for political outcomes. Harrington declared: 'as no man shall show me a commonwealth born straight that ever became crooked, so no man shall show me a commonwealth born crooked that ever became straight' (Harrington, 1977: 276). Yet, it was vital to frame the 'right' institutions from the beginning, because one could, as another republican Sidney explained,

'add' institutional provisions which were 'variable according to acci-
dents and circumstances' (Worden, 1985: 19).

As Blair Worden points out, seventeenth century republicanism
adhered to the doctrine of the autonomy of political activity, that
civic activity and virtue depended upon the skill displayed in the
designing and running of a State, that balance between opposing
forces was the key to stability and that institutions by enhancing
such a balance of powers could compensate for the tendency of
men/women to fall prey to vice and violent emotions (Worden, 1991:
443–75).

Republicanism is a strong current in constitutionalist thought. It
was no doubt nourished by the attraction of a few excellent examples of the republic: Sparta, Athens, Rome, Florence, Venice and
Holland. It is hardly a coincidence that all these republics were run
by a mixed constitution, at least during their most spectacular periods. Reference was made time and again to the balance of power
between the Doge, the Council of Ten and the legislative assembly
in Venice or between the nobles (populo grasso) and the people
(populo minuto) in Florence. A republic is superior to a monarchy,
declared Machiavelli. Yet, the prevailing form of State in western
Europe was the monarchy, a fact which any constitutionalist theory
had to face at that time.

In any case, republicanism had a strong bias for the oligarchical
type of government, as with Grotius and Althusius in their approval
of the Dutch republic and its States General of the United Provinces.
Republicanism, however, developed in an ever more radical direction
under the puritan influence in England in the seventeenth century and
on to the American revolution in the eighteenth century. Pocock in
The Machiavellian Moment (1975) traces the development of republican ideas from Machiavelli through Guicciardini and Giannotti to
Madison, Hamilton and Jefferson in the late eighteenth century.

At the same, constitutionalism was clearly also highly relevant in
monarchies, as a large number of theorists advocated a 'mixed', 'reg-
ular', 'limited' and 'legal' monarchy. The constitutionalist current in
republicanism was to surface both in Madison's great presidential
republic and in Montesquieu's constitutional monarchy. Where did
democratic ideas originate?

Democracy

The new religious orientation that surfaced in the Reformation was basically highly individualistic, focusing on the direct relationship between God and human beings. The crucial concept was grace, which involved a variety of conceptions that had political implications. The remarkable contribution of puritan sects in England during its civil war was their interpretation of the concept of grace in a democratic fashion (Wootton, 1991: 412–42).

Although they did not use the word 'democracy', the so-called Levellers agitated against monarchy and aristocracy, favouring some kind of democratic regime with a broadly based franchise. Their document *First Agreement of the People* (see Wooton, 1986) from 1647 also demanded that the representative assembly should have supreme political authority and that each individual had the right to freedom of conscience and freedom of expression (Wootton, 1986). Applying their own democratic practices in running their churches to worldly matters, these sects anticipated a secular theory of democracy and religious freedom. If all men/women were equal in the eyes of God, being all dependent upon his grace, then what allowed the magistrates to persecute people for their faith? Moreover, why would God have given certain divine privileges to kings?

It is apparent that Reformation theology could be employed in various ways in the development of constitutionalist thought. Both Luther and Calvin hesitated in drawing far-reaching political conclusions, rejecting extreme Protestant eschatology and the millenarians or Thomas Müntzer's anabaptism (Höpfl, 1991; Baylor, 1991). Yet the importance of Reformation theology for constitutionalism is apparent in several more or less radical ways. The so-called Diggers went one step further calling for a communist society or the abolishment of private property (Sabine and Thorson, 1973). The ideas of popular sovereignty and religious freedom emerged as cornerstones in the thought of political theorists such as Thomas Paine in the late eighteenth century. His democratic framework in the *Rights of Man* (1791–92) was argued from a distictly constitutionalist position.

Constitution and the State

The concept of a constitution as political institutions had been recognized early in the history of political thought by Aristotle. His types of rule have been discussed time and again in political thought. Typical of occidental political theory is the strong constitutionalist tradition that focuses upon special institutions that will prevent one form of debased rule in particular: tyranny.

The lack of such institutions is characteristic of governments out-side of western Europe. Whether we go to the Asian, African or American continent we always find a special kind of rule that Karl Wittfogel in his *Oriental Despotism* called 'total power'. He states:

> In these and other comparable instances the regime represents a definite structural and operational pattern, a 'constitution'. But this pattern is not agreed upon. It is given from above, and the rulers of hydraulic society create, maintain, and modify it, not as the controlled agents but as its masters (Wittfogel, 1957: 102).

Such rule was not uncommon in ancient times. Several Roman emperors may be labelled tyrants as indeed were many Greek tyrants. But tyranny was not typical of the Middle Ages, however dark these may have been. What made the difference? Germanic law and feudalism. This fortunate combination resulted in institutions which restricted government power and restrained the monarch. In the words of Marc Bloch:

> It was surely no accident that the representative system, in the very aris-tocratic form of the English Parliament, the French 'Estates', the Stände of Germany, and the Spanish Cortes, originated in states which were only just emerging from the feudal stage, and still bore its imprint (Bloch, 1965: 452).

At the same time the old Aristotelian notion of mixed government lingered on, especially well received in the few major republics. Con-stitutionalist notions were challenged by the revival of Roman law conceptions, the emergence of Papist canon law and the slow but steady expansion of the power of monarchs (Berman, 1983). At the same time the Papal claims were rejected by William of Ockham and the conciliar movement of the fourteenth and fifteenth centuries, during which time constitutionalist concepts were launched by Mar-silius, Gerson and Cusanus (Tierney, 1982; Black, 1991). The fight over royal absolutism came after the Renaissance and the Reforma-tion, when the new nation-states were founded.

Modern constitutionalism, much dependent upon medieval consti-tutionalism and receiving a strong stimulus from political thought in the Reformation, developed only slowly towards a democratic theory in the late eighteenth century, based upon natural law and social con-tract thinking. At the same time, the doctrine of a constitutional monarchy or a mixed government in a republic held out a less radical version of constitutionalism that attracted many. What the modern version of constitutionalism needed to separate it from the medieval version was the new concept of the state that emerged during the sixteenth century.

Scholars analysing the transition from Medieval political thought to political conceptions in the Renaissance and Reformation period disagree about the amount of continuity and change. A classic authority is J.N. Figgis who, in *Political Thought from Gerson to Grotius: 1414–1625* (1907), underlined the break between medievalism and modernism:

> The conditions for the growth of our modern politics were not afforded until the Reformation, or to be more accurate the intellectual revolution and practical catastrophe which destroyed the system of Middle Ages, both in the external framework of society and in the inward life of its members (Figgis, 1960: 35).

One of the basic notions in modern politics was the state in Figgis' interpretation. However, when constitutionalism is at stake with its characteristic ideas of limited government and the rule of law, then there is hardly any sharp break around 1500.

The concept of the State appears to be a novel idea emerging in continental political thought during the sixteenth century. In his *The Foundations of Modern Political Thought (I–II)* (1994) Quentin Skinner identifies the following conditions for the emergence of the concept of the State as 'the most important object of analysis in European political thought':

(1) Autonomy of politics, or the emergence of the study of statecraft as a discipline of its own distinct from religion or ethics in general.
(2) External sovereignty of a country, or the decline of the notion of an Imperium to which all countries belonged.
(3) Internal sovereignty of a country, or the emergence of the idea of one single source of all forms of political authority in a country.
(4) Natural ends of politics, or the decline of the notion that political organization was to serve non-worldly ends (Skinner, 1994: 349–52)

Notions such as (1)–(4) begin to appear in the sixteenth century, although words such as 'state', 'état' or 'stato' are not used consistently to refer to the State until the seventeenth century. The Latin word *status* simply meant condition and in medieval legal thought there figured a distinction between *status principis* or the ruler as a person and the *status regni* or the condition of the realm, although there was no sharp separation involved. It is not until the idea of a certain set of reasons of state is launched that continental scholars arrive at the notion of an impersonal or objective state. In 1589 Giovanni Botero published his *Reason of State*, which satisfies the above conditions (1)–(4). There he launches the doctrine about state interests or *ragione di stato*, which was to receive several interpretations by later theorists (Meinecke, 1984).

Actually, as Richard Tuck shows in *Philosophy and Government 1572–1651* (1993b) the development of a modern 'State' vocabulary took a long time after Machiavelli had published the *Prince* and Luther nailed his theses in Wittenberg in 1517, although there was a predecessor to the idea of State interests in ancient thought, viz. Tacitus. In Justus Lipsius' *Six Books of Politics* (1589) all the conditions (1)–(4) are present, but there is little mention of the State. Even Hobbes in *Leviathan* (1651) uses other words such as 'commonwealth' or 'soverainty', exactly as had Jean Bodin done in his *Six Books of a Commonwealth* (1576). However, whether political power was called 'la Republique' or *l'Etat*, 'state' or 'commonwealth' or 'government', it tended more and more to be analysed as public power or impersonal authority to be employed for social purposes. The concepts of medieval constitutionalism were as relevant to this new phenomenon of the state, but they had to be reinterpreted to fit to the new context. The major influences here are Locke and Montesquieu, who both stated the doctrine of limited government in a new way, although their approaches were radically different.

Locke and Montesquieu

When the first major constitutions were formally enacted in the eighteenth century, one finds references time and again to two constitutionalists, John Locke and Baron de Montesquieu. Their books were read by all those who pondered about the possibility and desirability of a constitution as the legal foundation of the state. Perhaps Locke played the major role in the Anglo-Saxon developments whereas Montesquieu afforded the model for continental European events. However, their constitutionalist inclination could not be more different.

Locke's theory is abstract, a priori and individualist. Montesquieu's approach is empirical, sociological and collectivist. Starting from such different bases they arrived at the same conclusion: the separation of powers doctrine. Locke deduces constitutionalist conclusions from natural law assumptions about the **ought** whereas Montesquieu surveys the existing States of the world at that time, ending up in inductive generalizations from the examination of the **is**. Locke presents a novel normative model based on the typical model of ethical argument at his time, the geometrical method of axioms and theorems.

Montesquieu makes crucial observations about which institutions actually enhance State stability and vitality. Their approaches are a world apart, but their conclusions are the same: the necessity of a separation of powers in the modern State based upon the rule of law or a constitutional set-up. If both Locke and Montesquieu were right on their own terms, then there were both deductive and inductive reasons, both normative and empirical reasons for accepting constitutionalism. Modern constitutionalism has not one key text, but two: Locke's *Two Treatises of Civil Government* from 1690 and Montesquieu's *The Spirit of the Laws* from 1748.

A key passage in Locke reads as follows:

> Men being, as has been said, by nature all free, equal, and independent, no one can be put out of this estate and subjected to the political power of another without his own consent, which is done by agreeing with other men, to join and unite into a community for their comfortable, safe, and peaceable living, one amongst another, in a secure enjoyment of their properties, and a greater security against any that are not of it (Locke, 1962: 164).

This quotation may be interpreted as containing two premises which result in a constitutionalist conclusion: (a) There is a natural law which provides mankind with certain rights – freedom, equality, independence and property; (b) any subjugation to political power restricting a person in exercising these natural rights will follow from consent to setting up a community for the protection of their natural rights; conclusion: (c) political communities are based upon the consent of people and exist to protect human rights.

This is a constitutionalist conclusion starting from contract theory assumptions. Political power derives from the people, their rational consent to set up a political community for the protection of funda-

mental rights. This is Locke's first step. The second step is to introduce a government. Locke's concept of government assumes that any
political community or commonwealth will have a government that
involves three powers: legislative, executive and federative. By the
latter Locke meant the power of war and peace, leagues and alliances.
However, where executive power is orientated towards internal
affairs and federative powers towards external affairs 'they are hardly
to be separated and placed at the same time in the hands of distinct
persons', because 'both of them requiring the force of the society ...
the force of the public would be under different commands', states
Locke (Locke, 1962: 192). But how about legislative powers on the
one hand and executive and federated powers on the other hand?

Locke's third step is to argue that both these powers should not
be in the hands of the same person(s). Locke favours a constitutional
monarchy:

> Where the legislative and executive power are in distinct hands, as they
> are in all moderated monarchies and well-framed governments, there
> the good of the society requires that several things should be left to the
> discretion of him that has the executive power (Locke, 1962: 199).

This executive prerogative, as Locke calls it, is necessary because the
legislators cannot anticipate all circumstances which may call for
action nor can they themselves meet but seldom. At the same time
as the legislative 'is the supreme power', Locke also holds that 'there
can be no judge on earth' between the executive power and the legislative power in conflicts over competences. Locke's emphasis is
upon the government as trust, as both the legislative power and the
executive prerogative are exercised on the basis of a trust that is for-
feited if either one of them does not implement the natural law
rights. Upon such forfeiture the people have the right of rebellion, if
such a step should prove necessary, which means that 'supreme
power' 'reverts to society, and the people have the right to act as
supreme, and continue the legislative in themselves or place it in a
new form, or new hands, as they think good' (Locke, 1962: 242).

Whereas Locke's constitutionalism was derived by means of a
deductive argument focusing upon the implications of government
analysed as a trust relationship, Montesquieu's constitutionalism is
empirical, arrived at by means of an inductive argument from a
number of critical observations. Montesquieu examined all kinds of
regimes for which he could obtain information. His first generaliza-

tion is that 'all states have the same purpose in general, which is to maintain themselves'. His second generalization reads as follows:

> In each state there are three sorts of powers: legislative power, executive power over things depending on the right of nations, and executive power over the things depending on civil right (Montesquieu, 1989: 156).

Montesquieu's way of presenting the separation of powers distinction differs somewhat from Locke's, because Montesquieu explicitly identifies the juridical branch of government. His third generalization links his first two about the State and its three powers to liberty. It reads:

> All would be lost if the same man or the same body of principal men, either of nobles, or of the people, exercised these three powers: that of making the laws, that of executing public resolutions, and that of judging the crimes or disputes of individuals (Montesquieu, 1989: 157).

Montesquieu explains his constitutionalist theory that liberty requires separation of powers by arguing that when legislative power is united with executive power, then those that make the laws will execute them tyrannically, and when legislative power is combined with judicial power, then those who adjudicate the law will enact arbitrary laws, and finally, when executive power is united with judicial power, then those who adjudicate will execute oppressively. Montesquieu backs his third generalization about separation of powers and the occurrence of liberty by putting forward lots of observations about old and contemporary regimes, monarchical or republican.

Locke's constitutionalism is the concept of limited government, political power restricted by the trust relationship between those governed and the governors. There are certain rights that government cannot forfeit unless it is prepared to break the trust and thus invite rebellion. Montesquieu's constitutionalism is the doctrine of the separation of powers, that liberty will probably survive in a state where executive, legislative and judicial powers are not in the same hands. By adding Locke to Montesquieu one arrives at modern constitutionalism as it was advocated in the wake of the great revolutions of the eighteenth century.

Conclusion

In the constitutionalist tradition the key question has always been whether it was possible to frame institutions that are conducive to good government. Such institutions may include customary rules and conventions such as in English constitutionalism or the adherence to an explicitly framed written constitution, such as in continental and Scandinavian constitutionalism. Constitutionalist notions date back to the beginnings of political thought in Greece and Rome, expressed in various ideas which all focus upon the exercise of government powers under the law, as it was argued time and again that institutions were needed to curb excessive political power.

One may distinguish between medieval and modern constitutionalism dating the borderline between the two to the Renaissance and the Reformation when the introduction of the concept of the state changed political philosophy. Medieval constitutionalism surfaced both in theory and practice. To start with the latter, one may observe constitutionalist practices in the Scandinavian monarchy, in continental feudalism as well as in constitutional development in England. Constitutional theory was advocated by radicals within scholastic philosophy, mainly Marsilius of Padua.

Modern constitutionalism emerges when there is a firm grip on the concept of the State. During the sixteenth century the term 'constitution' received the conceptual content it still has today meaning a set of institutions that limit the exercise of State power. Constitutionalist theory in the seventeenth and eighteenth centuries were expressed in different varieties of political thought. Locke and Montesquieu rendered the classical formulations of modern constitutionalism, Locke focusing on the trust or the obligation of government to uphold natural law rights and Montesquieu underlining the relevance of separation of powers by studying regimes, ancient and contemporary. Taken together Locke's and Montesquieu's theories could be employed for the actual making of constitutions by, for example, writing and enacting constitutional articles of various kinds.

3

The constitutional perspective

Introduction

Politics, everyone agrees, is the exercise of power. Yet, in order to be legitimate political power must be institutionalized. Politics in the State follows the rules of the game, meaning that it is connected with the rule of law. Politics in the international arena involves a greater degree of anarchy, but there are more and more institutions restricting the naked exercise of power by means of so-called international regimes. Politics consists of both power and institutions, as the State involves a claim to sovereignty, but government is also based upon the rule of law.

Old constitutionalism used to be the political theory that attempted to constrain State power and authority by means of special institutions, formulated in a so-called fundamental law. The development of constitutionalism over time has already been portrayed, but a new interpretation of constitutionalism would have to focus upon institutions that decentralize political power and authority in various ways as well as protect citizen rights. However, it is argued that constitutionalism may run into conflict with democracy (Elster and Slagstad, 1988). What is the general relevance of constitutionalism today?

The purpose of this chapter is to analyse a few constitutionalist notions and place them within the overall development of constitutional theory outlined in Chapter 2. Constitutionalism enters the normative parts of constitutional theory which are as important and relevant as the analytical or descriptive parts of constitutional theory. Constitutionalism raises a number of important moral and legal issues which are very relevant in modern political theory, although one may wish to raise objections against hard-line constitutionalism (Allen, 1993).

Constitutions and State power

All democratic States have constitutions of one sort or another. They may come more or less close to two ideal types: (a) the formal constitution in the shape of an explicitly laid down basic law protected by a special constitutional court – the German model; (b) the substantive constitution in the form of a tacitly understood set of customs and conventions that make up constitutional practice – the Westminster model. Democratic regimes tend to adhere to the doctrine of constitutionalism, i.e. the idea that there shall exist institutions that constrain the exercise of State power. But what, more precisely, is the relationship between democracy and the constitutional State?

The connection between the constitution and the State is so close that one may claim that a constitutional framework is necessarily part of the State, whether written or unwritten. States that do not adhere to the ideals of a democratic constitution may be said to have some form of a dictatorship, whether left-wing orientated or right-wing based. Authoritarian constitutions are not always explicitly laid down in a written document. Often dictatorships employ facade constitutions as when they suspend the constitution and rule by means of martial law. Dictatorships are never constitutional States.

A constitutional State has a constitution that really constrains the exercise of political power and protects citizens rights. Such a State need not be a democracy. Actually, the first constitutional States did not allow for a universal franchise. However, can a democracy fail to satisfy the requirements of a constitutional State, because constitutionalism involves institutional claims upon the State that come into conflict with the democratic notion of popular sovereignty?

The State has two faces: power and rule of law. The first is an expression of the State's capacity to take action. It is backed by one of the special features of government: the threat of or actual employment of physical violence. The State as power and authority is captured in the concept of sovereignty (Jouvenel, 1957; Hinsley, 1986). The second face of the State follows from the fact that the state cannot but act in terms of a legal order. The power of the State derives from its command over vast resources in the form of money, people and rules. How the State can employ these power resources tends to be regulated some way or the other by a system of institutions that may be identified either by statute law, customs or precedents and conventions. Or stated the other way around, the legal order comprises laws that regulate the State. There is an antimony built into the state in the form of a contradiction between these two faces of the state.

In political thought some scholars underlined the first aspect of the State, i.e. sovereign power, for example Bodin, Hobbes and Rousseau. Perhaps the clearest formulation of this perspective was launched by a legal scholar, Austin. Other political theorists placed the emphasis upon the second aspect of the State, viz. the rule of law, for example Althusius, Madison and Kant. Maybe Immanuel Kant's republicanism, laid out in various works such as the *Metaphysic of Morals* (1796), is an attempt to draw together the final implications of constitutionalism, as it reflects the ambitions towards creating a world order based upon the rule of law principle, i.e. by creating a regime which extends from the internal fabric of the sovereign States to an international law which secures peace and order between States.

Power and institutions for the rule of law have to coexist within the State, because one cannot do away with either one or the other. Niccolò Machiavelli vacillated between the two perspectives, favouring unrestrained state power in *The Prince* but advocating a constitutionalist position in *The Discourses*. The scholars who followed the reasons of State tradition stated that power takes precedence over the rule of law, whereas the constitutionalist scholars claimed that morality requires State power to be tamed by legal restrictions that bind the rulers (Pocock, 1975; Keohane, 1980; Viroli, 1991). The constitution would contain the most fundamental rules that structure and restrain State power.

Let us make a short overview of how the theme of State sovereignty and the rule of law in the State has been handled in political thought. It is impossible here to go into details or be accurate in relation to the 'Zeitgeist'. Following John Plamenatz's approach in *Man and Society I–II* (1967–68) we wish only to pinpoint the conflict between sovereign power and constitutionalist institutions inherent in the models of government of a few thinkers of major importance. We begin with Dicey's model.

Dicey: Sovereignty and constitutionalism

A well-known text at its time and published in numerous editions,

Albert Venn Dicey's *Introduction to the Study of the Law of the Constitution* (1885) claimed that English constitutionalism combined two guiding principles: (a) the sovereignty of parliament; (b) the rule of law. In addition, there was the principle (c) that constitutional conventions existed side by side with law. The critical question concerned the possible co-existence of these principles.

Dicey's model is an attempt to reconcile different strands in English political thought. The principle of legislative supremacy expresses the power aspect of the State, whereas the notions of the rule of law, in particular the relevance of constitutional customs and conventions, are orientated towards the institutional aspects of the State. The first strand had a strong advocate in Jeremy Bentham's *A Fragment on Government* (1776), while the other strand was formulated by Edmund Burke in *Reflections on the Revolution in France* (1790).

Dicey has been criticized because he did not fully understand that his model is contradictory (Jennings, 1967; Loughlin, 1992). If parliament has sovereignty, then how could it be bound by the rule of law, in particular customary law? If the rule of law is the foundation of the State, then how can parliament claim a power not bound by any legal restrictions? The problem involved reoccurs in any State, called the auto-obligation question. It implies that a political body that is sovereign cannot lay down institutions that bind itself. Ultimately, State sovereignty and the rule of law cannot be harmonized.

However, no State can escape this constitutional dilemma. Somehow the two faces of the State must be accommodated, because State power needs a legal framework and any legal framework requires State power for its implementation. Thus, we will see that several modern constitutions comprise both principles, on the one hand the sovereignty of the State and on the other hand the rule of law. What, more specifically, is involved in the two faces of the State? How can we define terms like 'sovereignty' and 'constitutionalism'? While the word 'sovereignty' refers to an absolute form of power or an unlimitable source of political control, the term 'constitutionalism' refers to such things as separation of powers, procedural stability and accountability.

Sovereignty models

In order to understand the conception of State sovereignty we look briefly at the models launched by Bodin, Hobbes and Austin. One has to bear in mind that focusing on a few key texts in political thought involves tremendous interpretation problems. Often political theorists are not consistent and they employ terms whose meanings are historically or culturally obscure. Here we try to isolate a few systematic properties by bypassing the historical context in which these conceptions were launched.

Bodin

Writing in the sixteenth century when the modern concept of the State was introduced in reality, Jean Bodin in *The Six Books of a Commonwealth* (1576) focused upon the conception of sovereignty. Political power being dispersed in the medieval society onto a large number of persons, corporations and estates, Bodin claimed that power in the modern State had to be conceived of as indivisible. This amounted to a most radical new concept, which was to play a major role in the new theories of the State. Bodin stated:

> I find that supremacy in a commonwealth consists of five parts: The first and foremost is appointing magistrates and assigning each one's duties; another is ordaining and repealing laws; a third is declaring and terminating war; a fourth is the right of hearing appeals from all magistrates in last resort; and the last is the power of life and death where the law itself has made no provision for flexibility or clemency (Bodin, 1955: 174–5).

One may look upon Bodin's conception of a commonwealth's supremacy as sovereignty as an early identification of the public power of a State. In contradistinction to medieval practices a number of powers, five in Bodin's interpretation, would be brought together under one heading – State sovereignty – which implied the creation of an organization with formidable resources.

Besides identifying State sovereignty as a practical legal construct, Bodin also proposed how and by whom this political supremacy was to be exercised. According to Bodin, the fact that State sovereignty must be conceived of as indivisible implied that the king alone could exercise such powers. Bodin also claimed that the king was bound by institutions derived from the laws of nature or customary practices. Bodin's consistency has been questioned as he may have falied to draw the logical conclusions of his detection of sovereignty (Franklin, 1991).

Hobbes

Thomas Hobbes delivered *Leviathan* in 1651 as a defence for the ambitions of kings towards absolutism. Yet, his influence on political theory stems not from this abortive idea. Instead, he stands out as the first political theorist who suggested a plausible theory of why government involves supremacy.

The commonwealth is created by a covenant, the essence of which is the election of a person who uses the strength and means of all parties to the covenant for 'their peace and common defence', writes Hobbes, concluding:

> And he that carryeth this person, is called Soveraigne, and said to have Soveraigne Power; and every one besides, his Subject (Hobbes, 1965: 90).

Sovereignty may be exercised by different bodies, but typical of State sovereignty is the making of law. Law derives its obligation from the obedience to the sovereign as the legislator. And sovereignty means the power to create law. Hobbes writes:

> The Legislator in all Common-wealths, is only the Soveraign, be he one Man, as in a Monarchy, or one Asssembly of men, as in a Democracy or Aristocracy. For the Legislator, is he that maketh the Law (Hobbes, 1965: 140–1).

Actually, laws in society are the rules that the State or the commonwealth lays down:

> And the Common-wealth only, prescribes, and commandeth the observation of thoses rules, which we call Law: Therefore the Commonwealth is the Legislator ... none can abrogate a Law made, but the Soveraign; because a Law is not abrogated, but by another Law, that forbiddeth it to be put in execution (Hobbes, 1965: 141).

Government supremacy expressed as the capacity of legislation is unbound by any kind of institutions. According to Hobbes, a State can at any time change the institutions of a country. The sovereign is free from any kind of restrictions. Customary law and constitutional conventions are binding only insofar as they have the tacit support of the state. Hobbes states:

> When long Use obtained the authority of a Law, it is not the Length of Time that maketh the Authority, but the Will of the Soveraign signified in his Silence (Hobbes, 1965: 141).

Hobbes model is that 'it is the Soveraign Power that obliges men to obey them [Laws]'. Here, there are four key elements involved, the first that the government possesses sovereignty, the second that sovereignty involves first and foremost legislation creating the only laws that men have to abide by, the third that law is the command of the sovereign and finally that the rationale of government is to avoid anarchy or *omnium bellum contra omnes*.

In effect, Hobbes launched the first truly consistent theory about the State as power, the sovereign commonwealth, by using a theory of law equating legislation with the issuing of commands. And as the law is the wish of the sovereign backed by the use of and threat of force, the sovereign cannot bind his or her own wishes, if indeed it is a question of sovereign commands. The origin of government is the contract between the sovereign and the population to set up a State, without which the life of man is 'solitary, poore, nasty, brutish, and short' as 'every man is Enemy to every man' (Hobbes, 1965: 64–5).

Rousseau

As long as the conception of the State as unlimited or indivisible power or sovereignty was combined with the ambitions of kings to retain or augment their power, the sovereignty approach to government was reactionary. However, Jean-Jacques Rousseau's *Social Contract* (1762) changed all this, because it brought out the revolutionary implications of the new construct. The principle of the sovereignty of the people was formulated in a succinct way by Rousseau and it had a tremendous impact upon politics.

Although Rousseau has frequently been accused of presenting an inconsistent concept of the 'General Will' as some kind of public interest that is above or beyond the will of the citizens, his identification of sovereignty is crystal clear:

> As nature gives each man absolute power over all his members, the social compact gives the body politic absolute power over all its members also; and it is this power which, under the direction of the general will, bears, as I have said, the name of Sovereignty (Rousseau, 1993: 204).

The state exercises sovereignty when it expresses what Rousseau calls the 'General Will'. There are several problems of interpretation with regard to this notion, especially how the General Will is forthcoming from the individual wills of each citizen. However, the difficulty in understanding how Rousseau conceived the process of aggregating citizen preferences into a collective choice is one thing, and the strong and unambiguous claims that Rousseau made for state sovereignty another.

The emphasis in Rousseau is on citizen participation with strong reservations about representative government. Government is simply administration. Rousseau states that when the General Will is declared, it is an act of sovereignty and constitutes law: in other circumstances government is a particular will, or act of magistracy – at most a decree (Rousseau, 1993: 201). Democracy as representative government is an illusion, as 'the Sovereign cannot act save when the people is assembled' (Rousseau, 1993: 261).

The Rousseau trinity – the people, sovereignty and the General Will – may be unpacked by asking whether these three entities always go together. If the General Will stands for what is best for the people, will democracy always identify the General Will? Should state sovereignty be without bounds when the people search for the General Will? The emphasis in Rousseau on sovereignty as indivisible and without restrictions receives tremendous practical force when it is identified with the General Will. The sovereign cannot make mistakes:

> Again, the Sovereign, being formed wholly of the individuals who compose it, neither has nor can have any interest contrary to theirs; and consequently the sovereign power need give no guarantee to its subjects, because it is impossible for the body to wish to hurt all its members (Rousseau, 1993: 194).

Whereas Bodin still maintained that the state as sovereignty must abide by customary law and Hobbes derived state sovereignty from the need to uphold law and order, Rousseau claims that the sovereign, although trusted with unlimited power, can never do wrong. When we move to Georg Wilhelm Friedrich Hegel, the identification of state power with ethics and justice becomes complete, as in his *Philosophy of Right* from 1821. The doctrine of the sovereignty of the people as formulated by Rousseau gave the notion of sovereignty a new direction, linking it up with democracy. The relevance of this new idea has been displayed already in the French revolution.

Austin

The power interpretation of the state received a strong foothold in modern jurisprudence in the work of John Austin. In the several editions of *The Province of Jurisprudence Determined*, first published in 1832, Austin launched the so-called command theory of law. It is intimately connected with the sovereignty approach to the concept of the State.

Making a sharp distinction between statute law and other kinds of law such as common law, international law or conventions, Austin claimed that positive law expressed the wishes of the sovereign, expressed, that is, in terms of general commands that are backed by State sanction.

To Austin sovereignty is a basic legal concept without which law could not be separated from ethics:

> Even though it sprung directly from another foundation or source, it is a positive law, or a law strictly so called, by the institution of that present sovereign in the character of political superior. Or (borrowing the language of Hobbes) 'The legislator is he, not by whose authority the law was first made, but by whose authority it continues to be law' (Austin, 1972: 193).

Consequently, Austin also ascribes illimitability and indivisibility to the sovereignty of the State. However, how to deal with constitutional rules, or the laws that regulate how State power is exercised? If constitutional law is truly law in the sense of positive law, then it must also constitute a set of commands that are valid due to the fact that they express the wishes of the sovereign. But how can the will of a sovereign State be bound by rules when its power is illimitable? And how can the constitution design a division of powers when there is legislative supremacy?

The sovereignty approach to the State implies a profound problem of how to interpret constitutional law and practices. Constititutional law, written or unwritten, codified or conventional, regulates State power, prescribing how State powers may be identified and exercised. But how, then, can they be derived from or be valid due to the power of the State? If the legal fabric of society expresses the commands of the sovereign issued legitimately in accordance with constitutional rules, then what makes a constitution valid in the first place?

Summation

The concept of sovereignty has been given a very prominent place in approaches to State and law both in political thought and legal thinking. To some the concept of the State implies a set of powers

that come in a most special dimension denoted by 'sovereignty'. If
sovereignty is the distinctive property of the modern State, then are
States bound by the rule of law? One major tradition in political
theory states *no*. Law in the form of constitutional statutes or custom
derives from or is made valid by the unlimitable powers of the State.
It is the State with its legislative supremacy that makes constitutional
law possible, not the other way around. There is one major drawback in the entire sovereignty approach to the State: is there really
something like a sovereign power? Are States today really sovereign?

The other major tradition takes an altogether different approach
to the rule of law in States. It argues that various types of law restrict
the exercise of State powers. Thus, constitutions regulate State
powers, i.e. constitutional law and conventions come first legitimating the making of laws and the issuing of directives in government.
International law sets definitive limits on State sovereignty, making
the theory of sovereignty as illimitable and indivisible mere rethoric.

Constitutionalist models

Generally speaking, 'constitutionalism' stands for an approach to the
State that underlines the importance of institutions for limiting State
power. Restrictions on the capacity of the State to act and employ
force derived from a rule of law framework lie at the heart of constitutionalism. It involves a requirement for the following State features: (a) procedural stability; (b) accountability; (c) representation;
(d) division of power; (e) openness and disclosure. What these
demands on the State imply has been much debated both in political
thought and in constitutional law and jurisprudence. Constitutional
thought, ancient, medieval or modern, enters much of the discussion
about government (Wheeler, 1975; Friedrich, 1968).

As long as there has been systematic thinking on the nature and
excerise of public power there has been constitutionalist thought. We
can trace constitutionalist ideas from modern constitutional law
through medieval ideas back to Cicero and Aristotle. The perspective
that the State is bound by the rule of law has been interpreted differently and we now look at five scholars within constitutionalism.

Althusius
In *Systematic Analysis of Politics* (1610) Johannes Althusius focused
upon two key concepts in constitutionalism, viz. consent and associ-

ation. Looking upon society as a network of associations, from the family to the State including communities and corporations, Althusius claimed that 'the efficient cause of political *consociatio* to be the consent and compact (*pactum*) of the communicating citizens'. This implied that political power derived from a contract between the rulers and those ruled, where the latter were prior to the former. The laws of the commonwealth derived from a covenant, in particular its 'fundamental law'.

Althusius used his contract theory to derive modest constitutionalist implications about the rights of various associations at different levels of government making him a forerunner of federalism, consociationalism and corporatism. In the end he advocated a mixed government blending Aristotelianism and Calvinist ideas. It was not until Locke that contract theory was married with a secular theory of natural human rights.

Locke

Major texts in the history of political thought have two ingredients, on the one hand ties to the milieu in which it appeared in time and on the other lasting features unaffected by time. Political thought as well as constitutional debate is replete with books and pamphlets that argue for one position or another in ongoing political struggle. Only a minor portion of all the ideas launched has a long lasting impact upon government.

John Locke's *Two Treatises of Civil Government* published in 1690 had an unmistakable practical intention, viz. to legitimate the so-called Glorious Revolution in 1688, when William of Orange was made King of England. It may be seen as a response to the major upheavals in the seventeenth century, the English civil war, the execution of King Charles I and the introduction of the republican commonwealth. Yet, Locke's ideas included a general constitutionalist theory that proved to be durable. The same applies to his *Letters on Toleration* from 1690, which advocated the separation of the State from the church against the background of the religious wars in seventeenth-century Europe, a message with a profound impact upon the secularization of the State in the eighteenth and nineteenth centuries.

Typical of constitutionalism is the notion that there exist somehow some restraints on political power. How these constraints are to be framed, or how they have been moulded as well as the rationale of a specific configuration of institutions are crucial questions in constitutionalism that may be answered in different ways depending upon theoretical assumptions and practical exigencies.

In Locke the validity of a constitutional dispensation follows from general principles about the nature of man/woman and the essence of the State. More specifically, government derives its power from the consent of its citizens, the people, you and me. The logic of the political contract is the foundation of the State and the powers of government. The rights and duties that derive from the political contract reflect innate rights of man, derived from natural law. Lockean constitutionalism is based upon the trust conception.

The fiction about a basic political contract giving the rulers the authority to govern the citizens is not enough to arrive at a constitutionalist argument, as is true with, for example, the great natural law scholars Grotius and Pufendorf, who ended up defending absolutism (Tuck, 1993a). Locke, however, adds to the idea of a covenant the idea of a trust, as any theory about government or 'political society' must recognize that ordinary people live in a state of nature before they make the agreement where there exists so-called 'natural liberties'. Locke writes:

> The natural liberty of man is to be free from any superior power on earth, and not to be under the will or legislative authority of man, but to have only the law of Nature for his rule (Locke, 1962: 127).

What Locke claims is not that man or woman in a stateless society will defend his/her self-interest. The basic behaviour assumption is not that man or woman is driven by self-preservation, which implies legitimate claims to the protection of life and property, as in Hobbes or Grotius. What Locke states is that everyone can claim certain liberties, because they follow from a law that is valid even before government is instituted. Here is the core of Locke's constitutionalism, viz. that since the rule of law applies to the state of nature it will also apply in everyday life, because the covenant confirms the liberties inherent in this natural law. The covenant is a trust to Locke, which implies that if the covenant is not kept by the ruler, then it is no longer valid. Locke states:

> The liberty of man in society is to be under no other legislative power but that established by consent in the commonwealth, not under the dominion of any will, or restraint of any law, but what that legislation shall enact according to the trust put in it (Locke, 1962: 127).

The idea of government as trust has a strikingly modern ring, as it touches upon the principal-agent model. The ruler is the agent of the population as the principal, and once the agent no longer sticks to the agreement, the principal will no longer have trust in him/her and the agent may remove him/her from power. If necessary, revolution is justified to protect the natural liberties of man or woman. In any constitutionalist framework the notion of reciprocity between the people and its government is basic. Constitutionalism implies that there are institutions constraining the exercise of state power. Locke identifies four constraints:

(1) Impartiality: 'They [governments] are to govern by promulgated established laws, not to be varied in particular cases, but to have one rule for rich and poor' (Locke, 1962: 189).
(2) The Public Interest: 'These laws also ought to be designed for no other end ultimately but the good of the people' (Locke, 1962: 189).
(3) Representation: 'They must not raise taxes on the property of the people without the consent of the people by themselves or their deputies' (Locke, 1962: 190).
(4) Accountability: 'Legislative neither must nor can transfer the power of making laws to anybody else, or place it anywhere but where the people have' (Locke, 1962: 190).

Locke's trust conception fits together with his idea of 'men being by nature all free, equal and independent' (Locke, 1962: 164). One of the great constitutionalist documents, the *Declaration of Independence*, declares:

> We hold these truths to be self-evident: that all men are created equal; that they are endowed by their Creator with certain inalienable rights; that among these are life, liberty, and the persuit of happiness. That, to secure these rights, governments are instituted among men, deriving their just powers from the consent of the governed; and that, whenever any form of government becomes destructive of these ends, it is the right of the people to alter or abolish it, and to institute new government, laying its foundations on such principles, and organizing its powers in such form, as to them shall seem most likely to effect their safety and happiness (Becker, 1942: 8).

The American revolution when taken further in the enactment of the 1787 constitution with its 1791 civil rights amendments created a constitutional republican State (Howard, 1990).

Montesquieu

In Montesquieu constitutionalism is based upon painstaking observations about comparative government. *The Spirit of the Laws* from
1748 is first and foremost a formidable empirical analysis of constitutions, their causes and consequences. Examining all forms of
regimes, ancient and modern, Montesquieu formulates the old doctrine of separation of powers in a novel fashion. His statement of the
idea that there are three basic state powers and the principle that
each of these state powers should rest with different state organs or
persons had a profound influence upon constitutionalism. As constitutions started to be enacted in one country after another during the
eighteenth and nineteenth centuries, there is reference time and again
to Montesquieu.

Constitutional government has taken two forms, observes Montesquieu. He warns against the third form of government, unconstitutional rule or despotism. Classifying various types of regimes on
the basis of how laws are made, he arrives at:

> There are three kinds of government: **republican, monarchical**, and
> **despotic** ... republican government is that in which the people as a
> body, or only a part of the people, have sovereign power, monarchical
> government is that in which one alone governs, but by fixed and estab-
> lished laws; whereas, in despotic government, one alone, without law
> and without rule, draws everything along by his will and his caprices
> (Montesquieu, 1989: 10).

Constitutional development in many European countries focused upon
the establishment of a constitutional monarchy, but one must not
forget republican constitutionalism, especially the American version.

Madison

American constitutionalism is closely connected with the country's
constitution. In the American debate we find no single great political thinker corresponding to European theorists such as Hobbes,
Locke or Rousseau. The political philosophy of American constitutionalism is stated in the well-known *Federalist Papers* (1961), edited
by Alexander Hamilton, James Madison and John Jay and published
collectively under the name 'Publius' at the same time the constitution was framed in 1787. Much attention has focused upon the sections written by Madison. His so-called factions theory outlines a
constitutionalist perspective upon the state (Dahl, 1964; Held, 1987).

Rule of law in the American context not only meant Montesquieu's theory about the necessity of making a sharp separation between the power of the three fundamental state organs: the executive branch, the legislative branch and the judicial branch. Rule of law in the new union not only implied the guarantee of a set of human rights, a list of such liberties were actually entered into the constitution by means of the first 10 amendments to the constitution, already enacted in 1791.

Rule of law in the American interpretation outlined by Madison comprised his core notion of checks and balances in order to minimize the impact of factions as well as reduce the risk of the tyranny of the majority. Creating a new state on the American continent called for an examination of constitutional models. Since a constitutional monarchy was not relevant for the American setting, Madison had to find some principles that could be employed to construct a republic (Pocock, 1975). As a matter of fact, republicanism has a long tradition in European political thought, but it was closely connected with small States such as the city-states of Greece (Athens and Sparta) and Italy (Venice, Florence). Madison launched the argument that big republics were more viable than small:

> Among the numerous advantages promised by a well-constructed Union, none deserves to be more accurately developed than its tendency to break and control the violence of faction. (Hamilton *et al.*, 1961: 41).

The key concept of a faction was defined by Madison in the following way:

> By a faction, I understand a number of citizens, whether amounting to a majority or minority of the whole, who are united and actuated by some common impulse of passion, or of interest, adverse to the rights of other citizens, or to the permanent and aggregate interests of the community (Hamilton *et al.*, 1961: 42).

This has a profound and a fresh ring. As a matter of fact, Madison launches a kind of public choice theory: factions are special organized interest groups that look more to their own advantage than to the public interests of all citizens. But if government attempts to suppress factions, then it will kill liberty.

The only way to handle factions is to employ a constitutional perspective in a large republic. States Madison:

> So strong is this propensity of mankind to fall into mutual animosities,

that where no substantial occasion presents itself, the most frivolous and fanciful distinctions have been sufficient to kindle their unfriendly passions and excite their most violent conflicts (Hamilton *et al.*, 1961: 43).

The detrimental effects of factions can be controlled by the creation of a federal constitution in a large union. The larger the republic the less the probability that one or two factions can dominate. And a federal constitution with checks and balances would ensure that various interests will be activited at different levels of government resulting in countervailing powers between the different factions.

Madisonian democracy is constitutionalism on a large scale, as it is based upon a theory of political motivation that warns about the possibility that the power of the State will be misused, and it builds up an argument about the importance of institutions in checking the self-interest seeking behaviour of élites. A constitution with checks and balances is necessary in order to restrict the State surge for supremacy.

The political theory launched in *The Federalist Papers* raises as many questions as it solves problems. Does republicanism imply democracy? Was the 1787 constitition democractic? Why were the rights of the black minority not acknowledged? Could too many checks and balances not reduce the capacity of the state to act in the interests of a political majority? Actually, Montesquieu warned against giving various veto powers to the three government branches. Yet, the American constitution is full of such checks and balances, resulting perhaps less from rational design than compromises between various interests at the constitutional convention (Jillson, 1988).

The basic tone in Madison's model is very modern. It starts from a kind of public choice hypothesis about the profound place of self-interest in politics. And it seeks a remedy in a rich institutional fabric with checks and balances and veto players. Vincent Ostrom argues that Madison's model is as relevant today as it was at the end of the eighteenth century (Ostrom, 1987), because it outlines a coherent constitutionalist alternative to the sovereignty interpretation of the State. In a sense constitutionalism takes the place of sovereignty in the American State (Miller, 1992).

Kant
A classical expression of European republicanism as constitutionalism was stated by Kant. Kant's formulation of a clear constitution-

alist position comes out nicely in the the philosophical sketch *Eternal Peace* from 1795. At the same time Kant formulated a number of constitutionalist ideas in his other major works (Riley, 1983). To Kant constitutionalism basically means government under the law. A constitutional state is a state founded upon what Kant referred to as public law, one part of which is the constitution.

Kant's constitutionalism involves more, however. He refers to his position as republicanism, by which he means the following constitutionalist principles:

> A republican constitution is founded upon three principles: firstly, the principle of freedom for all members of a society (as men); secondly, the principle of the dependence of everyone upon a single common legislation (as subjects); and thirdly, the principle of legal equality for everyone (as citizens). It is the only constitution which can be derived from the idea of an original contract, upon which all rightful legislation of a people must be founded. (Reiss, 1970: 99–100)

Thus, Kant embraces freedom, equality and popular sovereignty deriving these principles from the notion of an original contract which is simply 'an idea of reason', not a historical fact. However, Kant's republicanism is not revolutionary in one sense, as he rejects democracy and accepts a franchise that excludes women and persons without independent means. He actually accepts a kind of limited monarchy, where the king is supposed to work downwards for the introduction of a republican government. Yet, Kant's republicanism contains a most radical idea when he continues the above quote, saying:

> Thus, as far as right is concerned, republicanism is in itself the original basis of every kind of civil constitution, and it only remains to ask whether it is the only constitution which can lead to a perpetual peace (Reiss, 1970: 100).

Kant's answer to the question is **yes**, and he outlines a pacific federation (*foedus pacificum*) where the independent states commit themselves to an international regime based upon the following principles: (a) peace settlements should never comprise the material for a future war; (b) no states can be acquired by another state; (c) the abolition of standing armies; (d) no national debt can be assumed for the external affairs of a State; (e) no State shall interfere by force with another State's government; and (f) in war, States shall not commit acts of hostility that make mutual confidence impossible in peace. Kant derives these principles of international law from his republican form of government, because when States are founded upon the general will of the people, then it holds that:

> If, as is inevitably the case under this constitution, the consent of the citizens is required to decide whether or not war is to be declared, it is very natural that they will have great hesitation in embarking on so dangerous an enterprise (Kant, 1968: 100).

Could Kant's constitutionalist philosophy be more relevant than it is today with the explosive growth of international regimes, among which the European Union is a most important one? It may be noted that Kant rejected a federal state as the way to organize the internal affairs of a country favouring the unitary model. His proposal for an international regime has a rather loose format being generated from independent centralized states.

With Kant constitutionalism was based upon a highly complex theory of law and the legal order, including a variety of notions about republicanism and contractarianism (Kant, 1974). Although Kant's ethical ideas have retained their vitality and play a major role in modern theories about justice, his argument about the defects of democracy as necessarily involving the unrestrained rule of irresponsible majorities has restricted the overall relevance of his political writings. With Kant political theory is combined with legal thought in the form of a philosophy of constitutional law (Kant, 1965).

Constitutionalism today

When we enter the period when States begin to enact constitutions at large, then constitutionalism is the political theory that underlines the rule of law limiting State sovereignty by means of institutions that guarantee separation of powers and citizens rights. Today the problem of balancing this tradition in political thought with the other tradition that underlines government authority and supremacy reappears in several political science concepts and models as well as in constitutional discourse about human rights and public international law (Donnelly, 1993). The well-known democracy models by Arend Lijphart (Lijphart, 1977; 1984) may be seen as combinations of the aspects listed in Table 3.1. Moreover, the entire debate about government efficiency on the one hand and state ethos and government integrity on the other hand touches upon the very same aspects (Bovens, 1995). The tension between these two basic perspectives upon government was stated in a succinct manner by Neumann in his *Rule of Law* (1986), where he analysed the development of the rule of law notion from the thin idea that the state cannot act except by means of a legal order to the thick notion that the State must respect rights, citizen rights as well as the decentralization of government powers. On minority rights see Kymlicka (1995a, 1995b).

Table 3.1.
State Perspectives: power versus rule of law

Power	Rule of law
State sovereignty	Principle of legality, *lex superior*
Legislative supremacy	Separation of powers
Majority rule	Minority veto
Parliament sovereignty	Checks and balances
Unitary State	Federal State
Popular democracy	Consensus democracy
Government efficiency	Procedural accountability
Managerialism	State ethos and integrity

Legislative supremacy or the rule of law? *Machtstaat* contra *Rechtsstaat*. The constitution as a set of restrictions on State power or State command as the source of all legislation, including constitutional statutes and the validity of constitutional customs? The State cannot operate if it does not possess immense power resources. Anarchy prevails when the State can no longer issue commands that are obeyed by the people. Yet, State power unrestrained by constitutional principles and constitutional practice entails abusive authoritarian rule (Damaska, 1987). The constitutional State is firmly entrenched in many States today, in particular in the democracies. However, the question of whether constitutionalism is fully compatible with democracy remains a critical issue.

In order to display how the conflict between constitutionalism and democracy may arise, one could look at another great constitutional document, the *French Declaration of the Rights of Man and Citizen* from 1789. It lays down 17 paragraphs which reflects both constitutionalist notions but also expresses sovereignty ideas. Thus, it says on the one hand:

(1) Men are born and remain free and equal in rights; social distinctions may be based upon general usefulness.

(2) The aim of every political association is the preservation of the natural and inalienable rights of man; these rights are liberty, property, security, and resistance to oppression.

(16) Every society in which the guarantee of rights is not assured or the separation of powers not determined has no constitution at all.

(17) Since property is a sacred and inviolable right, no one may be deprived thereof unless a legally established public necessity obviously requires it, and upon condition of a just and previous indemnity.

These are the maxims of the constitutional state, but also in the famous declaration are the principles of democracy:

(3) The source of all sovereignty resides essentially in the nation; no group, no individual may exercise authority not emanating expressly therefrom.

(6) Law is the expression of the general will; all citizens have the same right to concur personally, or through their representatives, in its formation; it must be the same for all, whether it protects or punishes.

It requires little imagination to realize that the nation could express its general will by means of law (3 + 6) that goes beyond the restrictions laid down in (2 + 16 + 17). Or at least, there may occur different opinions as to whether laws expressing the sovereignty of the nation are in agreement with the listed constitutional restrictions. This is exactly what occurred in the confrontation between the socialist government under Mitterand and the French constitutional court exercising an *ex ante* legal review in the early 1980s. What is especially precarious with constitutionalism in relation to the principle of the sovereignty of the people is the sanctity of property.

However, constitutional documents may also be framed on the basis of the concept of positive liberties, commiting government to the establishment of a 'Sozialstaat' including a much more extensive list of human rights than those covered only by the concept of negative freedom. Actually, positive freedom may be interpreted as implying a right to employment, adequate housing and a decent standard of living in general, which positive liberties could come into conflict with one of the classical negative liberties, viz. property. In any case, any argument of the State and what it ought to do takes us into theories of justice, which will be discussed in Chapter 10.

It must be strongly emphasized that modern constitutional theory covers more than the traditional doctrine of constitutionalism or the rule of law theory. The core of constitutional theory includes first a theoretical part interpreting what kind of institutions constitutions are and what role they play in government; secondly there is an empirical part displaying the impact of alternative constitutional institutions on real life outcomes. In the chapters which follow we will elucidate these questions about the basic types of constitutions in the states of today: how do constitutional frameworks vary as a function of alternative patterns of State institutions (Chapters 5 and 6)? Does one framework matter more than another in terms of political, economic and social performance criteria such as liberty, equality and affluence (Chapter 9)?

One may distinguish between three broad sets of constitutions or institutional patterns: democratic, left-wing authoritarian and right-wing authoritarian regimes. And it is possible to distinguish a few distinct types of democratic regimes. What are the outcomes of these constitutions or patterns of fundamental State institutions?

Theoretically, the task for constitutional theory is to clarify the connections between the constitution and the state. One fruitful approach may be to employ the new economic organization theory in the new institutionalism as well as constitutional political economy, as is done in Chapter 8. Empirically, the task for constitutional theory is to show to what extent specific institutional patterns in the State have an impact upon real life predicaments of a social, economic or political nature. We test a couple of models taken from the contemporary debate that link major constitutional mechanisms with determinate outcomes such as affluence, economic growth, inflation, unemployment, equality, social order and political stability.

The politics of the late 1980s and the 1990s are focused upon the introduction and consolidation of democratic regimes. The number of countries that express adherence to some kind of democratic constitution has increased almost 100 per cent. This major trend raises critical questions about the nature of a democratic constitution. If democracy is government by the people of the people for the people, as Abraham Lincoln so accurately pointed out in his Gettysburg speech in 1863, then which rules do a democratic regime require to institutionalize these notions? In the next chapter we identify the major constitutional traditions since the end of the eighteenth century when democratic politics became a fundamental practical concern in politics.

Conclusion

In this chapter the task has been to try to analyse one part of constitutionalist history, viz. the doctrine of constitutionalism. Traditional constitutionalist thought was heavily normative in orientation. This does not mean that many of its conceptions are no longer relevant for modern constitutional theory. On the contrary, constitutionalism today may draw upon theories in political thought as well as in legal theory, while at the same time underlining the tremendous constitutional implications of the rapidly expanding international law framework.

Constitutional theory must come up with knowledge that is relevant to the understanding of the constitutional issues in the 1990s when many states search for a new constitution and other states reassess their constitutional records. The interpretation of constitutional design may be guided first by a discussion on the nature of the State and the reasons why a constitution in one form or another form is a necessity in a modern State, secondly by a survey of actually existing constitutions in the world, focusing on institutional variation, and thirdly by an assessment of whether crucial political institutions singled out in various constitutions matter for actual politics and social outcomes.

Constitutionalism today would comprise at least two distinct set of institutions, namely (a) human rights and (b) separation of powers institutions. Any interpretation of the relevance of such a weak form of constitutionalism in the twentieth century and in the future twenty-first century has to pay attention to the important developments in international law. However, constitutionalism may be interpreted in a much stronger fashion, including for instance legal review by the judiciary. Strong constitutionalism raises a number of issues in constitutional law which will be discussed in Chapter 7. In the concluding Chapter 11 we turn back to the problem of how democracy is accommodated within the constitutional state. It is now time to start examining constitutional documents.

4

Two great constitutional paths

Introduction

Having looked into the origins of the constitutional perspective in political thought and legal theory the time has come to start examining constitutional documents and constitutional institutions. The purpose of this chapter is to make an overview of constitutional diffusion since the drafting of two major constitutional documents in the eighteenth century, the American constitution from 1787 and the French constitution from 1791.

It is often stated that in the present constitutional setting there are two basic alternatives when new constitutions are to be enacted or old ones reformulated: the presidential model versus the parliamentary model. In this chapter we will describe how the parliamentary and presidential models have originated from constitutional history. One could label them the American model and the British model, if one so wishes, but they comprise two centuries of constitutional development in Europe and the United States.

Yet, let us start with the two major constitutions enacted when politics takes on a distinctly democratic ring. Table 4.1. outlines the developmental path that we set out to cover in this chapter.

The two constitutions that initiate the process of constitutional diffusion are the French 1791 constitution and the American 1787 constitution. One outlines a constitutional monarchy whereas the other comprises a republican constitutional State with democratic elements. Behind the scene of spectacular constitutional politics there is a third model – the mundane British constitutional model, unwritten and less visible, but more and more influential as it spreads parliamentarianism. Parliamentary institutions may be combined with both a constitutional monarchy and a constitutional republic (Bryce, 1905; Hawgood, 1939).

Table 4.1
Two major constitutional paths

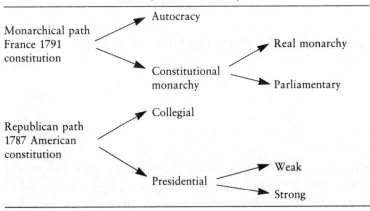

Constitutional monarchies

In the Europe of 1800 the prevailing type of constitutional government was the so-called constitutional monarchy, although there were also a few examples of small republics. The constitutional monarchy involved the combination of monarchical rule with some dispersion of power to other bodies, such as a national assembly of some sort and a system of courts. There was a clear ambition to identify the organs and the functions of the state in a written document. Actually, the early decades of the nineteenth century were a major constitutional period when a number of new written constitutions were enacted (Duchhardt, 1991; Bothart, 1993).

The idea of a constitutional monarchy was that the rule of the king or the queen was restricted in various ways. We find in the history of political thought several versions of mixed constitutions, of which the so-called mixed monarchy was one. In the seventeenth century there was talk about 'Monarchia Mixta', but the modern form of a constitutional monarchy was described by Montesquieu in *The Spirit of the Laws* (1748) – some say on the basis of an erroneous understanding of English practices.

Visiting Great Britain *circa* 1730, Montesquieu derived the vitality of the English State from its institutionalization of the principles of the separation of powers:

If there were no monarch and the executive power were entrusted to a
certain number of persons drawn from the legislative body, there would
no longer be liberty, because the two powers would be united, the same
persons sometimes belonging and always able to belong to both
(Montesquieu, 1989: 161).

However, it is questionable whether Great Britain was not at that
time already practising some kind of parliamentarianism.

In any case, in the eighteenth century it proved possible to restrict
royal power by means of a constitution, in some countries more so
than in others. The archetype of a constitutional monarchy is the
French 1791 constitution, which served as a model for constitutional
diffusion in the nineteenth century. Here, we may place the following constitutions: Sweden 1809, Spain 1812, Norway 1814, Portugal
1822, Brazil 1824, Belgium 1831, Piedmontese Statuto in Italy 1848,
Austria 1867 and Germany 1871.

The theory behind the conception of a constitutional monarchy
was brought out in its most modern form *circa* 1815 by Benjamin
Constant. He saw the king as the guarantee for the stability of the
State, having a veto against the legislative assembly, being able to
dismiss his ministers and having the right of pardon. In *Principles of
Politics* (1815) Constant remarks 'Constitutional monarchy creates
this neutral power in the person of the head of state', whose task it
is to ensure 'not that any of these powers (executive, legislative, judicial) should overthrow the others' (Constant, 1988: 184).

Yet, in some states a rather different form of constitutional monarchy was practised, which only legitimized the rules of royal autocracy: France: 1814; German States during the nineteenth century:
Bavaria, Würtemberg, Baden, Hessen-Kassel, Saxony and Hanover.
However, such regimes were at least not despotic, but were of a type
which can be institutionalized by means of a constitution. Typical of
many historically important regimes that were personalistic or sultanistic is the lack of stable rules for the exercise of power. A constitution does not have to embody a democratic regime, as was the
case with the constitutional monarchies, but there has to be some set
of restrictions or institutions.

The English constitution, a living unwritten constitution, can
hardly be classified as a constitutional monarchy at the beginning of
the nineteenth century. Its distinctive trait is parliamentarianism,
already institutionalized more or less clearly in the eighteenth cen-

tury. A parliamentary monarchy is not a constitutional monarchy, as in the former the queen reigns but she does not govern. Before we deal with parliamentary monarchies we will look at the second major constitutional tradition, presidential republicanism.

Presidential republicanism

The American constitution of 1787 initiates a worldwide spread of a specific constitutional model, whose practical relevance has not diminished after the Second World War. On the contrary, strong presidential government today is the main alternative to parliamentarianism.

Republicanism was hardly a novelty when the American colonies declared their independence in 1776. The idea of the republic as the ideal-type political system was cherished by many in political thought, pointing to well-known examples such as Holland and Venice. However, presidentialism was a true novelty. The existing republics were ruled by a form of mixed constitution involving one oligarchical body or another, which co-opted itself (Ketcham, 1986).

The American constitutional experiment favouring a big republic could not employ existing forms of republican government. After much deliberation over several alternatives the choice was a president, elected indirectly by an electoral college and entrusted with a variety of executive powers, sometimes subject to the approval of the Senate. As later on the electors in the various states precommitted themselves to voting for one presidential candidate, the American president is now in effect directly elected by the people, which further supports his powerful position, especially in times of war.

Various kinds of executives were discussed by the constitutional convention in 1787. One proposal was that Congress should elect the president, which could have meant a development towards parliamentarianism. Another suggestion was that the office of the president should be life-long, i.e. almost like a monarch. One proposal that was not discussed was to have a collegial executive, i.e. a republican government without a single head of State. Such an executive was employed during the French revolution in the form of the so-called directorate. Switzerland has had such a semi-presidential system; Uruguay tried it between 1918–33 and 1952–67 ('Colegiado').

The American model of strong presidentialism was exported to Latin America when these former Spanish colonies broke loose around 1820. Only Brazil, the Portuguese colony, chose the French model of a constitutional monarchy, but transferred to the American model in 1891. But the critical question is why presidentialism worked so differently in the USA and in Central and South America. Strong presidentialism invites opportunistic behaviour on the part of the president or the army when faced with severe political opposition. Then the temptation to resort to military government becomes quite considerable. And few of the checks and balances that are characteristic of the US political system have been institutionalized in Latin America.

In the twentieth century strong presidentialism became popular when the African and Asian States are formed following the colonies being broken up after the Second World War. In Europe, Finland in 1919 and Czechoslovakia in 1920 created a presidential republic. The most spectacular turn to presidentialism was made in France when De Gaulle introduced his new constitution in 1959. While several of the strong presidential systems in the Third World never came close to being a democracy, the Finnish and French version of presidentialism – semi-presidentialism, or presidentialism with a dose of parliamentarianism – have upheld the constitutionalist feature typical of the American constitution, the world's oldest constitution.

The French model of a constitutional monarchy and the American model of strong presidentialism are two basic modes of constitutionalist government. The third one is the English model of a parliamentary monarchy. Not until the creation of the Third French republic do we find an example of a parliamentary republic. The American model was copied in Latin America during the nineteenth century and in many places in the Third World in the twentieth century. It exercised a kind of spell over constitution makers, as the American political system appeared to be so successful in every way. However, few other countries achieved good results with this constitutional model. In Latin America it was a disaster, as it was replaced everywhere by military governments, either by the president himself or by means of a *coup d'état*.

Parliamentarianism

Constitutional diffusion in the early nineteenth century is dominated by the two models discussed above, the constitutional monarchy and the presidential republic. In the early decades another model becomes prominent, parliamentarianism or the English model. It actually spread rather rapidly, as it offered a simple solution to the problem of restricting the power of the King even further. In 1875 the first parliamentary republic was created in France. The French 1875 constitution became of model constitution of how to combine republicanism with parliamentarianism. It served as the source of much constitutional plagiarism in the early twentieth century.

In 1867 Walter Bagehot published *The English Constitution*. It comprises a most general analysis of parliamentarianism, setting out its distinctive traits in relation to other models, in particular the American constitution which Bagehot rejects as a composite model of government that is inferior to the simple constitution of England. Bagehot's statement of the principles of a parliamentary monarchy has maintained its freshness.

Bagehot starts by pointing out that many foreign commentators have failed to identify what is distinctive in the English constitution, because they have not probed behind its dignified parts to reveal its efficient parts. Its most spectacular features, such as an hereditary monarch reigning by the grace of God and an aristocratic upper house, the House of Lords, consisting of peers, amounts only to a theatrical show. Its real essence is its efficient part, the House of Commons which is government by public meeting, 658 members electing the cabinet that rules the country (Bagehot, 1993: 152–84).

The British constitution does not involve any doctrine about the separation of powers. The gist of parliamentarianism is the following:

> The efficient secret of the English Constitution may be described as the close union, the near complete fusion, of the executive and legislative powers. No doubt by the traditional theory, as it exists in all the books, the goodness of our constitution consists in the entire separation of the legislative and executive authorities, but in truth its merit consists in their singular approximation (Bagehot, 1993: 68).

The House of Commons has a number of crucial tasks, whereas the House of Lords only exercises revising and suspending powers. The Lower House is first and foremost an electing chamber, designating the Cabinet. In addition Bagehot (1993: 152–6) lists the following functions:

(1) Expressive, i.e. to give a voice to the British people.
(2) Teaching, i.e. to instruct the people on vital matters.

(3) Informing, i.e. to tell the rulers about events in the realm.
(4) Legislation.
(5) Financial, in particular the introduction of new taxes.

The peculiar contribution of English constitutional practice is the concept of the Cabinet as distinct from the Queen. Bagehot states:

> The connecting link is the Cabinet. By that word we mean a committee of the legislative body selected to be the executive body. The legislature has many committees, but this is the greatest. It chooses for this, its main committee, the men in whom it has most confidence. (Bagehot, 1993: 68)

The Cabinet is the 'hyphen which joins' or the 'buckle which fastens' the legislative part with the executive part of the State. By fusing the executive with the legislature the Cabinet offers distinct advantages over the presidential model and its dispersion of powers, viz: (a) elasticity; (b) continuity. By the first Bagehot means the capacity of Parliament to elect new leaders if changing circumstances so demand. And by the latter Bagehot has in mind the day-to-day interaction and reciprocity that takes place between the Cabinet and Parliament. Both these features contrast sharply with the immobilism of the American system, where it is very difficult to replace a president and where stalemate often occurs between Congress and the president.

At the time when Bagehot published his now classical analysis of a parliamentary monarchy the Queen's reign was in reality a 'government of disguise', where the role of the Queen was restricted to the rights: (a) to be consulted; (b) to encourage; (c) to warn. The Queen could be seen as a Grand Elector, when designating the person to be premier, but that task also had somehow been transferred more and more to the House of Commons.

The House of Lords had similarly seen their power being reduced. When the second edition of *The English Constitution* appeared in 1872 the powers of the Upper House had been confined to revising or suspending proposals of the Lower House. Both the Reform Acts of 1832 and 1867 and the Anti-Corn Law from 1846 involved a defeat for the House of Lords, reducing their esteem to the advantage of the House of Commons. The House of Lords enhanced the dignified part of the constitution by adding to it the prestige of the aristocracy.

Bagehot identified a number of conditions for the successful operation of parliamentarianism, internal conditions and well as external ones. Two internal conditions are considered as absolutely vital, the right of the Cabinet to dissolve Parliament and the right of the Queen to name new peers for the House of Lords. Only if these two internal conditions are satisfied, can parliamentarianism work, because they enhance the balance between the executive and the legislature.

No doubt, Bagehot here stated something very basic about the British model of government: there must be institutions that make for reciprocity between the Cabinet and Parliament. Once we broaden the perspective and look at the way parliamentarianism is practised around the world we will observe that not all parliamentary constitutions involve the right of dissolution.

Bagehot's external conditions are more diffuse, as he mentions the following: (a) mutual confidence of the members of the Lower House; (b) a calm national mind; (c) rationality (Bagehot, 1993: 160–1). These words can be interpreted differently, but what Bagehot has in mind is a 'deferential nation' run by an élite of 658 members, originating from the property class and the gentry. He vehemently rejected democracy by equating '*vox populi*' with '*vox diaboli*'. As we know there may be parliamentary democracies as well as parliamentary republics.

Looking around him Bagehot found four types of political regimes: (a) parliamentary; (b) presidential; (c) hereditary; (d) revolutionary. As an example of the presidential mode he cited the United States, where time and again Bagehot underlined the complexity and immobilism of its constitution; among the hereditary regimes he counted what we have referred to above as constitutional monarchies; and as examples of the revolutionary type he gave France with its frequent shift between various constitutions: monarchical, republican and imperial.

Despite Bagehot's lack of understanding of what was going on in broadening the electorate of the House of Commons – e.g. Disraeli's major election reform of 1867 – he clearly saw the problem of bureaucracy, pointing at the regime in Prussia. A parliamentary model could actually solve the difficulties with bureaucracy by providing politics at the top in ministries plus administration beneath. Ministerial rule means flexibility, change, superior ability and political control.

English parliamentarianism was well identified by Bagehot in his succinctly written text. But there is more to parliamentarianism than the amount Bagehot recognized. When we look at constitutional practices in the twentieth century, then we find other kinds of parliamentarianism, which do not involve a monarchy, a two chamber system or the right to dissolve. Moreover, there are parliamentary systems where Parliament and its committees are stronger than the cabinet (Döring, 1995).

Victory and defeat of parliamentarianism

Parliamentarianism became the constitutional device by means of which the powers of kings and queens could be abolished without the introduction of a republic. Parliamentarianism made it possible to make a peaceful transition from constitutional monarchy to constitutional democracy. At the same time parliamentarianism also attracted republican governments, where a distinction was made between the head of State, often a ceremonial president, and the premier as the true leader of the government. Actually, the British model of parliamentarianism proved extremely strong as an ideal model of how to structure the relationship between the executive and legislative branches of government. It was implemented in both monarchies – such as Belgium in 1831, the Netherlands in 1848, Norway in 1884, Sweden in 1917, Denmark in 1901 – and also in republics – such as Germany in 1919, Austria in 1920, Poland in 1921, Czechoslovakia in 1920 and in the three Baltic states of Latvia, Lithuania and Estonia between 1920–22 (Munro, 1926; Headlam-Morley, 1928).

The constitution in the 'Model' State of Belgium served as a type of constitutionalist parliamentarianism to be copied elsewhere. It not only contained the classical principles of constitutionalism expressed in the American Declaration of Independence and the French Declaration of the Rights of Man but also outlined a system of government where the 'the king, as the formal head of the executive, could possess and exercise only those powers expressly given him by the constitution, and could act only through his ministers' (Hawgood, 1939: 145). However, even after the First World War a few countries opted for retaining a constitutional monarchy, rejecting parliamentarianism, for example Bulgaria, Romania and Yugoslavia.

Yet the victory of the parliamentary model of government in 1919 proved to be fragile. In 1926 Pilsudski introduced a presidential regime in Poland which was legitimized by the 'ultrapresidential' constitution of 1935. In the same year Lithuania made a similar move towards presidentialism, confirmed in the revised constitution of 1928. Estonia and Latvia followed suit in 1934. In Turkey Kemal Ataturk had set up a strong presidential regime overthrowing the Sultanate in 1922.

The move towards strong presidentialism during the interwar years was part of the general crisis of democracy that actually started almost immediately after the Versailles peace – the peace that would, it was hoped, make the world safe for democracy. It began in Italy where Mussolini seized power in 1922. The Duce never launched a unified constitutional document to bolster his authoritarian regime. Instead the fascist Italian State was introduced in a piecemeal fashion by means of various separate legal acts. Between 1926 and 1928 a State corporatist system of representation and negotiation based upon economic categories was enacted and implemented. The Fascist Grand Council received legal recognition, although it had existed since 1923. The electoral law of 1928 strengthened the corporatist state under the control of the Fascist Party and the creation of a National Council of Corporations finalized the corporatist system involving a 'Chamber of Fasci and Corporations' instead of a people's assembly.

Adolf Hitler came to power by means of the parliamentary route. On 30 January 1933, Hitler was made Chancellor of the Reich by President Hindenburg. On 24 March Hitler already assumed unlimited emergency powers by means of 'das Ermächtigungsgesetz'. There followed a number of laws which concentrated all State power to the Reichspresident and Reichskanzler, both of which were offices Hitler held. The Fürher principle – 'all authority from above and all responsibility from below' – was carried through into the administration and the judicial system. But, again, there was not a formal constitution enacted that summarized the principles of the Nazi State.

In 1923 the Spanish 1876 constitution was set aside by General Primo de Rivera, who instituted an authoritarian regime, which was followed by the introduction of a republic in 1930, although this only lasted for nine years. The Spanish 1931 constitution was modelled on the format of the Mexican 1917 and German 1919 constitutions. However, this parliamentary republic was replaced by Franco by a new monarchy after the civil war. This was, however, a facade for the fascist regime that Franco inspired when he remained head of State and government with the Falange as the only legal political party up until his death in 1974.

Fascism in Portugal took on clear constitutional manifestations.

The democratic constitution of 1919 did not last any longer than until 1926 when presidential rule was introduced. In the 1933 constitution the new principles of *Estado Novo* under the direction of Dr Salazar were expressed in a State corporatist scheme with a one-party legislature. Just as in Italy, Portuguese fascism attempt constitutional recognition of its ideology, which the Nazi regime in Germany did not. The new Portuguese constitution was copied in Latin America, for example in Brazil by Vargas.

Fascism constituted one of the major challenges towards parliamentary democracy. Bolshevism was the other force that rejected the constitutional ideals inherent in the two constitutional traditions initiated in the French and American revolutions. The first constitution of the Union of Soviet Socialist Republics came into force in 1924, replacing the 1918 constitution of the Russian Socialist Republic. The well-known 1936 USSR constitutions provided for a federal framework, parliamentarianism, an independent judiciary as well as an extensive list of rights and duties of cities. However, it also stated: 'The right to nominate candidates shall be ensured to public organizations and societies for the working people; Communist party organizations; trade unions; cooperatives; organizations of youth; cultural societies' (Article 141).

Most interestingly, the first modern authoritarian constitution can be dated to the early stage of one of the constitutional paths portrayed above. The Jacobin constitution from 24 June 1793 is the first one that established a populist regime with some authoritarian tendencies, reminiscent of what was to show up during the interwar years. It is a short succinct constitution that expresses Robespierrian democracy, or the preference for popular sovereignty over constitutionalist restrictions. The 1795 constitution which replaced the democratic constitution of 1793 was a compromise constitution, the government being entrusted with an executive Directorate, a model of a collegial presidency that the French spread over Europe, along with the conquests of the French army, to Switzerland, among other countries. Actually, the Bonapartists' constitutions may also be interpreted in this perspective. They provided facade constitutions behind which authoritarian rule was the reality (Chevalier, 1993).

Return to democratic constitutions

In *The Third Wave: Democratization in the Late Twentieth Century*

(1991) Samuel Huntington identified three periods when democratic constitutions were introduced and flourished for a time: (a) 1828–1926, (b) 1943–62 and (c) 1974– (Huntington, 1991: 16). Such periodizations are always to some extent arbitrary, as one may emphasize different aspects of the development of events. Looking at constitutions one may in fact talk about four waves: (a) 1789–99, (b) 1914–26, (c) 1945–65 and 1989–.

Such a fourfold division captures well the fact that constitutional change is strongly related to major social upheavals such as revolutions and wars. The first democratic constitution is implemented in France by means of the Jacobin constitution of 24 June 1793, accepted in the first popular referendum in French history. The Jacobin constitution was a short compact constitution of 124 articles founded upon the sovereignty of the people expressed in universal suffrage. However, it was never implemented, as after Thermidor and Vendèmiaire, during which time also a democratic Girondist constitution was proposed, a compromise semi-democratic constitution was implemented in 1795 with a directorate as the government. The directorate model was spread by the French troops to the Batavian Republic, Switzerland, Modena, Milan, Genoa and Naples. The 1799 constitution inspired by Napoleon ended the first wave of democracy as a result of 18 Brumaire.

The second wave of democracy came around the First World War, when universal male suffrage was introduced either shortly before 1914 or during the war, and subsequently female universal suffrage was implemented at the end of the war or shortly afterwards. This applied in particular to a number of European countries. Another continent that moved towards democracy in the first decade of the twentieth century was Latin America, where female universal suffrage was introduced somewhat later, i.e. in the 1930s, 1940s and 1950s. However, democracy in Latin America proved to be as fragile as in Europe.

Universal male suffrage was introduced in Argentina in 1912 and a democratic regime was in place up until 1930, when a *coup* made way for the implementation of a restrictive democracy (Waisman, 1989). The military *coup* of 1943, however, established an authoritarian regime, continued by the Peronist dictatorship which lasted until 1955. Democracy was not restored until 1983. In Brazil the First Republic, introduced in 1891, was also ended by a *coup* in 1930, led by Vargas. The dicatatorial Estado Novo was put in place between

1937 and 1945 (Lamounier, 1989). Vargas' resignation at the end of the Second World War did not result in a stable democracy, as Vargas returned to power in 1950. In 1964 a *coup* led to military-authoritarian rule that lasted until 1984, when democracy was restored.

In Chile universal male suffrage was introduced in the 1910s on the basis of the long-lasting 1833 republican constitution, modelled after the American prototype. Chilean democracy is unique in Latin America, as it lasted for a long time, or up until the military *coup* in 1973, which brought Pinochet to power. Democracy was restored in Chile in the late 1980s (Valenzuela, 1989). Uruguay has been called 'Latin America's most successful polyarchy', because it had a democratic regime from 1918, when universal male suffrage was implemented, to 1973 when a military *coup* inaugurated an authoritarian regime that lasted until 1985 (Gillespie and Gonzalez, 1989).

Venezuela is different, as mass politics did not arrive until 1945, Venezuela having a personalist rule from 1903 to 1935 and a transitional military regime between 1936 and 1945. Between 1948 and 1958 there was again a military regime and the democratic regime that was set up in 1958 has been interrupted several times (Levine, 1989). Between 1910 and 1949 there was 'oligarchical democracy' in Colombia, when a military government was instated. Democratic institutions were installed in Costa Rica in 1913, the only country with an uninterrupted democratic tradition in Latin America (Booth, 1989). The major cause of the decline of democracy in Latin America was the same as in Europe, viz. the economic difficulties resulting in the great depression, which fuelled authoritarian movements.

The third wave of democratization is to be found after the Second World War, when democratic constitutions were introduced in a number of countries in Asia and Africa, in addition of course to the replacement of the fascist regimes in western Europe (Friedrich, 1950; Zurcher, 1951). Decolonization in Asia and Africa from 1945 to about 1965 had the consequence that formally democratic constitutions were written and enacted. However, few were really implemented but rather quickly became camouflage constitutions for dictatorships.

Perhaps the 1950 Indian constitution was the major event in the third wave of democratization. It gave to the second most populous country in the world a federal parliamentarian regime, which has proved to be long lasting, with the exception of a short period of emergency power rule under Indira Gandhi between 1975 and 1977 (Gupta, 1989). A stable democratic regime was also established in Japan in 1947 and in Papua New Guinea when it became independent in 1975, but constitutional developments in Pakistan, Sri Lanka, Malaysia, Indonesia, the Philippines and South Korea as well as Taiwan were less successful from a democratic point of view. In these latter countries there have been a series of constitutions replacing each other, often having been suspended by the declaration of martial law.

Thus, in 1971 Marcos declared martial law in the Philippines overthrowing the 1935 constitution. A fragile democracy was restored in 1986 when Corazon Aquino took office (Jackson, 1989). South Korea became an authoritarian regime lasting until 1987 after a military *coup* in 1961 (Han, 1989). Malaysia experienced what has been called 'democracy on trial' from its independence in 1957 to the *coup* in 1969, which suspended democracy. However, democratic institutions were reintroduced in 1971 to some extent: 'although fully democratic conditions have not been allowed, nonetheless there has been a sense of political participation, as exemplified by four general elections, and of continuity, as evidenced in two instances of constitutional leadership succession' (Ahmad, 1989). Sri Lankian democracy foundered upon the Tamil issue in the 1980s (Phadnis, 1989).

In the region of Asia Minor one cannot really speak of any democratic wave at all. Democratic constitutions were not on the agenda when traditional rule was dismantled or the decolonization process was begun. The Kemalist regime in Turkey, coming into place with the 1921 constitution, was a modernizing government based upon the single-party model, but after the Second World War attempts were made towards democratization. However these were crushed by the 1960 military *coup*. Democratization was attempted once more between 1961–80, but the military intervened again. The new 1982 constitution is democratic in its intentions, but there is little to resemble it in the constitutional practice of other states in Asia Minor except Israel.

The Fertile Crescent is clearly the area of the world where traditional rule still has a firm grip on the State. Written constitutions belong to a different kind of authority structure – what Max Weber referred to as legal-rational rule. Thus, it is little wonder that some of the Arab States lack a formal constitution, at least a secular one. An area expert notes:

At the end of the colonial period 19 Arab states or statelets had as their head of state a king, amir, shaikh, bey, or imam drawn from a family that had either established or been given hereditary right to rule. Five of these were then deposed in the 1950s and 1960s – in Egypt, Tunisia, Iraq, Libya and North Yemen – leaving 14 to survive until the present day – in Morocco, Jordan, Saudi Arabia, Kuwait, Bahrein, Qatar, Oman and the seven members of United Arab Emirates (Owen, 1992: 56).

In relation to these traditional regimes the key question is the extent to which they can be characterized as constitutional monarchies. Two candidates are Jordan and Morocco. According to the 1972 Moroccan constitution the powers of the King are substantial: sovereign head of state, appoints the Premier and other ministers, dissolves Parliament and approves legislation. The 1951 Jordanian constitution is somewhat less royalistic, as the cabinet is responsible to Parliament. Sharia law, i.e. Islamic legal practice based upon the Koran, the prophet's actions and early interpretations, makes up the constitution of Saudi Arabia.

Several of the Arab states getting independence from colonial powers choose the socialist one-party State regime. Here one may mention Egypt, Sudan, Syria, Iraq, Tunisia, Algeria, the two Yemens and Libya. Most of these countries have formally written authoritarian constitutions that concentrate power to one body or another. The 1977 Libyan constitution introduced the so-called Basic People's Congresses through which adults are supposed to share in policymaking all over the country. These local congresses elect the General People's Congress, which is the highest policy-making body, appointing the General Secretariat and the General People's Committee. The 1970 Iraqi constitution concentrates State power to the eight member Revolutionary Command Council. The Egyptian, Tunisian and Syrian constitutions establish strong presidential systems, founded more or less upon a one-party State model, whereas the Algerian and Sudanian constitutions have been suspended following civil war in those countries.

On the African continent there has been lots of constitution making, but the basic problem is that generally constitutions do not last very long. Actually, hardly any of the constitutions introduced when the African States became independent have not been either changed or suspended. Constitutional development has been disrupted to say the least in all but a few countries such as Botswana and Mauritius. Interestingly, the first constitutions put in place when the European powers left were heavily influenced by colonial heritage. However, only a few years after independence these English or French inspired constitutions had been either remodelled or suspended. As Larry Diamond notes: 'By the early 1970s, virtually all of the independent regimes in sub-Saharan Africa were either military or one-party' (Diamond *et al.*, 1988: 1). In some countries dictatorship constituted the real regime while the camouflage constitution had remnants of democratic features. In other countries authoritarian constitutions were introduced.

If one is interested in how constitutional documents can be revised rapidly, then the constitutional events on the African continent may be studied. A large number of constitutions have been enacted, suspended and omitted. When the first constitutions of the independent African countries were drawn up, there was an attempt to create a constitutional legacy in relation to the constitutional practice of the country to which the newly independent state had been a colony. After a rather short period, however, such constitutions were revised to reflect other constitutional images.

Thus, for example in the French Congo the constitutions of 1959, 1961 and 1963 were inspired by French constitutional practice, whereas the constitutions enacted a little later in 1970, 1973 and 1979 were of the Soviet kind. The first constitution of Tanganyika, enacted in the year of independence of 1961, was of the British type, i.e. on the Westminster model where the British Queen was the head of state. However, one year later a republic was introduced with a president empowered with real executive competences. The final step was to implement a one-part State in the united Tanzania in 1965. A quite similar constitutional path was followed by Kenya in a short time span from 1963 to 1964 as well as by Ghana during a slightly longer time span, from 1957, when it was the first colony in Africa to become independent, up until 1960. In French Cameroon the road to dictatorship also involved the introduction of a one-party State.

In British Nigeria dictatorship was introduced by means of a military *coup* in 1966, suspending the 1960 Westminster type constitution with a federal State. The conflicts over Nigerian federalism as well as over the structure of the executive has resulted in numerous constitutional changes. The 1979 constitution was modelled on the image of American presidentialism, but it has also been put out of effect by means of new military *coups*. In French Niger a one-party

State was put in place when the new state was declared, but its constitution was suspended in 1974 when military rule was implemented.

In the two countries which were not made colonies, Liberia and Ethiopia, constitutional development has been no less dramatic or chaotic. Liberia was ruled as a one-party State during most of its history since it was founded in 1847, but in 1980 there was a military *coup*. It has had a presidential type of executive while Ethiopia remained a traditional monarchy until 1974, when the Emperor was deposed and a Soviet type of constitution was proclaimed in 1987.

Botswana is the major exception, displaying constitutional stability since its year of independence in 1966. Is it a mere coincidence that Botswana has a Westminster type executive with parliamentary accountability when almost all the other African states with a presidential executive have been plagued by constitutional instability? A similar observation may be made of the other democratic state on the African continent, Mauritius, whose constitution dates back to 1968 and is of the Westminster type.

The fourth wave of democratization was initiated as a fresh start in 1989 when the East European Communist regimes faltered. This sets in motion a worldwide constitutional diffusion process whereby democratic constitutional principles replaced authoritarian ones in many countries. By the early 1990s many of the States in Eastern Europe had democratic constitutions, formally enacted and implemented with varying degrees of success. Only very few countries still have a Marxist-Leninist constitution: China with its 1978 constitution, North Korea with its 1972 constitution and Cuba with its 1976 constitution.

The democratization wave in Eastern Europe certainly reinforced democratic forces in Latin America, where in the early 1990s all countries now have a democratic regime, albeit a fragile one in a few countries such as Haiti and Peru (Berntzen, 1993). The other continent which was affected in the fourth democratization wave was Africa, where democratic institutions have been installed in the Republic of South Africa and where countries like Malawi, Zambia, Kenya, Zimbabwe and Ghana have attempted to introduce such institutions – although whether these institutions will comprise a sustainable democracy remains to be seen (Qadir *et al.* 1993; Clapham, 1993). The major exception is South East Asia where rapid socio-economic development goes hand-in-hand with weak attempts at

democratization in some countries but a straightforward affirmation
of authoritarian rule in other countries (Thompson, 1993).

Republics, monarchies, presidents and premiers

Constitutional developments since the two major democratic revolutions in the late eighteenth century, the American and the French revolutions, have followed two major paths, that of the constitutional
monarchy and that of the presidential republic. The French 1791
constitution provided the model for the first path and the American
1787 constitution afforded the model for the second path. In the
nineteenth century things became more complex, as parliamentarianism offered a constitution that could be combined with both a
monarchy and a republican form of government. What we need to
focus on are the institutions for the executive, which involves rules
about the head of State and the government, in particular the leader
of the government or the premier.

Today, almost all countries with a monarchical form of government are parliamentary democracies. Only a few real monarchies
remain, of which not all are constitutional monarchies in the first
place. Most States have republican forms of government, but not all
practise presidentialism, at least not in the form of strong presidential government. Several republics have weak presidents, because
they are parliamentary democracies. At the same time one must note
that many presidential republics are neither democracies nor constitutional states, as they are either ruled by emergency laws or by an
authoritarian constitution.

Which form of government is most viable, American presidentialism or parliamentarianism? The first form has an executive where the
head of State is also the leader of the government. The second form
implies an executive where the head of State, whether monarch or
president, is distinct from the premier and the premier conducts government activities. This question about the construction of the executive is one of the most debated issues in constitutional politics
today. In the new wave of democratization countries engage in constitutional policy-making (Hesse and Johnson, 1995), where one of
the choices concerns strong presidentialism versus parliamentarianism (Lijphart, 1992). There are critical constitutional choices in addition, the resolution of which may affect state stability and the
prospects of democracy. For example there is the problem of the

identity of the State – unitary versus federal – or the nature of the electoral system – majoritarian versus proportional. However, one may argue that presidentialism versus parliamentarianism is the most important issue in constitutional policy-making, reflecting to some extent the confrontation between the two historically given constitutional paths since the end of the eighteenth century.

The constitutional monarchies in Europe that survived the pressures for democracy transformed themselves into parliamentary regimes. The same may happen to the traditional monarchies that linger on outside of Europe today. The American model of a presidential republic has had an enormous attraction in constitution making all over the world. Yet, most presidential regimes have not been able to secure democracy, which makes American constitutional developments unique. Although many countries copied the American model, they failed to maintain its constitutional state characteristics.

European presidentialism must be recognized as of a special nature. It did not adhere to the American model, as it has always been combined in one form or another with a parliamentary form of government. European presidentialism involves either weak presidentialism where executive power rests with the premier, or strong presidentialism, where executive functions are exercised by both the president and the premier. The model of weak presidentialism is very close to the model of a parliamentary monarchy, but the European version of strong presidentialism is not really close to American republicanism.

The classical example of European presidentialism is France. Its 1958 constitution, including later amendments, provides for a mixture of presidentialism and parliamentarianism that is special. The presidential competencies include the following: (a) appoint the Premier and the ministers on the proposal of the Premier; (b) preside over the Council of Ministers, i.e. the government, and sign the ordinances and decrees of the government; (c) promulgate the laws coming from Parliament, which he/she may ask to reconsider; (d) submit to a referendum any bill on the proposal from the government or Parliament; (e) dissolve Parliament after consultation with the Premier; (f) make appointments to civil and military posts and accredit ambassadors and envoys; (g) be commander of the armed forces and have the right of pardon; (h) declare a state of emergency after consultation with the Premier, Parliament and the Constitutional Council (Stevens, 1992).

Besides these executive prerogatives the president is the head of state, which involves a number of ceremonial functions such as:

> The President of the Republic shall see that the Constitution is respected. He shall ensure, by his arbitration, the regular functioning of the public authorities as well as the continuity of the State. He shall be the guarantor of national independence, of the integrity of the territory, and of respect for Community agreements and for treaties (Title Two, Article 5 – see Stevens, 1992).

French presidentialism like European presidentialism in countries such as Finland and Portugal is reminiscent of American presidentialism insofar as the head of State is provided with not only ceremonial functions as in weak presidentialism but is also given important executive prerogatives. However, the head of State is not the same person who is the leader of the government, i.e. in European presidentialism there is, besides the president, a premier. Also De Gaulle's 1958 constitution comprises the institutions of parliamentarianism: 'The acts of the President ... shall be countersigned by the Premier and, should circumstances so require, by the appropriate ministers' (Article 19 – see Stevens, 1992). The premier must also have the confidence of Parliament.

The European version of strong presidentialism has built into its institutions a special tension between the head of State and the Premier which American presidentialism totally lacks. In this respect it is more in line with the constitutional developments of the first path – constitutional monarchy – than with the second path – the presidential republic. The typical feature of the constitutional monarchy is the institution of countersignature by the ministers, without which the decisions of the monarch would be invalid – the very same institution that became highly amenable to parliamentarianism, according to which the head of State always follows the advice of his government.

Thus, after having travelled along the two historical constitutional paths depicted in Table 4.1 involving the creation of hybrid forms of government we arrive at five models for executive institutions: (a) monarchy without parliamentarianism; (b) monarchy with parliamentarianism; (c) weak presidentialism or presidential parliamentarianism; (d) American presidentialism and (e) European strong presidentialism. It remains to be seen what is going to happen to model (a), whether it will survive at all by means of transformation into the form of model (b) or be replaced by a republican form of government.

Strong presidentialism creates a puzzle for constitutional research. It is true that model (d) is employed more frequently than the other two models involving a republican form of government, but it is also the case that model (d) tends to degenerate into various forms of dictatorship, or at least the regimes that harbour the American version of strong presidentialism tend to be highly unstable, with few exceptions like the United States itself and Costa Rica for instance. How come, then, that such a constitutional system is so often attempted? Why not move to some kind of parliamentary system, either weak presidentialism as in Greece, Austria and Italy or try the European version of strong presidentialism as in France, Finland and Portugal? What is the explanation for the sustained constitutional attraction of American presidentialism despite all its failures?

In *Presidents and Assemblies* (1992) M. S. Shugart and J.M. Carey defend the pure form of presidentialism with the argument that it 'offers the advantage of allowing the clearest possible choice to voters as to the constitution of the executive.' And they add: 'The checks and balances inherent in presidentialism are also desirable when majoritarian rule is opposed' (Shugart and Carey, 1992: 54). However, it still remains the case that there are two roles involved here with regard to the executive: (a) the role as umpire or the head of State; (b) the role as leader of the government or premier. The use of checks and balances in strong presidentialism typically involves creating various kinds of veto possibilities for the president and the national assembly in relation to each other. It is far from clear that such constitutional design promotes efficiency in policy-making. Actually, there may be so many veto opportunities that the basic distinction between the executive and the legislative functions become too blurred.

One observes in both the American and European versions of presidential rule a number of such institutions that marry the executive with the legislature. They can deal with legislative powers or budgetary power or they may involve the formation and dismissal of the cabinet and the dissolution of the national assembly and the proposal for a referendum (Shugart and Carey, 1992: 150). Here there is a source of institutional variation that has played a role in historical constitutions, but which also remains highly relevant today. These checks and balances may be found to varying extent in presidential systems. In legislative powers there may be either absolute power or suspensive veto, in budget-making a comprehensive veto or single item veto and a narrow or wide competence for the president to issue decrees. With regard to the appointment and dismissal of the cabinet as well as the competence to dissolve the national assembly or call a referendum there is huge institutional variation, not only among the Latin American presidential systems that are modelled after American presidentialism but also among the European strong presidential systems.

The question of the constitutional design of the executive remains highly controversial. The new democracies in Eastern Europe have either chosen weak presidentialism or the European version of strong presidentialism – both models give institutional recognition to the distinction between the umpire and the leader of the cabinet, a distinction which American presidentialism obliterates. Interestingly, the temporary new South African constitution enacted in 1994 comprises an executive where the same person is supposed to be both head of State and premier. Thus, the president in the Republic of South Africa has the executive powers of an American president but the South African president is elected by the national assembly, and needs the parliamentary confidence of the national assembly including the ministers in the cabinet. The South African president presides over the meetings of the government where the president takes decisions after consulting the ministers, who are supposed to countersign the decisions by the president. This is a unique combination in one institution of the two chief institutions for the executive today, the president and the premier, and in this case it goes back to the Boer constitution of 1983.

Conclusion

The concept of the regime as a political or legal constitution was recognized early in the history of political thought. Aristotle presented his grand scheme in his classic *Politics* and identified the importance of the constitution in the following way:

> For if a city is a community, it is a community of citizens; but if the mode of government should alter and become of another sort it would seem a necessary consequence that the city is not the same; as we regard the tragic chorus as different from the comic, though it may probably consist of the same preference. (Aristotle, Book 3, Chap 3, 1276b)

Aristotle's scheme of classifying numerous real life constitutions or *politeia* as he called them, was simple, as he combined the number of rulers with the quality of their rule as judged in terms of the concept of the public interest or moral criteria. Thus, he arrived at the classifications in Table 4.2.

Table 4.2
Aristotle's classification of regimes

	Rule of one	Rule of the few	Rule of the many
Dignified	Monarchy	Aristocracy	Polyarchy
Debased	Tyranny	Oligarchy	Democracy

The first major constitutionalist tradition, the constitutional monarchy was one such set of mechanisms that was recommended as a tool to enhance dignified rule. The second major constitutional tradition, the republic, was another such set of institutions, devised to harbour an aristocracy or a polyarchy. Both of these forms of government implied some kind of mixed government, i.e. one that would attempt to blend the three major forms. The first two model constitutions, the French from 1791 and the American from 1787, belong to these two constitutional traditions. Finally, parliamentarianism emerged in the nineteenth century as a mechanism for combining either a monarchy with an aristocracy or a democracy, where the monarch only figured as a symbolic head of State, power resting either with an oligarchy or a polyarchy, or a republic with a weak president, the exective functions resting with a Premier.

Today the major constitutional forms of government are either the strong presidential republic along the model of the USA constitution or the parliamentary form of a democracy, with either a monarch or a weak president as head of State – see *The Failure of Presidential Democracy* edited by Linz and Valenzuela (1994). European presidentialism is the very special mixture of strong presidentialism with a parliamentary regime. There are a few remaining examples of a constitutional monarchy. However, many States cannot be said to have a constitution, if one uses 'constitution' in the sense of a set of mechanisms that really restrain State power, either externally or internally.

Some States have suspended their written or formal constitution where the élite rules by means of martial law or by emergency powers. Other States employ a camouflage constitution. Finally, a few States have explicitly authoritarian constitutions which in one way or another do what a proper constitution should not do, i.e. they concentrate unlimited State power to certain organs or persons. These formally designed authoritarian constitutions introduce either a one-party State of a left-wing or right-wing version or a religiously defined state.

The basic divide today, following the constitutional paths elaborated upon in this chapter, is between two different institutions for the executive, the strong president versus the premier. Outside of European politics, this basic divide is upheld completely whereas in both Western and Eastern Europe there occurs the specific European version of strong presidentialism, namely constitutions that provide for both a strong president and a strong premier. Only in South Africa is there an institution where the president is the premier and vice versa. The problem with strong presidentialism, in either the pure American version or the mixed European alternative, is the blending of two separate roles, that of head of State as a neutral and impartial umpire and that of the premier or the politically active leader of the government or cabinet.

Since the two great revolutions in the end of the eighteenth century it has been practice for almost each and every state to have a written constitution of some sort. The concept of a constitution as a set of institutions regulating public power is to be found with Theodore Beza, who like his master Calvin, conceived of rules as mechanisms for structuring behaviour and handling needs and desires as in the latter's *Institutes of the Christian Religion* (1536). The first major treatise on political theory after the Ancient Period, *Policraticus* by John of Salisbury (1159) spoke of the difference between the prince and the tyrant thus: 'that the latter is obedient to law, and rules his people by a will that places itself at their service ...' (1995: 28). However, in order to prevent tyranny in whatever form, law may have to be **made**, namely constitutional law handing down institutional paragraphs for truly limiting the exercise of public power. Let us look more in detail at public power or public competencies.

Part III

Structures

5

The State – institutional elements

Introduction

Whenever we talk about politics the concept of the State is in the background. This is the case both when we speak of country politics and international politics. The former is focused upon the making of public decisions that are formally taken in the name of the State whereas the latter has States as the truly important actors. As a matter of fact, even when we trace the non-existence of a State in the occurrence of events such as civil war, anarchy or the establishment of war lords, then the concept of the State is in the background. We cannot do without it when we speak about politics. But how do we approach it conceptually? The purpose of this chapter is to pin down a few key properties of States. They all relate to institutions, i.e. to rules that govern the behaviour of States.

The literature on the State is huge, because political science wishes to understand how one State differs from another when moving from one country on the globe to another. There is talk about an 'Arab' State, as if it were fundamentally different from a 'Western' or 'European' State. It is argued that there exists a so-called Third World State with the implicit hypothesis that its shape has had a profound impact upon the overall social and economic predicament in such countries. Certainly, the Communist State was a special species, although it did not prove to be viable for any longer time period. If there is so much State variation, then how can we identify the common elements of all States?

In this chapter we first discuss a few salient properties that are present in all States. Then we take a look at a few general dimensions along which States may vary. Perhaps the most frequently employed paradigm for defining how States differ is the separation of powers. It may be interpreted functionally and territorially.

Elements of the State

The classical problem in the literature on the State concept is to compose a full defintion that contains the essence of the concept. A number of proposals have been suggested, but none have gained general acceptance within the community of scholars studying the State. For example we may mention: (a) sovereignty; (b) power; (c) monopoly on the legitimate use of physical violence; (d) the legal order; (e) organism; (f) the public interest; (g) reasons of State; (h) government; (i) political community; (j) nation.

Here we will not come up with another attempt at a definition. Instead we will point out a few interesting concepts in constitutional and international law that identify key properties of States. The emergence of neo-institutionalism in political science in the last decade has regenerated a tradition within political science that underlines the importance of teaching constitutional theory and law – covered well for example in George Jellinek's *Allgemeine Staatslehre* (1901) and Hans Kelsen's *Allgemeine Staatslehre* (1925). This very same title reflects the existence of an important tradition of scholarship in political science that should receive more attention. Its relevance for the new institutionalism is obvious.

The basic unit of the State is the State organ. A State organ is any person that performs a task in the name of the State. A public official, if paid by the State is a State organ of the so-called fisc. Let us quote from Kelsen:

> The organ is appointed or elected for a specific function; the performance of this function has to be his main or even legally exclusive profession; he has the right to receive a salary from the treasury of the state (Kelsen, 1961: 193).

The State disposes of its own revenues, the fiscus, which is a property of the State. The State organs constitute the machinery of the State, as it were, or the totality of all the actions performed in the name of the State. State organs may in their turn create new State organs by following specific institutions such as appointment or election. Thus, we have two fundamental elements of the State: simple and composite organs. When composite organs are connected in time, then we have a procedure. Thus, the American President would be a State organ whereas his cabinet would constitute a composite State organ. The process of legislation in the United States, involving both chambers of the Congress as well as the approval of the president with his/her suspensive veto, would on the other hand make up a State procedure. Kelsen goes on to introduce more complex properties of States that presuppose various kinds of combinations of State organs. Let us look at these State properties one by one.

Territory

Any State has a clearly delimitable space where it operates. In order to specify that area in detail it is necessary to consult international law. International law, whatever its shortcomings, may comprise rules for when an organization is to be called a 'state'. The basic institution is the control of the employment of physical force in a territory. What matters more is the *de facto* control than the *de jure* legitimacy.

Not all the surface area of the planet constitutes State territories. Very important areas are singled out as either high seas or no State's land. The oceans belong to the former set whereas the Antarctic or the North Pole are examples of the latter – see the Law of the Sea (Brownlie, 1993: 180–257). International law specifies a number of institutions that regulate open seas and no State's land which regulate or limit what actions States may take on those territories.

Time

No State exists for ever. Time is a crucial aspect of the State, because State stability and State longevity are fragile properties. States die and new States are born. Similarly, international law comprises institutions that identify the time aspect of the State. Again, the basic criterion is efficiency, or the probability that an organization can maintain law and order over a specified territory. The time and territorial aspects of a State are closely intertwined, as both derive their meaning from institutions laid down in international law.

People

One may believe that the people of the State are simply the persons that happen to stay on the State territory during one specific time period. However, things are far more complicated. Not only is there the institution of citizenship, which implies that the State implements specific rights and duties of certain people, but there is also the principle of exterritoriality, meaning that diplomats of foreign countries have immunity. Moreover, a State may take action in relation to people who stay on other territories, e.g. tax activity against its own citizens even though they reside in another State. What is excluded is a State engaging in actions involving physical violence on other States' territories.

Head of State

A State may be either monarchical or republican, depending on the institution that defines the head of State. Monarchies may be hereditary or the king, the emperor, the emir or the sheik may be elected for life-time service. Most of the monarchies that remain in the twentieth century – a period which has seen a dramatic increase in the number of republican states – are hereditary, although this does not preclude bitter rivalries as to who is the proper successor, as is often seen among the sheikdoms. It can happen that rulers declare themselves Emperor, as with Bokassa in the Central African Republic in the 1970s. Many monarchies are not real monarchies, i.e. the head of State does not govern the country, as in, for example, the Scandinavian countries, Japan and Spain. However, besides the facade monarchies there are real monarchies in a few Third World countries such as Morocco, Thailand, Jordan and the sheikdoms. The distribution of powers in the State is a complex matter, where one must separate between constitutional *formalia* and *realia*.

It may be pointed out that a republic does not have to have a president as the head of State. On the one hand, another official could be the head of State, as for example the Dodge in Venice, the Governor-general in Holland or the Führer/Duce/Caudillo in fascist regimes. On the other hand, there may be a collective presidency, where the government is the head of State, as in the Directorate during the French revolution and in Switzerland and Uruguay in modern times. In Switzerland with its limited presidentialism, the office rotates on a yearly basis among its seven-member Swiss Federal Council.

Powers

One may talk about both the powers of the State and the distribution of competencies between State organs. When considering the former aspect, one often focuses upon the rights and obligations of States and citizens versus each other. For example the constitutional protection of human rights is an important source of restriction upon the State's power if implemented by means of efficient institutions, as when ordinary or special courts are available for the filing of complaints. The special Scandinavian institution of an Ombudsman should also be mentioned in this perspective.

When considering the distribution of competencies between the organs of the State, one must distinguish between the functional interpretation and the territorial interpretation. The first involves the three categories of executive, legislative and judicial powers whereas the second covers the equally well-known categories of the unitary State versus the federal State as well as the pair of concepts of centralization versus decentralization. All of these concepts are crucial when understanding the State from a constitutional perspective. They have figured prominently within both political theory and historical political thought as well as within constitutional law and public administration. Yet, they are not clear or unambiguous.

Core ideas in constitutional law concentrate upon these two distinctions, on the one hand the functional separation of powers and on the other hand the territorial distribution of competencies. If we combine these two fundamental distinctions, then we arrive at a full scheme for the description of the power structure of the public sector with its division of executive, legislative and judicial competences between various levels of government, i.e. between the central, regional and local levels of government in a unitary State and between the federal government and the State or provincial governments in a federal State.

Whether an organization is a State depends, thus, upon the extent to which it maintains the five properties – territory, time, people, head of state, powers – specified above. There will always be marginal cases; not only do some States break down but sometimes new States emerge under circumstances when the characteristics listed above will only be more or less present. We also have a number of cases which function in a normal way, but which only satisfy the five criteria to a limited extent. Take the case of the Roman Catholic Church for instance. It has an order that it maintains all over the world, involving a distribution of powers both functionally and territorially. Admitting its power, one may still ask though whether it upholds a monopoly on the legitimate use of physical violence.

Functional separation of powers

The theory of separation of powers suggests ways to constrain State power by allocating specific competences to the main State organs at various levels of government such as the legislative assembly, the judicial bodies and the government, cabinet or administration, whatever it may be called.

Each and every written constitution employs the principle of division of powers meaning that it separates formally between the three distinct forms of State powers: (i) executive function, (ii) legislative function and (iii) judicial function. Where constitutions differ is in the allocation of these powers to the major actors in the State (Table 5.1).

Table 5.1
Functional separation of powers

State organs	Functions	Actors
Government	Executive Power	Monarch, President Premier
National assembly	Legislative Power	Elected representatives
Courts	Judicial Power	Appointed judges

Typical of the three basic State functions – legislation, execution and legal adjudication – is that it is impossible to strictly untangle them from each other. Consider the following ties:

(1) *Legislation – execution*: on the one hand it is difficult to make a sharp separation between laws and decisions meaning that there will be a struggle over what is to count as the one or the other between the national assembly and the government/administration. On the other hand, it is recognized that the legislative assembly could not possibly find time to handle all kinds of law making. Thus, most constitutions provide for the *delegation* of law making competence to the administration, in particular the making of regulations that substantiate major legislation, called variously 'ordinances', 'regulation', 'decrets-lois' or 'Verordnungen mit Gesetzeskraft'.

(2) *Execution – law adjudication*: on the one hand there are several activities that the administration engages in that are very similar to what the legal machinery does; on the other hand many countries employ a special system of administrative courts to handle

public law issues. Both these aspects tend to blur the borderline between the proper activity of the administration and the judicial State organs.

(3) *Law adjudication – legislation*: on the one hand the employment of legal review in several countries does imply that the judicial branch takes over legislative powers from the legislative branch, judge made replacing statute law; on the other hand there is a strong trend towards the introduction of more judicial review in many countries. Thus, there are now constitutional courts in several countries as well as special administrative courts.

The real allocation of powers onto the key persons and groups in the State – the State organs or the Communist Party or Rasputin fellows if power is exercised informally – may imply that one State organ such as the president or the party can control all three functions as in an authoritarian State. Or it may imply that one State organ maintains a close connection between two of the functions, as for example in parliamentarianism where the national assembly maintains a tie between the executive and legislative functions. A third possibility is that the three functions are allocated to different State organs, which cannot control each other, as in strong presidentialism.

The theory of checks and balances may be seen as an addition or almost a negation of the separation of powers theory. While the latter argues that each key State organ should have its distinct branch of government, the former claims that constitutionalism requires that special mechanisms be created that allow each State organ to keep each other in check. It was Montesquieu who argued for a pure model of the separation of powers in *The Spirit of the Laws* from 1748, while the checks-and-balances model was launched by James Madison in *The Federalist Papers* in 1787. The American constitution contains a number of such mechanisms: (a) presidential suspensive veto in legislation; (b) senate approval in the appointment of Supreme Court judges and a few other key federal offices as well as ratification of foreign treaties; (c) congressional approval of a declaration of war; (d) judicial review of federal legislation and administrative acts.

One additional device in the American model of checks and balances is the use of a federal system of government. What does federalism imply? It refers to the allocation of powers between various levels of government on a territorial basis. There are three State forms: the unitary, the federal and the confederal State forms. How do they differ from the point of constitutional law and in reality?

Territorial separation of powers

One often used classification of present day State constitutions focuses upon the distinction between a federal State and a unitary State. To that separation one would wish to add the classical conceptual pair of democracy versus dictatorship. We will deal with the institutions of democracy in Chapter 6. Here, we examine the concept of federalism.

Neither the distinction between a unitary State and a federal State or the separation between a democratic State and a dictatorship is easily made. To identify a State as a democracy is no doubt a value loaded enterprise, as many countries attempt to designate themselves as new democracies today, including the Republic of South Africa, Russia and Venezuela. One could make a distinction between stable democracies and would-be democracies, both sets counting some 30 cases.

Similarly with regard to federal States there are difficult borderline cases and various concepts may be drawn upon in order to arrive at these distinctions (Table 5.2). How are, for example, Spain and Italy to be classified? And is Austria really a federal State? Belgium has taken the step from a unitary to a federal State in 1993. Looking at constitutional law, the set of federal States is small, because one only counts the countries that call themselves 'federal'.

Table 5.2
Democracy and federalism

	Unitary State	Federal State
Democracy	UK, Scandinavia Holland, France, Greece, New Zealand, Hungary, Romania	USA, Switzerland Argentina, Brazil India, Australia, Canada, Germany,
Dictatorship	China, Zaire, Iran, Iraq, Burma, Indonesia, Peru, Haiti	Nigeria, Pakistan, United Arab Emirates,

Source: Derbyshire and Derbyshire, 1991.

As we see from Table 5.2 there are many examples of each category. The number of federal States according to strict constitutional law is small, although many of the federal States are huge States. If one equates federalism with regionalism and decentralization (Ostrom, 1991), then the federal model is much more frequent. But is federalism really the same as decentralization of State powers?

The distinction between a unitary State and a federal State may be approached in two very different ways, first from a legal point of view and secondly from a behavioural point of view. According to constitutional law, such States are federal as designate themselves as such, for example in their own constitution. Often the preamble of the constitution or its very first clauses declare the State to be a 'unitary' or 'federal' State. When it is an example of the latter, the constitution typically declares that the State is made up of States or provinces that are federated. However, is the actually employed constitutional language a true guide to the real constitution or institutional practices? Italy's constitution designates the Regions as 'autonomous bodies', but few would agree. And it has been claimed that the new South African State has a federal constitution, but the phrase 'federal' is not used.

According to the behavioural approach, legal formalism cannot be trusted. The crux of the matter is the degree of decentralization, because a distinctive feature of federalism is that power is dispersed between various levels of government defined on a territorial basis. One outspoken adherent of the behavioural approach is William Riker, who states in his *Federalism: Origin, Operation and Significance:*

> all that the principle of federalism requires is that there be a division of powers and some guarantee of the autonomy of each government in its own sphere (Riker, 1964: 11).

A major objection to Riker's defintion is that it blurs the distinction between unitary and federal States. A decentralized unitary State could most certainly satisfy the Riker criteria – for example the Nordic state with its strong commitment to local government autonomy. One must distinguish between the two conceptual pairs: federal versus unitary State on the one hand and decentralization versus centralization on the other hand. Each and every unitary State is not centralized and all federal States are not decentralized States.

One may identify a federal State with a number of characteristics which may not always go together (Wheare, 1966; King, 1982; Elazar, 1987; Elazar, 1991; Ostrom, 1991; Burgess and Gagnon,

1993). Actually when one surveys the occurrence of federal State characteristics, then one is amazed by the irregularities:

(1) *Origin*: The State may have been created by means of a federation act, in terms of which independent or semi-independent units come together and form a union. One example of this would be the 1900 Commonwealth of Australia Constitution Act, but not every federal States has been created in such a manner – consider Canada.

(2) *States as members*: A federal State consists of governmental units that are often designated as 'States', creating the typical tension between the federal State and the member States that is the core of federalism – so-called 'dual federalism'. The sub-units are not always denoted 'States', but may also be called 'provinces' as happens also in unitary States. Thus, the 1900 Australian constitution declares that the Commonwealth includes the former colonies as 'The States' (Article 6). The 1982 Canadian constitution speaks of 'provinces', as do the present Argentinian and Brazilian ones. The sub-units in unitary States are called either 'provinces' or 'regions'. The sub-units are called 'Länder' in Germany and Austria while in Switzerland they are called 'cantons'. Again, India talks about 'States' whereas Pakistan refers to 'provinces'. When Pakistan was broken up in 1971 and the new State Bangladesh was founded, that State choose a unitary framework.

(3) *A federal chamber*: A federal State has a two chamber system meaning that besides the national assembly it will also have a second chamber that is somehow connected with or represents the member States. According to some scholars federalism requires that all the States have the same representation in the federal chamber, as for instance the Senate in the United States or the Council of States in Switzerland. Yet, the construction of the second chamber varies among different federal States. German federalism gives different numbers of votes to Länder of varying sizes, while, at the same time, the Länder representatives in the Bundesrat vote in accordance with instructions from the Länder governments. The second chamber in Canada, the Senate, consisting of 104 members appointed for a life-time, is not a federal chamber at all. In Austria the Federal Council has 63 members who are elected by the provincial assemblies on a

proportional format representing the political parties.

(4) *Sub-national legislative bodies*: In a federal State the member States or provinces have legislative powers, not only executive powers. The parliaments at the State level have built up their own legal systems, involving a constitution and a supreme court. However, the extent to which States or provinces in a federal State are active varies – not only in whether they issue regulations based upon federal legislation or framework laws, but also in whether they create their own codes or systems of statutes. Clearly, one may speak of California law or Florida law, but do the Länder in Germany and Austria really have their own legal systems?

(5) *Financial powers*: The member States in a federation possess extensive rights to levy taxes of various kinds as well as to regulate the taxation powers of the lower tiers of government. Again, actual practice varies, as in some federal States most taxation is done by the central government, which then allocates grants to the provincial governments. Even in the United States massive federal government funding has weakened the fiscal powers of the States.

(6) *Constitutional court*: In a federal State there is a court of some kind that resolves conflicts between the federal government and the State governments about competences, against the background of the constitution. Typical of federal States is the problem of divided sovereignty which frequently occurs in the language of constitutional lawyers. Thus, there must be some mechanism for adjudication in conflicts about competences, which may be handled either by an ordinary court, a supreme court, or a special constitutional court. However, adjudication in conflicts about federal competences is not the same as strong judicial review (Chapter 7), i.e. a general right of courts to overturn federal legislation when it finds such unconstitutional. Strong judicial review is a prominent feature of American and German federalism, but is not allowed in Switzerland.

The crux of the matter is not only that these characteristics (1)–(6) take different forms in different federal States. When Belgium declared itself a federal State in 1993, it introduced special federal institutions with regard to both the definition of member States (language communities) and the composition of its second chamber. An important point is that unitary States may have all or some of these characteristics.

Unitary States consist not only of State regions but also of local governments of different kinds. Some unitary States have a second chamber that originates in the provincial parliaments. The extensive process of regionalization in Western Europe in the 1980s has meant that regional governments in unitary States often have legislative powers of some sort, as well as having financial powers. Whether regions and local government engage in legislation depends on what one means by 'legislation', for surely, these democratically elected bodies issue regulations and instructions? Several unitary States have a constitutional court, some of which may engage in strong judicial review. Thus, the new Czech constitution instructs the constitutional court to judge whether the central government respects the autonomy of the local governments (Article 87: 1k), which is also the case in the new Hungarian constitution (Article 43: 2).

Although unitary States typically adhere to the doctrine of the legislative supremacy of parliament, i.e. they designate the national parliament as the sole source of legislation, trusting other levels of government with administration, it is a fact that local governments in unitary States issue a large number of regulations. In unitary States, the regional or provincial governments do not have their own constitutions. Again, there are exceptions, such as Spain, Italy and France where some regions have a constitution or statutes of their own.

A distinctive feature of a unitary State, just as of a federal State, is the conflict of competences between the central government and the regions or local governments ('kommun', 'landsting', 'fylke', 'amt'). In unitary States the central government typically has agencies at the regional and local level which do coordination work outside of the framework of regional or local governments. Such regional State administrations, appointed from above, may collide with the autonomy of regional and local governments, elected from below, especially if they are explicitly instructed to supervise the activities or finances of local government units, either from a legal point of view ('Fylkesmannen' in Norway) or even more contentiously from a strictly political point of view.

The distinction between the federal and unitary State frameworks has become more and more blurred. The recent major developmental trends further erode any sharp separation between a set of federal States and a set of unitary States. Most unitary States have decentralized powers to their local governments or to regional parliaments, whereas several federal States have been centralized. Instead of dual federalism, there is intergovernmental federalism or organized complexity with reciprocities between the federal government and the States ('Politikverflechtung' by F.W. Scharpf). Instead of centralized unitary States with all powers exercised by the central government there is growing regionalization and increasing local government autonomy. A 'federal' State is perhaps only characterized by the fact that it is so designated.

Decentralization

In order to arrive at a sharp distinction between the federal State form and the unitary State form we have to resort to Weber's ideal-types construction (Weber, 1978). An ideal-type is a model that exaggerates certain features such that real-life phenomena come more or less close to the construct. A pure federal State would be one where the powers of the central government would be sharply limited as a result of a federation between States delegating certain minimum tasks to central government, with all remaining powers resting with the States. Such a sharp separation between federal exclusive powers and State or provincial residual powers is not easy to implement, partly due to the fact that it is impossible to specify once and for all the distribution of competences. The federal government is bound at one time or another to claim so-called incidental, implied, emergency or inferable powers besides enumerated powers, over which there may be conflicts of interpretation.

A pure unitary State would be one where there would be no local government tiers, or if there were governments elected from below at the regional or local level, then they would have all their powers delegated to them from the central government, which would fund and control how the local government functions were executed. France, during the period of the Napoleonic State, comes to mind as a State with the prefect system of government, but one must note that French regionalization has been substantial. Perhaps the recent developments of the Westminster State in the United Kingdom indicate a movement towards the centralization model (Jowell and Oliver, 1994).

Yet, realities do not conform to these two ideal-type constructs. One cannot take it for granted that a federal State is always less centralized than a unitary State. Actually, one of the major developments since the Second World War is the steady advance of decentralization claims and reforms within the unitary State. Some countries have undertaken extensive decentralization reforms increasing regional and local autonomy, trends that are referred to as 'regionalization'. Local government or regional government is the system of government at the regional or local level where the representatives have been directly elected in separate elections specifically to represent local or regional territorial communities.

'Decentralization' refers to the division of powers or competences between the central government on the one hand and directly elected sub-national levels of government on the other hand. The concept may be applied to both federal States and unitary States. Thus, in Table 5.3 we have tentatively placed a few democracies according to the two conceptual pairs: unitary–federal States versus centralization–decentralization. There may be disagreement with how countries are placed – the judgement about how centralized or decentralized a State is is open to various interpretations. It also depends upon the time period under consideration.

Table 5.3
State structure and division of powers

	Centralization	Decentralization
Unitary	United Kingdom	Nordic States
	Greece, Portugal	Spain, Italy
Federal	Austria	Switzerland

It is not difficult to give examples of all four possible types. It should be pointed out that scholars do not tend to agree about how various States are to be ranked in relation to the centralization–decentralization dimension. How far centralization has penetrated, for example, Germany (Hesse and Ellwein, 1992) and Australia (Lucy, 1993) is contested. The same applies to the United States (Zimmerman, 1992). There is no generally accepted scale that allows us to measure the degree of centralization or decentralization in an unambiguous fashion. If such a scale could be constructed at all, then it would have to take into account constitutional matters concerning the distribution of competences, as well as political realities relating to the amount of discretion exercised by various levels of government on different functions. Is there no easier way to measure the amount of decentralization in a political system?

One plausible approach is to look at the amount of resources that the central government allocates as a percentage of all public expenditures. Such a fiscal measure may not be totally adequate, as it is a rather simple indicator, but it is manageable. One may look at both the amount of resources that the central government raises and the amount of resources that it spends in relation to overall public sector figures. Table 5.4 gives such measures for a selection of countries.

Table 5.4
Fiscal measures of centralization: Share of central government in relation to general government in 1990

	Receipts	*Disbursements*	*Final consumption*
Austria	52.2	41.1	29.0
Belgium	62.2	52.2	65.3
Denmark	68.6	39.1	30.6
France	42.6	40.1	55.2
Germany	32.0	26.5	16.8
Greece	64.1	56.8	67.7
Ireland	82.6	62.4	50.2
Italy	72.4	48.2	54.3
The Netherlands	60.9	36.3	46.2
Spain	55.6	34.2	39.5
Sweden	52.0	41.9	27.3
Switzerland	28.5	17.0	23.0
United Kingdom	79.1	59.7	60.1
Canada	45.0	41.2	22.6
USA	42.7	41.7	43.7
Japan	44.5	24.8	24.3
Australia	73.8	56.5	31.6

Source: OECD (1992) National Accounts, vol 2.

One may note two things in Table 5.4. On the one hand, the information is not entirely consistent, as some countries score high on one fiscal indicator and low on another. On the other hand, one may observe that countries that are designated as unitary vary considerably on the indicators and that a few States designated as federal or quasi-federal are no more decentralized than some of the unitary States. Note in particular the percentages for the United States and the figures for unitary Japan as well as the high scores for federal Australia and Austria. The scores for Switzerland and Germany are truly low, while the United Kingdom and Ireland have very high percentages on all indicators.

The concept of decentralization should be separated from the concept of deconcentration. The latter refers to the transfer of powers or competences from the central government to its regional or local agencies, without involving the local government system or regional governments that derive their authority from regional or local political mandates. Concentration is the reverse trend, meaning the transfer of tasks away from regional and local agencies having their mandate from the central government to that level of government.

In the 1970s many countries initiated processes of both deconcentration and decentralization. Perhaps the most spectacular reform was the 1982 French abolition of the chief institutional symbol of the centralized unitary State, the prefects of the Napoleonic State. This reform involved first and foremost regionalization, or the transfer of functions to a system of regional parliaments allowing the expression of regional self-determination. However, developments in the United Kingdom involved the opposite trend, centralization by restricting the discretion of local government. In the Scandinavian countries there has been a great deal of both deconcentration and decentralization of competences in recent years.

The power of the central government to delegate tasks, or to instruct sub-level government units what to do and how to do it, is a contested issue in both unitary and federal States. In federalism the problem may be dealt with in two ways – either by specifying the exclusive powers of the central government, on the assumption that remaining competences rest with the States or provinces, or by specifying the powers of the States and provinces, on the assumption that central government can encroach upon those competences only under certain given conditions. In German federalism the central government, besides having exclusive competences, may engage in concurrent legislation and create framework legislation in vast areas, leaving implementation in principle to the Länder.

In a unitary system, the central government can easily transfer tasks from the central level to the regional and local level as long as it is a matter of deconcentration, but when it comes to issues of decentralization matters may be more complicated. Some unitary States have constitutional protection for the autonomy of their local governments. Certains functions or tasks are considered to belong to the local governments and the value of discretion is underlined. At the same time unitary States often employ local governments for the implementation of national policies, transferring huge block grants to pay for various programmes. Local government in a unitary State is ambivalent, as it is both an organ for self-determination and an implementation body of national policies. Perhaps the difference between a federal system and a unitary system simply boils down to the fact that in a federal system the State or provincial governments are more unambiguously the representatives of self-determination.

Confederal States and international law

The third State form, the confederated State, is often considered to be the marginal case. Firstly, there are few examples of confederated States in the real world. A confederation implies that a small collection of States set up a limited authority to which they all have to consent whenever action is to be taken and from which any State may leave, at any time, if it so wishes. The Commonwealth of Independent States (CIS) replacing the federal Soviet Union is an example of a confederation. Historically speaking, we find only a few confederations, for example the well-known Holy German Empire, which lasted exceptionally long for a confederated State, or the Hanseatic League. The State that preceeded the creation in 1787 of a federal United States of America was also a confederation as was the confederated South during the American Civil War.

Secondly, there is the theoretical argument that confederations, because they run counter to the unitary and federal frameworks, are inherently instable. Either they will be short-lived due to the danger of secession, or they will be profoundly weak due to the nullification rights of the separate States. Federal States do not accept the right to secession nor the right to nullification in order to empower the federal model and make it distinct from the confederal model. During the period up to the Civil War in the United States, a few southern States claimed such rights to nullification, interposition and secession, which were rejected by the federal government. In 1869 the Supreme Court ruled that the rebel South had in fact not discarded the federation, declaring: 'The Constitution, in all its provisions, looks to an indestructible Union, composed of indestructible States' (Fisher, 1990: 373–4).

Yet, one may look upon the confederal model from an entirely different angle. An increasing number of international regimes in the world can be interpreted as confederal States. Since the end of the Second World War there has been a virtual explosion in the number of and functions of international regimes. The most spectacular example is the European Union, which is in the process of developing towards a federal framework. The growth of international organizations is immense according to all conceivable measures (Archer, 1992). Let us mention just a few of them: ASEAN, ECLA, FOA, GATT, IEA, ILO, IMF, IWC, NATO, OAS, OECD, OPEC, UN, WHO and WEU. International law is rapidly beccomming as important as national law, as institutions laid down by, for example, the European Court of Justice of the European Union figure prominently in the legal orders of some of the European countries – see T.C. Hartley's *The Foundations of European Community Law* (1989).

The rise of the European Union presents a challenge to constitutional and administrative law: is the EU a federal or a confederal State? Actually, it is neither or both. The EU has federal characteristics but it is not yet a federal State. The differences between a confederal and a federal State involves:

(1) the decisions of the organization must be binding on all member States;
(2) there must be majority voting, meaning that no State has veto power;
(3) the decisions of the organization must concern the citizens of the member States directly;
(4) the organization must have powers to implement its decisions;
(5) it must possess its own financial resources.

The EU is federal with regard to (1)–(3) and (5) but confederal in relation to (2)–(4).

The tremendous growth in the relevance of international regimes, not only for the United Nations and its sub-organizations or for regionally created confederal customs unions and free trade areas in Europe, North America and South East Asia, but also for specific policy areas such as gas, fish and telecommunications, has the effect that the confederal model is a most important form of State today. The relevance of international law is clearly on the rise – see Ian Brownlie's *Principles of Public International Law* (1993). More and more, States enter reciprocal relationships by means of agreements setting up intergovernmental bodies. States are considered bound by bilateral and multilateral contracts, although intergovernmental agreements have to be ratified by each national assembly before such rules become laws in that country.

It is not possible to specify in an unambigous manner the contents of international law. It includes norms of various kinds such as (Brownlie, 1993: 3–31):

(1) international conventions;
(2) international custom;
(3) the general principles of law recognized by civilized States;
(4) judicial decisions and the teachings of the most highly qualified publicists of the various nations.

Among the first category, (1) international conventions, one includes so-called law-making treaties such as The Declaration of Paris on neutrality in maritime warfare from 1986, the Hague Conventions of 1899 and 1907 on the law of war and neutrality and the 1948 Genocide Convention. Moreover, here we also find the Resolutions of the United Nations General Assembly, as well as the conclusions of international conferences, fomulated in a 'Final Act'.

By the second category, (2) 'international custom', is meant a practice that is recognized among States as obligatory. Here we have a large number of institutions that govern how States interact, often laid down in statements by the International Court at The Hague. The Court employs a number of criteria in order to establish what is international custom: duration, uniformity, consistency, generality, bilateral relations and local customs.

The third category, (3) general principles of law, has a more vague content. It involves on the one hand the resort to arbitral tribunals, as well as acceptance of such very abstract norms as the principles of consent, reciprocity, equality of States, finality of awards and settlements, the legal validity of agreements, good faith, domestic jurisdiction and the freedom of the seas.

Category (4), judicial decisions, is even more questionable, as judicial decisions can only be regarded as the evidence of the existence of law. The decisions of the International Court and arbitral tribunals are only binding for the parties concerned and in respect to the particular case. Moreover, the Court does not observe a strict doctrine of precedent. The teaching of international law includes what is referred to as 'la doctrine', but it is an open question as to how specific its contents are. It covers abstract equity principles, i.e. considerations about fairness, reasonableness and the interests of humanity as well as attention to legitimate interests.

In legal theory there are two positions with regard to the relationship between the national legal order – municipal law – and international law. Dualism implies that one of the two is more fundamental than the other, either so-called municipal law or international law. Monism is the position that municipal law and international law are so strongly interconnected that it is impossible to say which one is more primary or superior. While there used to be a strong emphasis on the priority of municipal law, recent decades have witnessed a growing relevance for international law. Thus, many countries have incorporated international law documents, such as the The European Convention on Human Rights from 1950, into their legal order. If the protection of human rights in a country is not in accordance with the rulings of the European Court on Human Rights (being part of the Council of Europe), then it is often not considered to be adequate. A few countries adhere to the monist principle that international treaties are *ipso facto* part of municipal law, while most countries employ the dualist position that international agreement cannot constitute law in the country until introduced by separate municipal legislation.

Conclusion

The literature on the State is tremendous (Vincent, 1987; Dunleavy and O'Leary, 1987). This is hardly surprising since it seems to be one of the most pervasive and powerful organizations or set of institutions ever devised by mankind. In political thought the State starts to receive attention from the end of the Middle Ages and it has just increased ever since. It is actually not until after the Second World War that one may see signs of the twilight of the State. The growth in the number and powers of international regimes has had the consequence that it is hardly adequate to speak of sovereign States in the world of today, if 'sovereignty' means unlimited power. More and more public international law sets limits upon States, in particular if they enter into agreements setting up international regimes orientated towards the implementation of agreed upon rules.

The structure of the State is typically analysed by means of notions taken over from the separation of powers doctrine. One such basic distinction in State theory refers to the territorial dimension, i.e. to the concepts of unitary and federal States, which were discussed at length above. Not only is it difficult to make a sharp separation between unitary and federal States, but one may also identify cases which do not neatly fit any of the categories. Spain is a special blend, as Articles 1 and 2 of its constitution introduce, without doubt, a unitary State, but the Spanish State has a few of the federal State characteristics, in particular the system of autonomous regions as outlined in articles 140–158, including the extensive competences in article 148. It should perhaps be labelled 'semi-federal', if there were such a term in constitutional law. On the contrary, Italy may be designated 'quasi-unitary', because although its constitution lists the country as a 'republic, one and indivisible' (Article 4) it recognizes regions as 'autonomous bodies with their own powers and functions' (Article 115) and in addition attributes 'particular forms and conditions of autonomy' to certain regions such as Sicily, Sardinia, Trentino-Alto Adige, Friuli-Venezia Giulia and to Valle d'Aosta (Article 116). Both the Spanish and the Italian constitutions recognize that autonomous regions will have a special autonomy statute, resembling to some extent the fact that each separate State or Länder in a federal State has its own constitution besides the federal one.

When one takes a closer look at the fundamental building stones of the State, then one can confirm the thesis launched by the new institutionalism, viz. that institutions matter. Each and every element listed above – territory, time, people, head of State and powers/competences – derives its identity from rules that lay down rights and duties in an often complicated framework. Typically, formally written constitutions are employed to structure such institutions. Let us make a survey of the constitutions of the world today in order to pin down some major country differences.

6

Mini or maxi constitutions in the world

Introduction

When one sets out to map the constitutions of the world, then one may employ the image of a Russian doll, containing within itself a number of additional smaller Russian dolls. Each doll would be a set of institutions. The larger the formal skeleton of the constitution, the more specific institutions it contains. We are talking here about written constitutions as they are assembled in *Constitutions of the Countries of the World* (1972–), edited by Blaustein and Flanz.

Some States have formally drafted constitutional documents that are not actually employed in the real-life operations of the State. Either the constitution has been suspended in terms of an explicit decision as part of a *coup d'état* or the written constitution is simply not being implemented. Some States of the world have small compact constitutional documents whereas other States have a huge document with hundreds of articles and paragraphs. A few States have authoritarian constitutions whereas many States have democratic constitutions covering a range of institutional varieties.

In this chapter we make an overview of the constitutions of the States in the world today, trying to address questions of how constitutions differ so tremendously in shape and content. What are the pros and cons of mini and maxi constitutions? How much variation is there among democratic constitutions (Finer et al, 1995)?

Elements of written constitutions

A written constitution consists of rules for the following four objects: (a) the nature of the State; (b) the rights of individuals; (c) the powers of the State and (d) the process of changing the constitution. These are the elements of each and every written constitution. What varies are all the different institutions through which these rules are given concrete substance.

The first articles of a constitution set out what kind of state the country has, whether it is a unitary or federal State, whether it is a secularized or religiously neutral State. Then, the constitution regulates the relationship between the State and the individual, i.e. introducing human rights if any. Identifying the basic powers of the State is the next part of the constitution: executive, legislative and judicial powers. At the same time an equally important task is to outline how these powers are to be distributed onto the chief players, the occupants of the State organs. Finally, there are the rules for changing the constitutions, which may introduce a degree of constitutional inertia, protecting the constitution against sudden changes.

A written constitution is a set of institutions that regulate the external powers of the State in relation to society as well as allocate the internal state powers to the key political actors. Constitutions empower State organs to do certain things by means of its three state powers – executive, legislative and judicial powers. Moreover, constitutions allocate these competences to the political players by means of rules for their interaction. The key political players include the following persons: (a) the citizens; (b) the representatives of the people in parliament; (c) the members of the cabinet or government; (d) the head of state; (e) the judges who make up the judicial system.

However different constitutions may be, they outline institutions for the allocation of executive, legislative and judicial powers onto the persons that are State organs. The two crucial problems in writing a constitution involve: external State powers or the delineation of the overall powers of the State in relation to the individual; internal State powers or the allocation of State powers between the major players with regard to executive, legislative and judicial powers. Constitutional variation reflects to a considerable extent the choices made in relation to the structuring of the external and internal powers of the State. Authoritarian constitutions differ mainly from democratic constitutions along these two dimensions as do various democratic constitutions from each other.

It is true though that written constitutions may also differ with regard to the institutions for the identification of the State and the institutions that govern how constitutions may be changed. Yet, these different rules, however important they may be, do not differentiate between authoritarian and democratic constitutions, nor do they identify special democratic constitutions.

Written constitutions identify the nature of the State by indicating whether the State is a unitary State or a federal State. The difference in wording becomes significant when we contrast a few federal (F) constitutions with some unitary (U) ones. Look first at the following federal ones:

(F1) We the People of the United States, in Order to form a more per- fect Union, establish Justice, insure domestic Tranquillity, provide for the common defence, promote the general Welfare, and secure the Blessings of Liberty to ourselves and our Posterity, do ordain and estab- lish this Constitution for the United States of America (Preamble).

(F2) ... the German people in the Länder Baden, Bavaria, Bremen, Hamburg, Hesse, Lower Saxony, North-Rhine-Westphalia, Rhineland- Palatinate, Schleswig-Holstein, Würtenberg-Baden, and Würtenberg- Hohenzollern, has, by virtue of its constituent power, enacted this Basic Law of the Federal Republic of Germany ... (Preamble).

(F3) Belgium is a federal State, composed of communities and regions (1994: Article 1).

(F4) It is the will of the Mexican people to organize themselves into a federal, democratic, representative Republic composed of free and sov- ereign States in all that concerns their internal government but united in a Federation established according to the principles of this funda- mental law (1988: Article 40).

(F5) The Federative Republic of Brazil, formed by the indissolvable union of the States and Municipalities and the Federal District, is con- stituted as a democratic state of law upon the following premises ... (1988: Article 1).

(F6) India, that is Bharat, shall be a Union of States (1949: Article 1).

Here, either the act of federation is referred to or the outcome of such a process is mentioned, i.e. a union or federated State. The building blocks of federal States are not simply the people of the country but there is also mention of regional units, coming together in a state. In many federal constitutions these regions are listed by name. Such wordings are almost completely lacking in unitary State constitutions. See the following unitary ones:

(U1) France shall be a Republic, indivisible, secular, democratic, and social (1946: Article 1).

(U2) Romania is a sovereign, independent, unitary and indivisible National State (1991: Article 1).

(U3) The Czech Republic is a sovereign, unified and democratic law-observing state, based on the respect for the rights and freedom of the individual and citizen (1992: Article 1).

(U4) Ecuador is a sovereign, independent, democratic and unitary State (1978: Article 1).

(U5) Gabon is an indivisible, secular, democratic and social Republic (1991: Article 2).

(U6) Bangladesh is a unitary, independent, sovereign Republic to be known as the People's Republic of Bangladesh (1993: Article 1).

(U7) The Indonesian state shall be unitarian and with a republican form of government (1959: Article 1).

Here, the emphasis is upon the words 'indivisible', 'unified' and 'sovereignty'. Although the use of key terms is not always consistent, one can tell a federal constitution from a unitary one simply by looking at the way the nature of the State is identified in the preamble or in the first articles of the constitution. Thus, it has been discussed whether the new constitution of the Republic of South Africa harbours a federal or unitary State. Look at the first article in this provisional constitution, to be finalized at a later date:

1. (1) The Republic of South Africa shall be one, sovereign state. (2) The national territory of the Republic shall comprise the areas defined in Part 1 of Schedule 1.

Now, these words do not enter the federal language. The Republic of South Africa is a unitary State, according to constitutional language. However, whether it is a centralized or decentralized unitary State or even some kind of semi-federal State is an altogether different question. One cannot equate a federal State with decentralization and a unitary State with centralization, as was argued in Chapter 5. It may well happen that the final constitution of South Africa will be a federal one, but then the provinces of the country must be spoken of in another way in Article 1. The Nigerian constitution is special in the way that it mixes languages, employing both federal words and unitary ones:

Nigeria is one indivisible and indissolvable Sovereign State to be known by the name of the Federal Republic of Nigeria. Nigeria shall be a Federation consisting of States and a Federal Capital Territory (1979: Article 2).

Written constitutions lay down a specific process for the change of the constitution, the more specific the rules the greater the incidence of constitutional inertia. If constitutional law is considered as a special kind of law, then the constitution will contain rules that require a special decision process for amending the constitution. The amount of constitutional inertia entrenched in the constitution reflects the weight given to constitutionalism, or the belief that the State needs to be governed by a superior law that cannot be changed as easily as ordinary law.

Institutions guaranteeing constitutional inertia involve at least six types: (a) no change; (b) referendum; (c) delay; (d) confirmation by a second decision; (e) qualified majorities and (f) confirmation by sub-national government. Many countries employ a few of these mechanisms in various combinations.

A constitution could lay down certain articles that it may consider unalterable. Thus, the 1949 German constitution rules that

> An amendment to this Basic Law affecting the organization of the Federation into Länder, the basic participation of the Länder in legislation, or the basic principles laid down in Articles 1 and 20, is inadmissible (Article 79: 3).

The German constitution not only requires a two-thirds majority in both the Bundestag (lower chamber) and the Bundesrat (federal chamber), but it explicitly rules out certain changes in the constitution. More specifically, it gives to certain rules about basic rights, a democratic regime and the federal nature of the State eternal constitutional protection. How long such strong constitutional protection may last depends though upon political realities. Incidentally, the Portuguese constitution contains such no change provisions.

Such no-change rules are not frequent, because it is not considered advantageous to bind the State too closely to already existing constitutional rules. There must be constitutional flexibility. Constitutional inertia is more frequently achieved by means of rules about a second confirmation. Thus, for example, the Italian constitution requires two positive decisions within both chambers of the national asssembly within three months. And the Swedish constitution stipulates that constitutional change needs two positive decisions by two Parliaments, where there has been ordinary elections to Parliament in between the decisions. The Norwegian constitution only requires delay, i.e. that a proposal concerning a change of the constitution can only be decided after a new Parliament has been elected through ordinary elections every fourth year, but there must also be a qualified majority of two-thirds.

Actually, the requirement of a voting majority on a decision ruling to be larger than a simple majority is frequent when it comes to constitutional decisions. In France there is requirement of a majority of 60 per cent in both chambers of the national assembly, or a simple majority decision in each chamber combined with a referendum. The Portuguese constitution stipulates a two-thirds majority, which is also the case in Finland. However, the Finnish constitution requires both delay and confirmation: the first positive simple majority decision has to be confirmed by Parliament by a second positive two-thirds majority decision, with elections having taken place in between, or, if there is no time for such a long process of constitutional change, then one five-sixths majority decision in Parliament is enough.

Similarly rather complicated schemes can be found in the Netherlands and Belgium. The Dutch constitution involves both delay, confirmation and a qualified majority vote: first a positive majority decision in both chambers of the Staaten-Generaal is required, after which there will be a dissolution of Parliament with elections, whereupon there has to be a second positive decision taken with a two-thirds majority. In the former Belgian constitution there first had to be a decision that a constitutional revision was needed, then Parliament would be dissolved after which new constitutional provisions could be enacted with a two-thirds majority. In the new federal constitution in Belgium the same procedure is employed.

Perhaps the most complicated scheme resulting in high constitutional inertia is to be found in the American constitution, where there are both qualified majority requirements, confirmation and outside involvement. First, there must be a positive decision about constitutional change in both the Senate and the House of Representatives with a two-thirds majority or a single majority decision in two-thirds of the legislatures of the States and then there has to be a second confirmatory single majority decision by three-quarters of the legislatures of the States or a constitutional convention in the States. Thus far, 26 amendments have been made to the constitution of the United States, which is not many given the fact that the constitution has been in place for so many years. However, several of the amendments have been very important in shaping the politics of that country.

Another type of constitutional inertia derives from the use of the referendum mechanism for constitutional changes. Obligatory referenda may be combined with the other institutions of delay, confirmation and qualified majority voting. In the Swiss, Austrian and Irish constitutions any constitutional change requires an obligatory refeceredum, in which a simple majority is enough. The Danish constitution outlines a process of constitutional revision that is truly complicated: first a positive decision in Parliament, then dissolution of Parliament and an election to Parliament, then a new positive decision by Parliament and finally confirmation by a referendum where there has to be at least 40 per cent of votes for the decision among all those elegible to vote, besides of course that **yes** must defeat **no**.

One may find similar variations in the institutions of constitutional revision outside of the West European framework, with its strong constitutionalist tradition. Thus, in the new Eastern European constitutions one finds a variety of provisions. The Czech Republic with its rules about a three-fifths majority in the lower chamber and three-fifths of the senate and the Slovak Republic with a three-fifths majority of the national assembly are rather uncomplicated. However the Romanian constitution with a two-thirds majority decision in the lower chamber and the senate, to be confirmed by a referendum within 30 days is more complex, especially as there is a no-change area relating to the unitary and republican form of the Romanian State. Yet, in the Bulgarian constitution amending or adopting a new constitution requires a highly elaborate change processes. The standard case is that amendments need a three-quarters majority in the national assembly in three ballots on three different days, but there are more complex ways to change the constitution. In relation to certain crucial articles in the constitution there has to be a special Grand National Assembly, elected specifically for the purpose of deciding upon constitutional amendments, and it has to come up with a two-thirds majority in three ballots on three different days.

Constitutional inertia takes different forms in various country constitutions. The argument for constitutional inertia is often considered so obvious that it is hardly reflected upon. The pros of constitutional inertia are that certain laws are singled out as being of special importance, their existence guaranteed by special procedures for changing or amending the constitution. This is the *lex superior* argument, which one often finds in constitutionalism. However, the question is whether inertia is really part of the core of the constitutional state. The cons of constitutional inertia are that it comes into conflict with two other valid principles, on the one hand democracy as the sovereignty of the people and on the other the doctrine of parliamentary sovereignty. Why should a sovereign legislature or a sovereign people choose to restrict its power to make and change constitutions in accordance with the will of the majority? Constitutional inertia may be employed by minorities to protect their vested interests. Here we have a conflict of principles, constitutionalism colliding with democracy interpreted as simple majority rule or the sovereignty of parliament.

In British constitutionalism there is little understanding for constitutional inertia. Parliament today cannot bind Parliament tomorrow. It is up to Parliament to change constitutional practice in the United Kingdom by its unlimited power to enact statutes, if Parliament so wishes. If Parliament has legislative supremacy anyway, why enact a written constitution with rules concerning constitutional inertia that Parliament can choose to sidestep? British constitutionalism is as a matter of fact rather plastic, although the standard conception of British constitutional practice is of a rigid allegiance to a large set of established customs and conventions – see Rodney Brazier's *Constitutional Texts* (1990). In *The Changing Constitution* (Jowell and Oliver, 1994) it is shown that constitutional practice has changed substantially during the last ten to fifteen years and that the Parliament increasingly has to cope with the introduction into UK law of legislation and precedents from the European Union, weakening the doctrine of legislative supremacy in the Westminster model of government.

What are authoritarian constitutions like?

Can we speak of dictatorial or absolutist constitutions? How do we classify the few cases of sultanistic or personalistic rule that the world has seen since 1945 in Africa: Amin (Uganda), Bokassa (Central African Republique), Nguema (Equatorial Guinea), Mobutu (Zaire), Eyadema (Togo) and Banda (Malawi)? Did dictatorships like those in Latin America have constitutions: Papa Doc Duvalier

(Haiti), Casto (Cuba) and Pinochet (Chile)? Authoritarian rule is prevalent in Asia. Were the rule of the following dictators based upon a constitution: Saddam Hussein (Iraq), Ayub Khan and Zia-ul-Haq (Pakistan), Mujibur Rhaman (Bangladesh), Mao-Zedong (China), Chiang-Kai-Shek (Taiwan), Suharto (Indonesia), Syngman Rhee and Park Chung-Hee (South Korea) and Marcos (the Philippines)?

If the word 'constitution' means simply a set of institutions governing the major political players, then all States have a constitution. The real constitution may be very far off from the written formal constitution, but no rule can do without institutions. Typical of Communist states is the huge distance between the *de jure* constitution and the *de facto* constitution. Thus, the various constitutions in the Soviet Union (the 1936 and 1977 USSR constitutions) and China (the 1954 and 1982 Chinese constitutions) all underline individual rights and due process of law, political expression and privacy, at the same time as they contained a clause about the leading role of the Communist Party. Typical of Communist constitutionalism is the dualism between the formal State framework and the party's real political grip as well as the parallelism between the State and the party, meaning that the structure of the party mirrored that of the State.

A State without a set of institutions governing the three State powers – executive, legislative and judicial powers – would be so instable that it could not survive for a substantial period of time. Even in extreme authoritarian states like in Hitler's Germany and Stalin's Soviet Union there were operating institutions, although they were sometimes overriden by the whims of the dictator. In the Soviet Union the institutionalization of the control of the Communist Party over the State stabilized the unpredictability of totalitarianism, whereas in Germany the established institutions such as the bureaucracy and the army dampened the erratic decision-making of the Führer.

Actually, in every State there is a gulf between the codified constitution and the real constitution. No State lives to 100 per cent in accordance with its written documents. Customary law plays a major role in every State constitution of the world. This is true of democratic countries, especially if their constitutions are old, which would make several of their articles obsolete. How large the gulf is has a profound impact upon the legitimacy of the state.

However, in dictatorships and authoritarian States there is typically a tremendous distance between the formal constitution and the real constitution. Often such States enact one constitutional document which, however, has no connection whatsoever to institutional practices in the country. It is only a camouflage constitution.

If we mean by a 'constitution' a set of institutions that somehow restrict State powers, either by limiting the overall power of the State or providing for a true separation of powers between independent State organs, then authoritarian States cannot have a constitution. Such regimes, if driven to extreme power concentration in the hands of a single ruler, a single party or a military junta, can only have camouflage constitutions, which they typically have suspended, explicitly or implicitly.

Not all those countries that do not have a democratic regime have camouflage constitutions, but it is just as important to note that not all democracies have written, codified constitutions. There exist written authoritarian constitutions which attempt to legitimize dictatorial rule. Thus, not all dictatorships are based upon naked power in the form of martial law or emergency powers. Among the written authoritarian constitutions one may distinguish between the following types: (a) Monarchical constitutions; (b) one-party State constitutions and (c) revolutionary or religious constitutions.

A number of States which have real monarchical rule or a strong presidential non-democratic rule have constitutions that legalize such institutional practices: the 1969 Bhutan constitution providing for a 'democratic monarchy', the 1959 Brunei constitution (partly suspended), the 1951 Jordan constitution (partly suspended), the 1961 Kuwait constitution (partly suspended), the 1980 Morocco constitution, the 1951 and 1962 Nepal constitutions (abolished 1990), the 1991 Thailand constitution and the 1875 Tonga constitution.

The real monarchical constitutions in the world today often employ a language that reminds one of the constitutional monarchies in Europe in the nineteenth century. The Jordanian constitution sounds constitutionalist:

> The Hashemite Kingdom of Jordan is an independent Arab State. It is indivisible and no part of it can be ceded. The people of Jordan form part of the Arab nation. The form of government shall be parliamentary with hereditary monarchy (1984: Article 1).

The Jordanian constitution really outlines institutions that belong to parliamentarianism. Thus, we have:

> The King shall exercise the powers vested in him by Royal Decrees. Any such Decree shall be signed by the Prime Minister or the Ministers concerned (1984: Article 40).

Moreover, there is not only the institution of ministerial countersignature, but there is also the rule about parliamentary confidence:

> The Prime Minister and Ministers shall be collectively responsible before the House of Deputies in respect of the general practice of the State (1984: Article 51).

Real constitutional practice in Jordan differs from ordinary parliamentarianism, as the King exercises far more power than is typical of European parliamentarianism.

The monarchical constitutions of Bahrain and Kuwait differ from the constitutionalist ring of the Jordanian one, as their formal constitutions legitimate more or less dictatorial rule, albeit in a contradictory fashion. The 1973 Bahrain constitution starts out by declaring:

> The system of government in Bahrain is democratic, under which sovereignty lies with the people, the source of all powers (1973: Article 1).

To the principle of popular sovereignty the constitution adds talk about the separation of powers:

> The system of government shall be based on the principle of separation of the legislative, executive and judicial powers (Article 32.a).

However, the gist of Arab monarchical rule becomes clear in the following clause:

> Legislative power shall be vested in the Amir and the National Assembly in accordance with the Constitution and the Executive power shall be vested in the Amir, the Cabinet and Ministers. Judicial decrees shall be passed in the name of the Amir, all in accordance with the Constitution (Article 32.b).

Furthermore, Articles 33 to 40 specify the Arab institution of the Amir with competences that cannot be defended on the basis of Montesquieu's separation of powers doctrine. The same steps to legitimate monarchical autocracy are used in the Kuwait constitution.

In the Islamic world constitutions with a strong religious flavour are put into practice, restricting both democracy and constitutionalism. What is referred to as 'shar' or 'shariah' constitutes Muslim law, and comprises the duties and rights of a Muslim, derived from the following four sources: (a) the Koran; (b) the Sunna or the traditional behaviour of the Prophet; (c) the ijma which is the consensus of the Muslim community; (d) the kiyas or the juristic reasoning by analogy (David and Brierley, 1985: 457). As substantial parts of the Shariah or Islamic law were laid down during the second and third centuries of the Muslim era, i.e. the eighth and ninth centuries, the constitutional implication of the Shariah is rigidity, although there remains scope for variation in interpretation. Since Shariah does not say much about constitutional matters, it allows for a certain amount of malleability.

In Saudi Arabia for example the constitution is derived from Shariah law legitimating monarchical autocracy. Yet, in no other country is religion so dominating a force in constitutional matters as in Iran after the Khomeini revolution. The 1979 Iran constitution provides supreme power to the Spiritual Leader while there is also a popularly elected president who appoints the ministers. Article 110 enumerates the prerogatives of the leader:

(1) delineate the systematic policies of the Islamic Republic of Iran;
(2) supervise the efficient execution of such policies;
(3) issue decrees for national refendums;
(4) assume leadership of all the armed forces;
(5) declare war or peace;
(6) appoint and dismiss members of the Council of Guardians, highest ranking official of the judicial branch, president of the radio and television network, joint chief of staff; commander of Revolutionary Guards and military and law enforcement forces;
(7) resolve the differences and harmonize relations among the three branches of government;
(8) resolve extraordinary and unconventional problems;
(9) confirm the appointment of the President after election by the people;
(10) dismiss the President;
(11) pardon or commute the sentences of the convicted.

Besides introducing a Leader institution which is exceptional in constitutional history, this constitution also specifies the criteria that are to be employed when a person is designated the Leader. The criteria involve the principles of Islamic Fundamentalism:

The qualifications and attributes of the Leader are: (1) Scholastic competence, in order to deliver formal decrees in matters related to questions of theology. (2) Justice and piety necessary for leading the Moslem Ummah. (3) Correct political and social insight, resourcefulness, courage, administrative capability, and sufficient strength for assuming leadership (Article 109).

The 1973 Pakistan constitution with its 1986 amendments identifies the Koran and the Sunna as the foundations of State law though it is true that it contains democratic institutions. The 1971 Egyptian constitution claims that the country is a part of the Arab nation with Islam as State religion but the State is 'an Arab Republic with a democratic, socialist system'. Yet, in some of the Islam countries there is dictatorship with a camouflage constitution, such as in Indonesia, or with a total suspension of the constitution under martial law, as in Bangladesh, where the 1991 constitution reintroduced the 1972 one. Yet, some of the Arab constitutions differ extensively from Western constitutional language, which is also true of the Marxist-Leninist constitutions.

Left-wing authoritarian rule often employs constitutions where power is confined to the leading party, such as in the 1973 Syrian constitution which singled out the Arab Socialist Renaissance Party (Baath), or as in the 1980 Vietnam constitution which declared the State as a proletarian dictatorship in the Marxist-Leninist spirit, or as in the 1975 constitution for Madagascar which only accepted the National Front for the Defence of the Revolution as the legal party, having the task of 'guiding the revolution and inspiring the actions of the State', or finally as in Cuba where the 1976 constitution declared that the working people wield political power through legislative and politico-administrative assemblies in alliance with the peasants through the Communist Party, which is the only party in the country adhering to Marxism-Leninism as state ideology.

Perhaps the most odd Marxist-Leninist constitution is the Socialist Constitution of the Democratic People's Republic of Korea. In the version issued in 1991 it lists a number of articles that expresses Marxist ideology with almost no connection to prevailing principles in constitutional law. Thus, we have:

The Democratic People's Republic of Korea is a revolutionary State power which has inherited the brilliant traditions formed during the glorious revolutionary struggle against the imperialist aggressors and for the liberation of the homeland and the freedom and well-being of the people (Article 3),

Yet, the constitution is more down to earth when it comes to specifying where power is placed in the State:

All State organs in the Democratic People's Republic of Korea are formed and run in accordance with the principle of democratic centralism (Article 9).

Left-wing authoritarian regimes need not embrace all the features of a Marxist-Leninist constitution, as for example party-state parallelism or democratic centralism. It is sufficient to have a rule that introduces the one-party state. Look at Tanzania:

(1) The Union Republic is a democratic and socialist nation with one political party. (2) The party exercises Executive powers over all matters in accordance with this Constitution and the Constitution of the Party. (3) The Revolutionary Party, in short 'CMM', is the only political party in the United Republic (1986: Article 3).

At the same time one must remember that such a one-party institution has often also been used in right-wing authoritarian regimes. Take the example of Kenya:

There shall be in Kenya only one political party, the Kenyan African National Union (1988: Article 2a).

Right-wing authoritarian regimes tend to employ more of camouflage constitutions or they simply suspend the existing constitution ruling with martial law. The constitutional developments in Pakistan, South Korea and Nigeria involve a series of new constitutions, *coup d'états* and declarations of martial law or a state of emergency. In Argentina the basic constitutional framework remains the 1853 constitution as amended up to 1898, although the country has experienced military rule for several years. In Brazil, on the contrary, the unstable political climate is reflected in the introduction of no less than eight constitutions since the country's independence from Portugal in 1822, the present constitution dating from 1988. The Republic of South Africa did not employ a camouflage constitution, as its 1983 constitution explictly endorsed apartheid.

Due to the relevance of constitutionalism there are limits upon how authoritarian or absolutist regimes may attempt to legalize their rule in terms of a written constitution. A formal constitution can only confer legitimacy upon political authority, if it, at least to some extent, is in agreement with basic constitutionalist ideas. When the real constitution diverges strongly from constitutionalist notions about human rights and separation of powers, then it may be more effective simply to rule the country without a formal constitution or suspending the existing one. As a matter of fact, left-wing authoritarian regimes have been more prone to try to legitimize their dictatorial rule in formal constitutional documents than right-wing authoritarian regimes, in particular military regimes who often promise a return to civilian rule in the future, restoring the original constitution.

The importance of the written constitution may be seen not only in the *formalia* that surrounds a constitution, but also in how it actually works in the politics of a country. There are two possibilities: either the constitution effectively binds the political players restricting both state powers and the powers of the different State organs, or the constitution does not bind. Even in the latter case, a written constitution may play a profound role, as the examples of Thailand and Indonesia testify.

The political struggle in Thailand has very much focused upon the written constitution(s). From 1932 to 1987, Thailand experienced 13 constitutions, 13 general elections, 16 *coups*, of which 9 were successful, and 43 cabinets (Samudavanija, 1989: 320). The country experts classify these constitutions thus: 'Out of 13 constitutions, only 3 can be classified as "democratic" while 6 have been "semidemocratic" and 4 have been "nondemocratic" ' (Samudavanija, 1989: 321). Indonesia, on the other hand, experienced only one formal constitution – the democratic 1945 constitution which was implemented continuously except between 1950–57. Instead, the real constitution has been either martial law (1957–59) or various regimes called 'guided democracy' (1959–66), 'Early New Order' (1966–73) and 'Late New Order' (1974-87) under first the Sukarno and then the Soeharto dictatorships (Sundhaussen, 1989: 453).

When the written constitution is out of tune with the real one, then one constitutional strategy is to rewrite the constitution until it matches the realities, while another constitutional strategy is to bypass the written one for as long as possible. Thailand has engaged heavily in constitutional politics:

> In Thailand a constitution does not normally provide for the general
> and neutral rules of the game to regulate participation and competition

between political groups. On the contrary, it has been used as a major tool in maintaining the power of the grip that created it (Samudavanija, 1989: 320).

We are back to the problem of what a constitution really is. Can constitutions be employed to legitimate authoritarian rule?

Human rights

If stating principles for the separation of powers between State organs and political players is the first chief task of a constitution, then the second – and equally important – task of a constitution is to lay down limits on the exercise of overall State powers in relation to individual citizens. This second chief task, according to constitutionalism, deals not with the internal structure of the State but with its external relationships, in particular with regard to the individual and his/her rights and duties. We have here the standard concept in modern constitutionalism of fundamental human rights. However, it is a complex concept with several ingredients that may be unpacked into different rights, exemplified in the following paragraphs with reference to the new constitutions in Eastern Europe.

Talking about human rights one may start with the due process rights. The kind of individual rights that originate in the famous English Habeas Corpus Act of 1679 include institutions that protect the individual against arbitrary arrest, detention and prosecution. Thus, we find in the Czech constitution: every citizen may do whatever is not forbidden by law, and no one may be forced to do what the law does not conjoin (Article 2, paragraph 4). And the Hungarian constitution states: persons suspected of the perpetration of a criminal offence and detained, must be released or brought before a judge as soon as possible. The judge is bound to give a hearing to the person brought before him, and must produce a written decision adducing his reasons for setting the detained free or keeping him in custody (Article 55, paragraph 2).

Such protection under the law may be enlarged by providing free legal services such as the right of an attorney. Closely related are rights that a convicted persons may enjoy. Consult the Romanian constitution: (1) The right to life, as well as the right to physical and mental integrity of a person are guaranteed. (2) No one may be subjected to torture or any kind of inhuman or degrading punishment or treatment. (3) The death penalty is prohibited (Chapter 2, Article 22).

Political rights have always been considered important when human rights are discussed. Here we include the exercise of certain freedoms that are closely connected with political activity such as the right to vote, to freedom of thought, religion, association and the freedom of the press. The Czech constitution contains: (1) Every person shall have the right to associate freely with other persons to protect their economic and social interests. (2) Trade unions shall be independent of the State. (4) The right to strike shall be guaranteed. And the Romanian constitution stipulates: Citizens may freely associate into political parties, trade unions and other form of association (Article 37, paragraph 1).

Economic rights are much more controversial than political rights in the human rights framework. They include both the right to private property and the rights of employees to, for instance, employment and influence in working life. The Slovak constitution lays down that: everyone has the right to own property. The property rights of all owners shall be uniformly construed and equally protected by law. The right of inheritance is guaranteed (Article 20, paragraph 1). The Hungarian constitution says: (1) Hungary has a market economy in which public and private property are to receive equal consideration and protection under the law. (2) The Republic of Hungary recognizes and supports the right to enterprise and the freedom of economic competition (Article 14). And the Romanian constitution: (3) No one may be expropriated, except on grounds of public utility, established according to the law, against just compensation paid in advance (Article 41.3). Property is not always considered part of the human rights framework, because it may come into conflict with social rights.

Under social rights we include a number of obligations that may be laid down upon the State such as providing education, health care and housing to the population. The Slovak constitution says: (3) Citizens shall have the right to work. The state shall guarantee, within reasonable limits, the material welfare of those who cannot enjoy this right through no fault of their own (Article 35). The Romanian constitution stipulates: (1) The state shall be bound to take measures of economic development and social protection, of a nature to ensure a decent living standard for its citizens. (2) Citizens have the right to pensions, paid maternity leave, medical care in public health establishments, unemployment benefits, and other forms of social care, as provided by law (Article 43). And the Bulgarian constitution declares: (1) Citizens have the right to work. The state shall take care to provide conditions for the exercising of this right. (Article 48).

While due process rights and the political rights are relatively easy to police and implement in court, the economic and social rights are far more slippery. How much shall the State do to promote full employment, universal health care and free education? While private property rights used to be highly contested, it is now widely accepted that the State has the right to expropriate property when necessary (the eminent domain principle). What is still open to debate is the level of remuneration that the State should pay.

There are conflicts between these various individual rights towards the State. Thus, comprehensive rights for employees such as a minimum wage and the regulation of working conditions may come into conflict with private property rights. How central are economic and social rights in modern constitutionalism? Connecting constitutionalism with democracy it seems difficult to do away with political rights in both, but how about a number of the economic and social rights?

Another difficult area concerns minority rights. By this we mean not the institution that guarantees that everyone is equal under the law, but that minority groups in the country have special rights. Thus we have, on the one hand, in the Romanian constitution: All citizens enjoy the rights and freedoms granted to them by the Constitution and other laws, and have the duties laid down thereby (Article 15.1.). (1) Citizens are equal before the law and public authorities, without any priviledge or discrimination. (2) No one is above the law (Article 16). On the other hand, we have in the same Romanian constitution: (1) The State recognizes and guarantees the right of persons belonging to the national minorities, to the preservation, development and expression of their ethnic, cultural, linguistic and religious identity (Article 6). And the Slovak constitution says: Protection measures...(a) right to be educated in minority language, right to use minority language in official communications, right to participate in decision-making in matters affecting the national minorities and ethnic groups ... (Article 33, paragraph 2).

How the rights of minorities are to be balanced against the principle of majority rule in democracy comprises one of the most difficult problems in modern constitutionalism. Are individual human rights not sufficient? Should there also be group rights? In any case, without a legal machinery for the interpretation and implementation of human rights (of whatever content they have), no sharp border-lines between the State and the individual have been drawn. Such legal protection may be institutionalized in different ways, either in terms of weak judicial review or strong judicial review – see Chapter 7. How can the relations between the three branches of government be structured from a constitutional point of view?

Separation of powers

Although many constitutions employ the language of the separation of powers doctrine, few now follow Montesquieu's original model. As noted in Chapter 2 Montesquieu did not outline any institutional mechanisms by which the State organs could keep each other in check. The executive function is to be vested in some kind of government, monarchical or republican; the legislative function is to be handled by the national assembly and the courts will deal with the judicial function. However, Montesquieu was explicitly against any mechanisms that would allow each State organ to meddle with the others' functions. The theory that, in addition to the separation of powers, constitutionalism also requires an explicitly drawn up system of checks and balances between the major political players – the king, the president or the cabinet, the national assembly or Parliament and the judges – was launched by James Madison when drawing up the American constitution in 1987, as outlined in *The Federalist Papers* (Hamilton et al, 1961).

So although Montesquieu advocated separating the allocation of State powers, he did not take the next step and make the doctrine of judicial review a part of his model. Judicial review entails the courts having a form of veto in relation to laws made by the national assembly and decisions and directives taken by the government. And Montesquieu certainly did not adhere to the doctrine of parliamentarianism, according to which the national assembly not only exercises the legislative powers but also controls access to the executive powers. It was not until Walter Bagehot in his *The English Constitution* in 1867 presented a coherent argument for parliamentarianism as a constitutional framework that it was clearly identified as an alternative to the Montesquieu framework.

A full scale separation of powers model is only to be found in countries where the constitution clearly separates the three state powers from each other: executive, legislative and judicial powers. However, this is not the case in countries where the constitution contains some kind of parliamentarianism connecting the executive with the legislature or where there is a constitutional court that can engage in judicial review, connecting the judiciary with the legislature. Actually, complete separation of powers is only to be found in constitutions with a presidential system of government where there is at the same time no judicial review, as for example in Argentina and Brazil or in a constitutional monarchy where the king still has executive powers.

Judicial review has become increasingly popular. Several constitutions today provide for some kind of constitutional court that has the task of reviewing whether laws or decisions are in accordance with the constitution. What differs from one country to another is the scope of the judicial review as well as the specific institutions that handle judicial review. Of equal importance is the set of institutions that govern the allocation of executive powers to the monarch, the president or the premier.

Note that presidential constitutions are not the only non-parliamentary regimes and that some parliamentary regimes include a weak president as the head of state. Traditional rule as exercised in a few countries with kings or sheiks (Amir) is an example of a non-parliamentary constitution. Strong presidential constitutions may be either democratic or non-democratic. Monarchical as well as presidential rule may be either restricted, a constitutional monarchy or a constitutional presidency, or absolutist as in sultanistic and patrimonial rule or as in authoritarian regimes. When a State practises parliamentarianism and the head of State is a president, then we have weak presidentialism. When a president is the head of State and also exercises real State power, then there is strong presidentialism, which need not be constitutional or limited in scope.

One may argue that the separation of powers doctrine tends to be invaded from various corners. On the one hand, there is parliamentarianism that ties the executive to the legislature. On the other hand, there is strong judicial review which bends the legislature to the judiciary. Finally, there is the checks and balances doctrine that connects all three branches or functions of government with each other, creating countervailing powers as it were.

The difficulties in implementing a pure separation of powers model is further augmented by the tendency of such constitutions to become camouflage constitutions. Since they erect a strong executive branch of government, especially in the form of strong presidentialism, there is always a temptation for the president to meet difficulties created by the other branches of government by bypassing their constitutional powers, thus establishing a dictatorship or an authoritarian regime. Time and again this has happened with the constitutions that have introduced presidential government in Latin America, Africa and Asia.

Coming back to the distinction between the judicial branch of government and the legislative, one should note that the 1787 American constitution did not endorse the kind of judicial review that we think about today in relation to American practices, as they developed during the late nineteenth and early twentieth centuries. The constitution does invite one kind of judicial review, viz. deciding on the division of powers between the federal government and the States. However, it hardly authorized judicial review in the sense that the Supreme Court can declare acts by Congress unconstitutional.

It is one thing to have a federal court checking that governments at lower tiers act in accordance with the constitution. Actually, it is difficult to see how a federal system State could do without some such court, be it a general supreme court as in the USA or a special constitutional court as in Germany. Unitary States also may employ special administrative courts, including a constitutional court, as is the case in France and Italy for example. When judicial review is confined to strictly legal matters about intergovernmental relations and the overall legality of acts and decisions at lower levels of government, then we can speak of the weak version of judicial review.

It is another matter when the courts can engage in strong judicial review, i.e. to test from a political point of view whether legislation is in accordance with the constitution as interpreted by the court. It becomes especially controversial when the highest federal court can declare acts and decisions by the federal government as unconstitutional and thereby not to be implemented. Few states have strong judicial review in the American sense.

Judicial review in the sense that the Supreme Court can declare legislation by Congress invalid or decisions by the President as not to be implemented is derived from precedents in the United States. The first precedent is the well-known case of Marbury versus Madison in 1803, where the Supreme Court under Chief Justice Marshall ruled a so-called mandamus against the President. 'Mandamus' describes a situation where the Supreme Court orders that something should be done, in this case that appointments made by the former president had to be implemented by the incoming president. Judicial review became a spectacular political event in the twentieth century for the first time when a conservative court declared much of the welfare state and the New Deal legislation unconstitutional and secondly when a liberal court reinterpreted the constitution in favour of radical political demands beginning with the desegregation decisions in the 1950s.

The distinction between dictatorship and democracy if often taken as the starting-point for screening the constitutions of the world. Although its importance and validity cannot be questioned, it remains the case that there is more to constitutional variety than this separation. The set of democratic constitutions harbour many different mechanisms for the aggregation and translation of citizen preferences into social choices. Here, we focus on the formal constitutions of the countries that qualify as stable democracies.

There are a few key distinctions that always crop up when analysing the constitutional variety among stable democracies. As a matter of fact, constitutional variety very much boils down to two key aspects. First, there is the referendum institution, which may be framed in very different ways. Secondly, we have the questions related to parliamentarianism, i.e. the kind of connections that prevail between the government and the national assembly. Democratic countries may or may not have institutions for referenda and parliamentarianism, and those that have these institutions frame them in different ways. Let us point out the basic constitutional alternatives involved here.

The referendum

The constitutional status of the referendum raises many problems about the nature and form of democratic government. Here we enter a field of political theory that has been much debated and where many issues still remain unresolved. There is confrontation between the adherents of participatory democracy and those who favour representative democracy. There is disagreement about the nature of democractic representation, whether the representative mandate is an open or bound one and whether representation implies ideas of social composition. Finally, there are different views about how referenda should be conducted and what the role of key political players such as the political parties should be.

The extent to which the referendum is recognized in written constitutions in democratic countries differs from one state to another. In a few countries referenda are obligatory, such as in Switzerland, Austria and Denmark, while in most countries they are facultative as in France, Italy, Sweden and Norway. In some countries the outcome of referenda are decisive, as in Switzerland, while in a few countries they constitute advice to the national assembly, as in Sweden and Norway. Finally, in a few countries there is a constitutional recognition of the people's initiative (Butler and Ranney, 1994).

Only about half of the West European democracies recognize the referendum in their constitutions. This does not mean, however, that only these countries employ the referendum. Other countries have had referenda regulated only by means of ordinary law, such as the United Kingdom, Belgium and Norway. It should be pointed out that the number of referenda is low in most democratic countries during the post-war period with the exception of Switzerland, Denmark, Italy, Ireland and France. It is also noteworthy that the Federal Republic of Germany, the Netherlands and Portugal neither recognize nor employ the referendum. In the United States referenda occur frequently in local politics, but not at the national level. In Canadian politics referenda have played a role, but not so in Australia, New Zealand or Japan.

In Switzerland there are two forms of peoples' initiative. If at least 100,000 citizens petition that a proposal concerning constitutional change should be put to a referendum, then Parliament has to accept that. And if at least 50,000 citizens petition that an ordinary law proposal be put to a referendum, then that also has to be done. Another type of peoples' initiative is to be found in Austria where at least 100,000 citizens or 59 per cent of the electorate in three Länder may petition Parliament to accept a proposal for a new law.

Democratic States differ in terms of their representative institutions as well. Here there are two sources of institutional variation, the type of chamber system and the electoral formula employed. While electoral technicalities tend to be regulated in ordinary laws, the structure of the chamber system is very much a task for constitutions. There are three possibilities: (a) unicameralism as in the Nordic countries, Portugal and Greece; (b) symmetrical bicameralism meaning two chambers with equal powers as in Germany, Switzerland, Italy and Belgium; and (3) asymmetrical bicameralism where the lower chamber is stronger than the senate, as in the Netherlands, France and the United Kingdom. We will not enter into all the variation in electoral systems here – see e.g. Arend Lijphart's *Electoral Systems and Party Systems* (1994a).

Parliamentarianism

Basically, parliamentarianism implies that the persons who handle the executive powers of the State must have at least the tacit tolerance of the persons who make up the national assembly, and who have been entrusted to take care of the legislative power. Parliamentarianism is thus a kind of fusion of the executive and legislative powers. In British parliamentarianism the persons who recruit one of the two key State organs, the government, also participate in the other, the national assembly, whereas in other countries ministers cannot sit in parliament as long as they are members of the government.

Parliamentarianism involves a number of institutions governing the relationship between the people that handle the executive and legislative powers. It involves among other things: (1) the vote of no-confidence on the part of parliament towards the cabinet; (2) the right to dissolve parliament on the part of the premier; (3) the right to call a vote of loyalty towards the cabinet on the part of the premier; (4) the right of parliament to appoint or accept a premier; (5) the right of the premier to appoint ministers in the cabinet.

Parliamentarianism comes in different shades in various countries. Not all of these institutions are present in all the democracies that practise parliamentarianism, and the emphasis placed on various mechanisms differs from country to country. In some parliamentary regimes one or two of these crucial decisions (1)–(5) above rest with the head of state. The archetypal parliamentarianism is British parliamentarianism which satisfies all the criteria above, but continental parliamentarianism and Nordic parliamentarianism are not always in agreement with the British model.

For example, German parliamentarianism emphasizes the constructive vote of no-confidence, meaning that the German Bundestag can only bring down a government if it can simultaneously designate a new Kansler. It is the head of State who dissolves Parliament after a vote of no-confidence. The Prime Minister may at any time dissolve Parliament in Canada, Denmark, Ireland, Spain and Sweden. However, in Norway Parliament cannot be dissolved. In Belgium and the

Netherlands the right to dissolve Parliament is not an instrument in the hands of the Premier, as dissolution only takes place when there is a constitutional revision or as in Greece when Parliament has failed three times to elect a President. One may distinguish between two types of parliamentarianism, so-called ministercaesarism versus committee parliamentarianism. The first type means that the premier dominates the parliament while the other implies that parliament dominates over the cabinet by means of its committees where crucial decisions are hammered out.

From a constitutional point of view, the European version of strong presidential government implies that there is a hybrid form of parliamentarianism where the head of State competes with parliament about the decisions on recruitment and dissolution of governments. Thus, in the semi-presidential systems in Europe such as France, Finland and Portugal, it is the president who appoints and dismisses the premier at the same time as the premier must have the confidence of parliament. The Romanian and Polish constitutions have the same kind of parliamentarianism or semi-parliamentarianism as it were. The other side of the coin is, of course, presidentalism or semi-presidentialism.

The only case of a stable democracy that has fully fledged presidentialism is the American constitution. Presidentialism combining democracy with separation of powers has been tried over and over again, but it has failed everywhere except in the United States. Some argue that the explanation for the American success is that American presidentialism is mitigated by several so-called checks and balances, making the constitution of the United States more Madisonian than truly of the Montesquieu format.

However, in Europe there are several cases of presidential rule and stable democracy, but European presidentialism is different from the American presidentialism from a constitutional point of view. Presidential government in Europe is of the semi-presidential type, adding to presidentialism a strong dose of parliamentarianism (Shugart and Carey, 1992; Döring, 1995).

Conclusion

When one sets out to map the formal constitutions of the world, then one immediately observes a couple of puzzling things. First, many States have formally drafted constitutional documents that are not actually employed in the real life operations of the State. Either the constitution has been suspended by an explicit decision as part of a *coup d'état* or the written constitution is simply not being implemented, being a camouflage constitution. Actually, very few States altogether lack a formally drafted or codified constitution.

Secondly, looking at the written constitutions of the States of the world some States have small compact constitutional documents whereas other States have a huge document with hundreds of articles and paragraphs. Does it really matter for constitutional practice whether a constitution is short and succinct as the American one or huge and complicated as the Indian one? Both states are real federal democracies.

Thirdly, only a few countries have a constitution that is altogether different from what is normal or usual in constitutional law. One of the most special constitutions is that of Libya, which in its 1969 version comprises only 37 articles. Its size is thus similar to that of the American constitution, but its tone could hardly be more different:

> The Revolutionary Command Council constitutes the supreme authority in the Libyan Arab Republic. It will exercise the powers attached to national sovereignty, promulgate laws and decrees, decide in the name of the people the general policy of the State and make all decisions it deems necessary for the protection of the Revolution and the regime (Article 18).

To find something similar one has to go to the Iraqi constitution and its institutions for The Revolutionary Command Council. However, the Iraqi constitution is a camouflage constitution, as it lists a large number of constitutionalist principles such as Fundamental Rights and Duties, the independence of the judiciary as well as the democratic notion of popular sovereignty.

When one reads the written constitutions in the countries of the world, then one is struck by the firm grip that Western constitutionalist ideas have, even when the real constitutional institutions fall far short of the written formal ones. Only a few countries have enacted totally different constitutions. They are to be found either in the Arabic-Islamic culture or in the Marxist-Leninist tradition. Typical of Western constitutionalism is the strong integration of constitutional and administrative law in order to create stable and accountable institutions in the public sector. Let us discuss what this means more concretely in the next chapter.

7

Constitutional law and the legal order

Introduction

Constitutions are either written documents comprising a set of rules about the State, or real life institutions that regulate how political power is exercised within the public sector and how individual persons and governments interact. In both the literal and the real interpretation of the concept of a constitution the key element appears to be the rule or the set of rules, as it were. Constitutions typically contain written rules that are supposed to govern the creation and maintenance of institutions. Laws have a similar function.

Since laws also introduce rules for behaviour one may expect that constitutions are closely connected with the legal order. The constitutional order as well as the legal order consists of rules which have been institutionalized, meaning that they are upheld by a system of sanctions. Constitutional law is considered to be a discipline within the legal sciences, which again indicates how close a state constitution is to the legal order in a society. Yet, however strong the similarities may be, constitutions are not merely just a part of the legal order, because constitutions have distinct features, which after all comprise the basis for the distinction between constitutional or administrative law on the one side and other forms of law on the other side.

The purpose of this chapter is to place the constitution within the legal order. Actually, this task raises profound questions within legal theory and philosophy. What is the nature of a legal rule and how should one identify a legal order? Is the constitution somehow the basic foundation for the entire legal order meaning that constitutions require separate protection by special mechanisms or courts? How do we make a separation between public and private law? Let us begin this overview of key issues in constitutional law and legal theory by attempting to pin down what constitutional law refers to. Rules and institutions, yes, but rules and institutions for what?

Rights

Constitutions are part of the legal order because they consist of the same elements. The building blocks of a legal order are rights. The rules of the legal order may be of four kinds:

(1) statute rules or laws;
(2) judge-made rules or precedents;
(3) customary rules or custom;
(4) rules of reason or equity.

Whatever the source of the rule, it introduces rights which regulate the conduct of persons. Constitutional law deals with special sets of rights, whereas other kinds of law deal with different sets of rights. The legal order is the distribution of rights between individuals, generally speaking. Now we must ask what is a right and what kinds of rights are there?

A democratic constitution comprises rights of various kinds. It establishes citizens' rights in the form of negative and positive liberties. To the former belong the freedom of conscience and religion, the right to association and to vote as well as the freedom of thought and expression. Among the latter are the rights to work and housing, the right to health care as well as to respect and dignity. In addition to such rights, a constitution lays down citizens' duties, or more specifically what individuals have to do.

A democratic constitution contains a number of rights for public officials, including among these both politicians and public employees. The constitution, we can say, empowers certain persons to do certain things which have consequences for other people. Among these powers we find the right to enact legislation and the right to execute rules such as in the bureaucracy and within the judiciary. These competences create citizen duties and they are the sources of political power. The constitution regulates such competences, defines which competences they are and how they may created.

A constitution specifies the rights of citizens as well as the competences of public bodies such as the legislature, the government and its bureaux as well as the various judicial bodies. Citizen rights and duties as well as public powers or competences are the basic building stones of a constitution. All the rules of a constitution whether written, judge-made, customary or reasonable, specify rights, duties and competences.

The principle of legality requires that major rights, duties and competences be specified in explicitly laid down rules. Supremacy of law implies that rights and powers be documented in rules, be these of different kinds. Constitutions contain such basic rights and powers and they lay down rules for how additional rights, duties and competences may be introduced and implemented. Constitutions are part of the legal order, because the legal order is the general system of rights and duties in a country. What, more specifically, is the legal order? This is one of the key problems in legal philosophy, a subject which is characterized by fierce competition between alternative theories about the nature of law and jurisprudence (Friedmann, 1967; Lloyd, 1991; Harris, 1992).

What is the legal order?

Legal theory comprises a number of alternative models of the legal order and the tasks of jurisprudence. It debates a large number of issues in relation to both what the subject matter of law is and what its special methodology amounts to. On the one hand there is disagreement about what a legal system is or consists of – the ontological issue. On the other hand there is conflict about what the proper methodology of jurisprudence should be – the epistemological issue. The two established doctrines in the twentieth century, legal positivism and legal realism, have come under increasingly intense criticism. Both doctrines argue that the concept of rights is a muddled one and that it cannot be employed to state what the legal order is.

In legal positivism, the legal order is approached as a system of norms. Since there exist many different kinds of norms, a legal positivist lays down a criterion for the identification of the legal norms in a society. According to H.L.A. Hart's *The Concept of Law* (1970) the legal order consists of two kinds of norms: (a) primary legal rules or legal obligation rules and (b) secondary legal rules or rules of change, adjudication and recognition, i.e. power conferring rules. Now, a norm is part of the legal order in a country if it meets the criteria of recognition laid down by a special rule of recognition. Such a rule of recognition is, for example, that the norm enters a statute enacted by Parliament or enters custom. If a norm cannot be said to meet with any of the identification criteria of belonging to the legal order of a country, then it is not a legal norm in that country. Another very influential model within legal positivism was launched by Kelsen, who stated that the ultimate criterion of identification is the Basic Norm, i.e. the constitution of a country. Both Hart and Kelsen argued that it is the task of jurisprudence to describe and analyse what the law of a country is and not what it ought to be, as legal positivism is typified by a sharp distinction between law and morals. Only positive meaning existing norms are the subject matter of jurisprudence, not values (Kelsen, 1967).

In legal realism, the emphasis is upon the behaviour of the officials who handle the legal order. What judges and bureaucrats actually do is the legal order. There are two versions of legal realism, the Scandinavian approach and the American approach. According to the former, to speak of rights is simply to employ a mode of expressing legal facts which always refers to the behaviour patterns that constitute the legal machinery, i.e. a state's public administration, the courts and the tribunals – see e.g. Alf Ross' *On Law and Justice* (1974). When words like 'rights', 'duties' and 'powers' are employed in legal language, they are working as directives or 'independent imperatives' to the key persons in the legal machinery to take action, and that legal machinery is founded ultimately upon feelings of obligation among the population (Olivecrona, 1971). The task of jurisprudence is simply to analyse this legal machinery or special legal language and not to engage in values.

In American legal realism the focus is upon the judge and his/her interpretation of the law. The most famous expression of legal realism is that of Justice Holmes: 'The prophecies of what the courts will do in fact, and nothing more pretentious, are what I mean by the law'. Realist legal philosophy in American jurisprudence is connected with K. Llewellyn, J. Frank and R. Pound, who emphasized that law is what judges do about disputes.

It is not possible to read the law from statutes or code books or to state what the law is apart from how it is interpreted in actual court proceedings. Whereas legal positivists underline norms, legal realists emphasize behaviour, because rules in themselves do not determine court decisions. Law becomes real in court proceedings, where norms and facts are interpreted. Jurisprudence is the science that analyses such court decisions, as before the court has made its deliberations about a particular subject, law on that subject does not exist. Thus, jurisprudence is an empirical science, making predictions about the behaviour of judges.

Legal positivism and legal realism are in agreement in their rejection of rights as the basic element of law. Talking about rights involves a strong moral tone, which confuses the distinction between the legal order as an existing phenomenon and political philosophy as a discourse about how society should be changed in order to satisfy the demand for justice. To legal positivists and legal realists alike there is a sharp gulf between law and morals, between the legal order and the requirements of justice.

R.M. Dworkin reopened the whole issue about rights and the legal order in his *Taking Rights Seriously* (1987). He argues that legal positivism in its philosophy of law has failed to recognize that jurisprudence involves more than simply applying the correct rules to a case. Deciding and reflecting upon legal issues typically involves more than finding and applying the relevant statutes or precedents, as what Dworkin calls standards are involved, or principles relating to rights. When legal issues are simple and clear-cut, then the positivist analysis is correct. But when matters are contentious and difficult, then standards play a major role. Since these principles about rights express moral considerations about what people deserve in various circumstances, a sharp separation between law and justice cannot be made.

Dworkin's criticism of legal positivism applies equally well to legal realism. If judges, when considering what the law is, are deliberating about rights, then much more is involved than simply predicting what judges normally do. Legal positivists have replied to the Dworkin attack by somehow upholding the distinction between jurisprudence and morals (Denning, 1979; Coleman, 1988; Waluchow, 1994).

There are two different questions involved in this debate about rights, jurisprudence and ethics, one epistemological and one ontological (Table 7.1). The latter problem raises the whole issue about what law is about: norms, behaviour or rights? The former question deals with whether morals are necessarily a part of jurisprudence or whether law is a science that may shun values. Note that the expression 'law' stands for both the discipline and the subject matter of jurisprudence. Various combinations are possible as shown in Table 7.1.

Table 7.1
Rights and jurisprudence

	Ontology	
	Rights exist	*Rights do not exist*
Epistemology		
Jurisprudence is different from morals	I	II
Jurisprudence involves morals	III	IV

A radical legal positivist would take stand II, which is also the position of the legal realist, whether of Scandinavian bent or American. Dworkin's position is III, but positions I and IV are also logically possible.

In order to invoke the relevance of rights in understanding constitutions and the legal order, it is not necessary to become engaged in the debate about the **is** and the **ought** in law that Dworkin raises. Early in this century W.N. Hohfeld presented an analysis of the legal order based upon the concept of rights, viz. in his *Fundamental Legal Conceptions as Applied in Juridical Reasoning* (1946), Hohfeld presented a systematic scheme for handling various rights, stating clearly how they were related to each other.

Hohfeld's scheme allows us to present the two key components in a constitution – citizen rights and public competences – in a web of concepts that cover the legal order. The building blocks are as follows (Table 7.2):

Table 7.2
Variety of rights in Hohfeld

Left-hand		*Right-hand*	
Claim	Duty	Power	Liability
Privelege	No-Right	Immunity	Disability

Note: Within these two squares the horizontal relationship stands for a correlation whereas the diagonal relationship denotes an opposition.

Source: Harris, 1992: 77.

On the left-hand side we have the citizen rights, where a claim for one person may imply a corresponding duty on the part of another person or it may be a matter of a privilege meaning that he/she has no duty towards the other person. On the right-hand side we have the public competence, where a power of one person implies a liability on the part of another person or an immunity towards the other person. Hohfeld's basic insight was that the concept of rights covered all these entities and that, although they were related to each other, they were partly distinct. Human rights as entrenched in constitutions involve both of what Hohfeld refers to as immunities and privileges. And constitutions typically also regulate competences, which cover both powers and duties.

Rights are real phenomena to the same extent as legal systems are real. Not only is there a system of human rights including both negative and positive liberties, besides private property rights, there is also a system of rights in relation to public bodies such as the right to legislate, to govern and to adjudicate. Constitutional law is the analysis of such rights in the constitutional setting, whereas law in general encompasses a much larger range of rights.

According to Dworkin, any statement about rights must include a reference to moral standards, which amounts to a very controversial claim. It suggests that the distinction between **is** and **ought** should be blurred in law. Can we not describe and analyse the existing constitutional rights in a country without passing judgement on what those rights actually ought to be? It seems possible to speak about different constitutions as well as alternative legal systems without at the same time launching a moral theory of rights (Dworkin, 1986).

If constitutions comprise citizens rights and public powers, then how can these constitutional elements be regulated? Besides rights and competences a constitution must specify procedures in terms of which matters relating to rights and competences may be decided. Rights, powers and procedures may be regulated in various ways, relating to the various modes of entering such rights, powers and procedures into the legal order. In some countries there is an explicit public law framework – what does it amount to? Let us first say a few words about the basic legal systems of the world.

Legal systems

When there is talk about types of legal systems, then the basic divide is that between the Romano-Germanic family and the common law family. It is so basic that it crops up everywhere in all kinds of law, constitutional law as well as private law. However, it is not an exhaustive classification, as other types of legal systems exist. R. David and J.E.C. Brierley, in *Major Legal Systems in The World Today* (1985), add the following: Socialist law, Muslim law, Hindu law, Chinese law, Japanese law and African law. It is not quite clear what these categories stand for from a systematic point of view. Muslim law and Hindu law are examples of religious legal systems whereas Chinese law and African law represent customary legal systems.

From a constitutionalist point of view the two major Western categories of legal systems, the Romano-Germanic and the common law types, are the most relevant. Within religious legal systems constitutional law is suppressed by religious dogma which has an anti-constitutionalist bias, especially in Muslim law where the basic foundation is the so-called Shariah law. Legal systems based on custom may also counteract constitutionalism, if customs give a large leeway for rulers to act, as in China and Africa. Finally, Socialist law was really an instrument of the Communist party to wield power in a hegemonic fashion. Interestingly, Japanese law as it developed after the Meji restoration in 1868 has been more Western-like in its emphasis on due process and the protection of citizen rights, particularly so after the Second World War.

The distinction between the Romano-Germanic type of legal systems covering continental Europe, including Spain and Portugal as well as the Scandinavian countries on the one hand, and common law type, including the United Kingdom, most Commonwealth countries and the United States on the other hand has a long historical tradition behind it. In the analysis of the history of constitutionalism we have already come across this divide in the development of law. What are the distinctive properties of these two types of legal systems?

The Romano-Germanic legal systems, or the civil law family, emphasize *codification*, meaning the establishment of general and abstract principles of law. In ancient times when Roman law and canon law were practised there was an ambition among legal scholars such as Bartolus (1313–57) and Baldus (1327–1400) to establish, amidst compilations of legal materials, a consistent bulk of legal principles, applicable to a wide array of situations. In modern times there has been a concentration upon the systematic enactment of statute law, e.g. in the form of so-called codes (Stein, 1991).

The most well-known of codes are the five Napoleonic codes, enacted between 1804 and 1811. However, there are earlier codes such as Denmark in 1683, Sweden in 1734 and Prussia in 1794. It was not until 1900 that the German Civil Code came into force. These codes systematized mainly private law, but in the Romano-Germanic legal systems the distinction between private and public law is firmly entrenched. Thus, public law has expanded tremendously in the twentieth century, as legislation has become the principal tool for systematizing law in the countries that belong to this family of law.

The common law type of legal systems underline judge-made law, pointing at the crucial importance of how laws are interpreted in the courts. Precedents are more important than statutes, and case law goes before legislation. Legislation does not really become law until it has been interpreted in specific cases giving judges and lawyers a major role in determining what the law actually is. The common law type of legal system does not recognize a sharp distiction between public and private law. Instead there is a hesitation to accept special forms of public law, such as administrative law, as somehow different from ordinary law. At the same time there is a realization that there has been an expansion of public law in the form of new statutes in, for example, the United Kingdom and the United States.

Any classification of legal systems is open-ended. Alternative frameworks are possible (Schmidhauser, 1987) and new distinctions may be introduced with such broad types as the Romano-Germanic versus the common law types, referring to the possibility of legal review, the place of constitutional law and the existence of multiple sources of legislation within one country as in a few federal states. In any case, Table 7.3 isolates a couple of crucial distinctions from the constitutionalist perspective that cut across the main divide between Romano-Germanic systems and Common Law systems.

Table 7.3
Formal constitution and legal review

	Written constitution	Unwritten
Legal review	USA, Germany	–
Non-legal review	The Netherlands, Sweden	United Kingdom

Note: Legal review implies a capacity on the part of a court to rule upon the constitutionality of a legislative act or an executive decision (Volcansek, 1992).

Interestingly, in terms of a few properties of the legal order that are relevant from a constitutionalist point of view, countries from each of the two families – the Common Law tradition and the Romano-Germanic tradition – may have much in common. Thus, both the United States and Germany allow for extensive constitutional review, in the case of the former to its main chief ordinary court, the Supreme Court, and in the case of the latter, a special constitutional court in Karlsruhe. Similarly, the United Kingdom and Romano-Germanic law countries such as the Netherlands and Sweden reject extensive legal review, all three adhering to the principle of Parliamentary sovereignty.

When it comes to classifying legal systems, then one has to be aware of the possibility of mixtures. Thus, several countries have elements from different kinds of legal systems. One such blend is the use of Dutch law and English law in South Africa – Roman-Dutch law. Another mixture is the employment of either a Romano-Germanic type law or a common law type law in countries which have either religious law or customary law. The Romano-Germanic type of law has been adopted more or less in Latin America, parts of Africa, the Near East, Japan and Indonesia.

At the same time, one must not overemphasize the internal coherence of the Romano-Germanic type and the common law type. It is often argued that the Romano-Germanic legal systems are weak in terms of public law. Thus, David and Brierley state:

> In the Romano-Germanic family, public law has attained a degree of development and perfection certainly inferior to that of private law (David and Brierley, 1985: 83).

This overall characterization is true of the early development of Roman law, where constitutional law was almost non-existent. When we searched for the sources of medieval constitutionalism in Chapter 4, we had to look elsewhere in other legal frameworks such as custom and feudal law. However one may talk about a Romano-Germanic type of legal system, there is more public law in this category than David and Brierley recognize. We are referring to Scandinavian law where constitutional rules were laid down early when customary law was transformed into statute law. It is hardly an accident that major constitutions emerge in the eighteenth century within the Romano-Germanic tradition, because there was always a tension within this category between the absolutist bent of Latin law and the constitutionalist tendency of Germanic law. Today public law has a very strong position in the Romano-Germanic legal systems, as it is the fundamental division in the civil law family. What is public law all about?

Structure of public law

Martin Loughlin in *Public Law and Political Theory* (1992) points out that there are two basic perspectives underlying the framing of public law in various countries. He calls them the 'normativist style' and the 'functionalist style', the distinction between them being very interesting from the points of view discussed in this book. The former style is associated with constitutionalism whereas the latter style is connected with the power perspective – see the introductory chapter.

Loughlin examines these two public law styles both from an historical perspective and from a systematic point of view. Let us quote from his presentation of these two styles:

> The normativist style in public law is rooted in a belief in the ideal of the separation of powers and in the need to subordinate government to law … . The functionalist style in public law, by contrast, views law as part of the apparatus of government. Its focus is upon law's regulatory and facilitative functions and therefore is orientated to aims and objectives and adopts an instrumentalist social policy approach (Loughlin, 1992: 62).

In reality, public law has both of these two components: legality and power. On the one hand there is the set of rules that regulates the relationship between the citizens and the state from the point of view of the former, introducing citizen rights versus government. On the other hand, there is the set of rules that empowers governments in relation to their citizens or inhabitants and foreign visitors, stating duties and competences.

One may see the tension between the normativist style and the functionalist style as an expression of the conflict between negative and positive freedom. When public law institutions aim for the protection of human rights, such as the classical negative liberties, then the normativist style is resorted to in order to set limits to what government can do. However, when the purpose is to empower governments to take action in order to promote positive liberties, then the functionalist style is employed. It is true, as Loughlin argues, that liberal scholars fearing a large public sector have favoured the normativist style, as, for example with Friedrich Hayek and Michael

Oakeshott. Collectivist thinkers, on the other hand, tend to enhance the functionalist style, such as Leon Duguit and Harold Laski. Yet, both styles have to be integrated into the public law framework in a constitutionalist democracy.

The two approaches to public law, the normativist and the functionalist, are based on different philosophies of what is characteristic of the legal order. The differences between these perspectives may be tapped by looking at a few contributions to the debate about state and society in this century. In his books *The Constitution of Liberty* (1990) and *Law, Legislation and Liberty* (three volumes, 1982) Hayek starts from the assumption that the legal order comprises two very different sets of rules, *nomos* versus *thesis*. *Nomos* is the same as spontaneous order, or the institutions that evolve gradually in an evolutionary and adaptive process. *Thesis* stands for legislation, i.e. statute rules made by parliaments. His argument is that *nomos* is superior to *thesis*, because *thesis* involves all the difficulties inherent in rational design. A similar theory had already been expressed by Hayek in 1944 in *The Road to Serfdom*, which is an attack on the possibility of planning.

A slightly different distinction is offered by Oakeshott in *On Human Conduct* (1975), where he focuses upon two different interpretations of the basic role of the state. On the one hand there is the state as *societas* or a civil association and on the other hand we have the state as *universitas* or a managerial enterprise. A state orientated towards the *societas* model is an association that is held together by impersonal rules which regulate how the different interests of its equal members may interact to their mutual benefit. A state based upon the *universitas* model is an association with a common purpose, but if this common purpose is to be accomplished the government will require the citizens to perform particular roles.

Both Hayek and Oakeshott view the growth of government in countries with an advanced economy, such as in Western Europe, as an unfortunate victory for one model – *thesis* or *universitas*, while in reality from a political or moral point of view the other model is the superior one: *nomos* or *societas*. To some extent this is a correct observation, as the expansion of public law has meant a tremendous increase in legislation and public management. Whether the evaluation of these scholars is also correct is open to further discussion.

For an evaluation of the growth of government that is quite different we may turn to Harold Laski, claiming in *A Grammar of Politics*

(1925) that 'a working theory of the state must, in fact, be conceived in administrative terms' (Laski, 1967: 35). The making and implementation of administrative law and the setting up of administrative courts was not defended by Laski by rejecting Hayek's belief in the spontaneous order or Oakeshott's trust in civic association; instead Laski viewed the legal order as closely connected with social forces, to which legislation plays a major role by giving it expression, since:

> It is a function of the whole social structure and not some given aspect of it. Its power is determined by the degree to which it aids what that whole social structure reports as its desires (Laski, 1967: 287).

Such an approach to public law implies that the gulf between *nomos* and *thesis* as well as between *societas* and *universitas* is bridged. Administrative law which makes delegated legislation and bureaucratic discretion possible simplifies processes of change in society, reacting to citizen needs. Legislation is a necessity in a society that consists of multiple groups interacting in a complex way.

That law is simply the organization of a group of people and that individual persons cannot survive without belonging to a group had been pointed out by French legal scholar Leon Duguit in *Law in the Modern State*, originally published in 1901 and translated in 1921. Groups cannot survive without their members accepting duties, the regulation of which expresses group solidarity. A State is one such group whose laws follow from social solidarity. Individual rights stem from duties which are simply the result of the organization of society. Freedom and solidarity are mutually compatible in a decentralized State which accepts the existence of other groups and associations.

A somewhat similar view on law was propagated in the pragmatist movement in the United States. The philosophers James and Dewey as well as the legal scholars Pound and Llewellyn advocated what was called 'legal realism' above, or the doctrine that law is a tool for social change. By means of legislation practical objectives can be achieved, or better still accomplished in a piecemeal fashion where each step calls for a revision of the objectives in a never ending fashion.

Thus, public law may be employed for the purpose of constraining the State. Or public law may be used to enable the State to engage in activities. These two faces of public law can only be reconciled with each other to a certain extent. In the final analysis the orientation of public law in relation to the normativist and functionalist styles will reflect one's political values. What creates the ten-sions between various positions as to the nature of public law is the form and scope of administrative law which besides criminal law constitutes the bulk of public law. Why is this so?

Administrative law

Administrative law is vast in advanced countries, corresponding to the large number of public policies that governments conduct in various fields such as the environment, energy and communications, the infrastructure, education and health, culture and research, social security, not to forget law and order. The eleventh edition of Wade and Bradley's *Constitutional and Administrative Law* has the following identification of the concept of administrative law which is right to the point:

> A formal definition of administrative law is that it is a branch of public law concerned with the composition, procedures, powers, duties, rights, and liabilities of the various organs of government which are engaged in administering public policies (Bradley and Ewing, 1993: 603).

Administrative law starts in constitutional law and ends with all the minute regulations which are laid down by means of delegated legislation. Often one may observe a distinction between general administrative law and special administrative law. To the former belong the general rules that all sections of public administration have to follow when making and implementing decisions, including the possibility of citizen remedies and the judicial control of the administration. Under special administrative law falls the separate legislation that regulates areas such as water legislation, electricity legislation and social security legislation.

Public law is contested, because there is a variety of opinions as to how far the State should go in regulating society by means of administrative law. It has been argued that too much administrative legislation makes it difficult for individuals to handle problems by negotiating solutions. It may well be the case that certain problems in society could be handled by means of voluntary agreement between citizens, searching for efficient outcomes by bargaining until mutually beneficial contracts are reached. Administrative routines may simply impose unnecessary transaction costs upon society, delaying the resolution of conflicts and failing to implement first-best solutions (Coase, 1988).

In his *Economic Analysis of Law* (1992) Richard Posner argued that the common law method offers the most efficient method for settling legal disputes involving property rights and claims of compensation. A common law approach is to be preferred to a public law approach, because it offers the institutions that lower transaction costs. Statutes need administrative agencies which deliver rules and outcomes that are inefficient and high on transaction costs. The use of tort law and the imposition of a duty to pay compensation according to liability for damages, as established in ordinary courts, minimize the joint costs of all parties involved.

Public law is also contested for another reason, namely its form. On the one hand, there is the French approach to administrative law – *droit administratif*, which is an uncodified law distinct from private law involving a separate system of courts from the lower Tribunal Administratif to the highest Conseil d'Etat. There is a set of rights, duties and privileges that public officials have in relation to the citizens of the country which stem from principles of law that are entirely different from the rights and duties that citizens have in relation to each other, i.e. to be ruled over by special courts as ordinary courts should have no jurisdiction over issues involving the State and its citizens. On the other hand, there is the English approach to administrative law in which there is no sharp separation between public and private law, where the ultimate legal control over the administration and the large number of special tribunals rests with the common law courts ruling over the actions of public officials in terms of the same principles of natural justice or fairness that ordinary courts apply in issues involving citizens versus each other (Foulkes, 1990).

In a public law perspective, administrative law is basically different from private law, since it regulates the state and private citizens. However, in a common law tradition there is only one single law in a society. Developing a special administrative law was explicitly rejected by Dicey – see Brown and Bell: *French Administrative Law* (1993), who became very influential in orientating English practice. It was even stated that there was no need for a special administrative law, which has been rejected by the growth of administrative law alongside the growth of government and the welfare state.

The structure of administrative law may be explained by separating between general administrative law and special administrative law. While the former deals with administrative procedures, the latter covers the special topics in administrative law, regulating a policy area.

Administrative law is the law of public administration, as David Foulkes points out. He states about administrative law:

> It is concerned with the legal forms and constitutional status of public authorities; with their powers and duties and with the procedures followed in exercising them; with their legal relationships with one another, with the public and with their employees (Foulkes, 1990: 1).

Administrative law regulates the operations of the administrative authorities, their powers and procedures as well as the control of their activities. Since administrative law is closely connected with the institutions of the public sector which differ from one country to another reflecting different constitutional practice, it will differ in form and content. But there are certain universal themes in administrative law, in particular in those countries which adhere to the idea of constitutionalism or the notions covered by the concept of the rule of law.

To administrative law in a constitutionalist country belongs the specification of:

(1) The rules for the identification of the public authorities, from the ministries to sub-national level government including public enterprises and semi-public boards.
(2) The rules that public authorities may create covering the distinctions between statutes, delegated legislation and administrative rules.
(3) The rules of procedure in public administration including decision-making, sanctions, enquiries, consultation and participation.
(4) The rules of control, whether administrative remedies or strict legal control, covering administrative tribunals, ordinary courts, ombudsmen and auditors.

The overall objective of administrative law is to ensure legality in the activities in the public sector. Foulkes states:

> Administrative law is therefore concerned with the way powers are acquired, where the authorities get their powers from, and what is the nature of those powers (Foulkes, 1990: 2).

Empowerment is one crucial aspect, but even more important is the qualification that the powers be employed according to rules or institutions:

But administrative law and indeed other branches of the law, is to be seen also as an instrument for getting things done by the creation through legal processes of institutions and granting them powers and imposing on them duties (Foulkes, 1990: 2).

The notion of the rule of law or legality is indeed a broad one. It involves a number of requirements upon the administrative powers and procedures. In a constitutionalist approach legality in public administration demands:

(1) Supremacy of the law, meaning the exclusion of arbitrary powers.
(2) Equality before the law, or equal treatment under the laws.
(3) The existence of citizen rights and liberties versus the State.
(4) Predictability in administrative processes: fair hearing, the duty to give reasons, remedies, public liability in tort, compensation, openness in procedures, legal review.

The rule of law may be institutionalized in different ways in various countries. The French approach is based upon the public law approach whereas the English approach stems from the common law approach. Various combinations of these two approaches are possible. Thus, the complaint process in public administration may be handled exclusively by special courts – administrative courts as it were – or ordinary courts may play a crucial role. Finally, some countries have two complaint processes, one process via the standard administrative system where a higher authority may correct the decisions of a lower authority and another process that runs through the judicial system, involving either administrative courts or the ordinary courts system.

It is an open question which institutional approach is the most suitable one for protecting the crucial objective of legality and securing the possibility of remedies. The crux of the matter is not the legal technique used but the implementation of the objective, viz. to safeguard that demands (1)–(4) are met. It has been argued that the rule of law requires a special institution, viz. judicial review. What is legal review?

Judicial review

One must observe the difference between weak and strong judicial review. Weak legal review only implies that judges may try cases involving a dispute between administrative officials and citizens whereas strong legal review is based upon the examination by judges of the constitutionality of legislation by parliament or acts by governments. What is contested is strong legal review. The French penal codes of 1791 made judicial review a punishable offence and similar provisions may be found in other countries such as the Netherlands and Belgium that were under French legal influence and belonged to the Romano-Germanic law family. However, at the same time one must recognize that the country that has been most vehemently opposed to strong judicial review is the United Kingdom, which enters from the common law family (Tate and Vallinder, 1995).

To clarify the distinction between weak and strong legal review one may refer to the distiction between legal review of legislation and legal review of administrative action (Cappelletti, 1971). The latter is strongly entrenched in countries which uphold the principles of the rule of law but at the same time negates strong judicial review, as for instance the United Kingdom. Various courts, including in the last resort the ordinary courts can review the legality and validity of actions and decisions by persons or bodies having administrative powers. A number of principles are involved, including the *ultra vires* rule and the so-called principles of natural justice. The remedies against administrative action include *certoriari, mandamus*, prohibition, injunction, declaratory order and damage.

Another kind of quasi-legal review of administrative action is the use of the ombudsman institution, i.e. a person appointed preferably by the national assembly, to look into complaints about administrative incompetence or injustice, although not strictly illegality. The ombudsman institution is a Scandinavian invention, coming first from Sweden (1810) and then from Finland (1919), Denmark (1954) and Norway (1962). Several countries which acknowledge the principle of a Rechtsstaat now have some corresponding institution, called sometimes 'Parliamentary Commissioner' or 'Public Protector' and such officers deal mainly with public administration.

However, some would argue that the rule of law or legal justice requires more than weak judicial review. Constitutionalism, it is stated, implies the real existence of a written and rigid constitution, which can only be guaranteed by allowing judges or a court to test the constitutionality of any new legislation. One may make a few distinctions between various forms of strong judicial review, which are highly relevant when constitutions are drawn up or revised.

First, there is the diffuse and the concentrated types of legal review, referring to whether judicial review may be done by all judges or whether it belongs in a special court. Secondly, we have *ex ante* and *ex post* legal review, depending upon whether judges are supposed to rule upon the constitutionality of a law before it has been enacted or after. Thirdly, there is the distinction between legal review based upon international law and legal review as part of the country's legal order.

The classical case of legal review is the American system, as it has developed after the famous Marbury versus Madison case in 1803. The American constitution contained an explicit procedure for the Supreme Court to test the constitutionality of State legislation, as is typically the case in federal States where there has to be a legal umpire resolving matters relating to the division of powers and competences between the levels of government. What Judge Marshall introduced in 1803 was a much broader concept of legal review, viz. the right of the Supreme Court to strike down federal legislation if it was not considered to be in line with the constitution and its amendments.

The American judicial review is of the diffuse type and is exercised *ex post* in relation to concrete cases on the basis of principles derived from American law. All the courts in the country from the lowest to the highest level are permitted to engage in judicial review. Such a diffuse type of legal review process is to be found in a number of countries such as Argentina, Mexico, Greece, Australia, India, Japan and Norway. Final judgement in matters concerning the constitutionality of legislation and executive action would, however, belong to a Supreme Court, as is the case in the United States which does, of course, practise the strong version of judicial review while, for example, Sweden, Denmark and Finland practise the weak version.

The concentrated type of judicial review has been called the European model or the Austrian system of judicial review, because it was first introduced in Austria and Czechoslovakia in their new constitutions from 1920 and it has since the Second World War been adopted in Italy, Germany, Spain, Portugal, the Czech and Slovak Republics and Hungary. As a matter of fact, the idea of a separate constitutional court that would be the only court to handle judicial review was suggested by Hans Kelsen (Kelsen, 1928). The concentrated model is also employed in Chile, Ecuador and Peru.

The concentrated model of judicial review may be seen as a com-

promise solution to the problem of reconciling the doctrine of constitutional supremacy on the one hand with either the separation of
powers doctrine or with the notion of the sovereignty of the national
assembly on the other hand. Having a written constitution implies that
there is a procedure through which the constitution may be upheld. At
the same time the Montesquieu principle of *trias politica* has most
often been interpreted as a requirement for a sharp separation between
the three branches of state power – the executive, the legislature and
the judiciary – meaning that strong judicial review is excluded under
the Montesquieu principle. Similarly, the doctrine of the sovereignty
of Parliament in the British constitutional tradition has always been
claimed to imply that strong judicial review is out of the question, as
judges are not allowed to challenge Acts of Parliament.

Yet, Kelsen argued that a concentrated type of judicial review
could offer a compromise solution, because the special constitutional
tribunal would somehow complement the national assembly. Allan
Brewer-Carías states in his *Judicial Review in Comparative Law*:

> legislative power was, for Kelsen, divided between two bodies: the first,
> Parliament, the holder of political initiative, the positive legislator; and
> the second, the Constitutional Tribunal, entrusted with the power to
> annul laws which violate the Constitution (Brewer-Carías, 1989: 192).

However, it can be argued that there is a conflict between strong
legal review and democracy, as it seems rather difficult to accept that
there could be a second chamber on a par with the national assembly but not popularly elected and therefore not under direct popular
control. The kind of difficulties that strong legal review have given
rise to may be exemplified by looking at the development of judicial
review in the United States.

Before that, it should be noted that judicial review may also take
the form of *ex ante* control of legislation, as with the French constitutional court. The Constitutional Council in France belongs to the
concentrated type of judicial review, but it exercises its power exclusively a priori and in an abstract manner. Moreover, this constitutional court is detached from the French legal system, because it does
not hear cases or instruct on appeal from the judiciary. What it does
is examine new pieces of legislation before they have been enacted
on the basis of norms taken from the 1789 Declaration of the Rights
of Man and the preamble to the 1946 Constitution which was
reasserted in the preamble to the 1958 constitution.

Judicial review has occupied a very prominent place in American politics. Major decisions by the Supreme Court have been given an attention that hardly has any correspondence elsewhere, although it is true that the German constitutional court in Karlsruhe has also exercised considerable political influence. Fundamental to the operation of American judicial review is that the principle of *stare decisis* does not apply to the rulings of the Supreme Court. This means that the Supreme Court is not bound by its earlier rulings, but may reverse its decisions from case to case. Constitutional development in the United States has been intimately connected with such major reversals in the way the constitution has been interpreted by the Court.

In a federal State there has to exist some form of judicial review, because there are bound to occur conflicts about the proper competences of the federal government versus the State governments. Since the distribution of powers between the central and the regional governments in a federal State is to be resolved on the basis of constitutional provisions, there will be an urgent need for constitutional interpretation. It is thus no surprise that we find that the Supreme Court has declared unconstitutional as many as 1,058 State statutes, presumably because the State legislatures have overstepped their competences.

The Supreme Court has also overturned 130 Acts of Congress. Here we have the core activity in strong legal review, a national court striking down central government legislation, invoking constitutional provisions concerning basic citizen rights. Actually, the number of statutes overturned is not the essence of activist judicial review. A few crucial decisions may have tremendous legal impact, because the Supreme Court decisions operate as precedents for how inferior courts are to interpret the constitution. Key rulings by the Supreme Court are major policy decisions that neither the federal government nor the state governments can neglect. The Supreme Court may also act by simply clarifying how certain constitutional rules are to be interpreted without at the same time squashing statutes – statutory construction.

One may identify a few major trends in the activity of the Supreme Court (Fisher, 1990). In the early decades of the nineteenth century the court expanded federal powers in various ways, increasing congressional power under the Necessary and Proper Clause of the constitution as well as defending federal policy of national economic integration. The infamous Dred Scott decision in 1857, which denied citizenship to blacks and opened up the possibility that slavery could spread to the territories in the west, is considered as a major mistake in the history of the Supreme Court, as, rather than settling a divisive issue, it provoked a civil war. After the civil war the constitution was amended in order to undo the implications of Dred Scott, as Amendments 13, 14 and 15 prohibited slavery and guaranteed all persons born or naturalized in the United States equal human rights, including the rights to vote.

However, the period 1870 to 1937 is called the substantive due process era in the history of the Supreme Court. It refers to the fact that the court frequently employed the Due Process Clause of Amendment 5 and Amendment 14 to strike down economic legislation that could threaten the prevailing *laissez-faire* regime. The clause that 'no person be deprived of life, liberty, or property without due process of law' was interpreted as prohibiting interference by State governments with individual and corporate rights derived from the principles of economic liberty and property as well as blocking federal economic legislation derived from section 8 of the constitution, enabling Congress to regulate among other things interstate commerce. When the court struck down pieces of the New Deal legislation initiated by F.D. Roosevelt, there followed a constitutional crisis including the threat of a Court-packing plan. The crisis was resolved by the Supreme Court reversing its position on economic legislation in 1938.

Instead the Supreme Court turned to the protection of civil liberties and individual rights. The major decisions concerning individual rights came under the Earl Warren Court (1953–69) and they include: Brown versus Board of Education (against racial segregation of schools), Baker versus Carr (reapportionment of electoral districts), Engel versus Vitale and Abington Township v. Schempp (religious freedom), Gideon versus Wainwright (protection of criminal defendants), New York Times versus Sullivan (freedom of the press) and Grisvold versus Connecticut (right of privacy). The strong endorsement of the rights of individuals and minorities versus State or federal governments has been based upon the Bill of Rights ratified in 1791, i.e. Amendments 1–10, as well as the 13th, 14th and 15th Amendments, in particular the Equal Protection Clause: 'No state shall ... deny to any person within its jurisdiction the equal protection of the laws'.

In the 1970s, 1980s and early 1990s constitutional litigation has produced less radical decisions. However, in Roe versus Wade the Supreme Court upheld the right of a pregnant woman to obtain an abortion during the first two-thirds of her pregnancy. But in Regents of the University of California versus Bakke the court ruled against affirmative action in college and university admissions. David G. Barnum points out in *The Supreme Court and American Democracy*:

> The years since 1969 have been characterized by a fitful but inexorable decline in the Supreme Court's willingness to support the constitutional claims of underpriviledged minorities. An increasing proportion of the Court's plenary docket consists of cases that are being reviewed at the government's request. Moreover, an increasing proportion of the Court's decisions are favourable to government (Barnum, 1993: 100).

Barnum discusses the principal problem involved in strong judicial review, viz. the potential conflict between the political power of the Supreme Court and the requirements of majoritarian democracy. Acknowledging that judicial review may be counter-majoritarian, he states:

> we argue that the United States is an example of a 'constitutional democracy', rather than a 'majoritarian democracy' (Barnum, 1993: 195).

This is hardly an acceptable solution to the problem of reconciling strong legal review with democracy, because we would designate those countries that are democracies and recognize only weak legal review as 'constitutional democracies', for instance the United Kingdom which rejects strong judicial review. While it seems that weak legal review is easily accommodated with almost any concept of democracy, it is difficult to harmonize strong judicial review with democracy. The overwhelming experience of strong legal review is that sooner or later there is bound to be a conflict between the court and the national assembly as to which body exercises legislative powers. Moving from weak to strong judicial review has the consequence of 'judicializing' politics, which restricts political democracy. The same lesson can be seen in from Europe, for example Germany, Italy and France (Volcansek, 1992; Vallinder, 1994).

Constitutional review has been much discussed, both with regard to its techniques and its ultimate justification. There are two opposing positions about how far judicial review can/should go: judicial restraint versus judicial activism. A prominent spokesman for the latter was Earl Warren with his social-liberalism whereas Felix Frankfurter can be mentioned as an example of the former.

How judicial review should be done is a contested question. One may distinguish between four standpoints: (a) literalism; (b) natural law; (c) historical development; (d) ecclecticism. Each one of these methods has its pros and cons. Literalism, or the doctrine that the court shall follow as closely as possible to original intention in the constitution, is difficult to apply, because all judicial concepts require interpretation. Seeking out the intention of the original constitutional 'fathers' may be impossible as the meaning of words change depending upon the context. Leaning on natural law principles is equally contested, because one may have conflicting views about what the so-called 'Right Reason' entails in different situations. It may be just as valid to simply refer to the fact that present day society is different from that of the founders, meaning that the wordings of the constitutions have to be reinterpreted to make sense.

It should be pointed out that in countries with weak judicial review the established method for legal interpretation involves a focus being placed on what is called the 'Lawmaker'. The purpose is to find out what the Lawmaker intended with the legislation. Thus, one critical source for legal interpreters is to go back to the supporting documents which surround the mere text of the legislation: government initiatives, public investigations and the deliberations of parliament. Such a restricted form of legal interpretation is rejected as a matter of principle in the US judicial review tradition.

There are a few key sources of judicial review in the American constitution. The 5th (1791) and the 14th Amendment (1868) speak about 'due process', 'equal protection', 'unreasonable searches and seizures' as well as 'cruel and unusual punishments', which have been used by the Supreme Court as arguments when declaring Congressial legislation and administrative acts unconstitutional. Just as famous is the clause about 'interstate commerce' in the original constitution, section 8, as it was used for removing state legislation and administrative decisions.

The judicial review of the American federal Supreme Court must be placed in its context of American politics and the fundamental role that political litigation places at all levels of government. Thus, also the State courts engage in judicial review, where each State has a supreme court that interprets each State constitution. Political litigation has a scope that is not matched in any other political system, complementing the activities of the legislative branch of government. Another country with strong judicial review is Germany under its 1949 constitution – see the country overview in *Comparative Judicial Review and Public Policy* (Jackson and Tate, 1992).

Conclusion

Understanding constitutions means seeing how they enter into the legal order. Constitutional law is generally looked upon as a *lex superior* in that all other kinds of law presuppose the existence of a set of fundamental laws that regulate how laws may be made and how they should be implemented. However, regarding constititutional law as a part of general law raises a number of difficult questions about the nature of law and the legal order.

We have in this chapter attempted to find common ground between constitutions and other kinds of law by focusing upon rights, duties and powers or competences. This route led in turn to an examination of the nature of rights in general as that concept is understood in legal theory. One body of law is of special interest from a constitutionalist point of view, namely administrative law, regulating the relationships between public authorities and citizens in a large number of policy areas.

Speaking in terms of ideal-types, there are two approaches to creating and upholding administrative law, the public law approach and the common law framework. Much discussion has dealt with the pros and cons of the two approaches, especially since the public law framework belongs to the Romano-Germanic type of legal order whereas the common law approach enters the Anglo-Saxon type of legal order. However, from a constitutionalist point of view the decisive point is not the legal technique used but whether the administrative law in a country safeguards the basic requirement for legality in the public sector. One should distinguish between weak and strong judicial review, as a constitutional state requires necessarily weak legal review but may also cover strong judicial review.

We discussed the nature and form of public law. Public law regulates the rights, powers, immunities, duties and liabilities of the state, the government and its departments and agencies as well as all organized political communities. It may include for example constitutional law, administrative law, local government law and police law.

Criminal law may be part of public law but is sometimes regarded as distinct from both public and private law. In all countries with an advanced economy and a democratic political system there has taken place an expansion of public law. Formally written constitutions are almost everywhere used to structure public law and its various modes of administrative law. Why? What are constitutions all about? 'Constitution' is a word with a strong legal ring, but when it comes to analysing the *raison d'être* of constitutions, we must turn to the new economic theory of organizations, as discussed in the next chapter.

Public or administrative law is more and more employed to regulate rights. The meaning of 'rights' has been a contested matter, it is a much debated question whether a radical separation between existing rights and ideal rights (George, 1994) is possible or desirable. The nature of rights is a source of contention, although the Hohfeld scheme makes the crucial distinctions. Whether there are collective rights besides individual rights is also a matter of sharp dispute (Kymlicka, 1995b). Should the state recognize group rights in addition to the ordinary human rights? If so, under which conditions? Only for special underprivileged minority groups or for all kinds of ethnic or religious groups? Is affirmative action or quota systems a mechanism for enhancing group rights? Group rights actually involve a whole spectre of mechanisms or competences: minority veto, minority representation, autonomy, fiscal support and recognition.

Administrative or judicial bodies are more and more involved in implementing rights. The Ombudsman institution is spreading around the world, either in its Swedish model version or in its Danish version. In the former, the Parliamentary Ombudsman may take legal action as prosecutor against any public official who does not respect citizen rights. In the latter, the Agent of the Parliament only makes recommendations to the administrative agencies in order to persuade them to change their practice. The attraction of strong judicial review is on the increase, either by the ordinary courts or by means of a special constitutional court. New constitutions in constitutional states often contain rules about both Ombudsman and legal review.

Part IV

Rationale

8

Why constitutions?

Introduction

The neo-institutionalist literature in political science states that institutions have not been given enough attention in the prevailing approaches to politics, the structural approach originating in sociology and the rational approach stemming from economics (March and Olsen, 1989). Neo-institutionalist theory includes a number of attempts to show that institutions matter. Crucial questions about the possibility of a civil society and the necessity of a polity cannot be addressed without an institutionalist perspective, it is claimed by the neo-institutionalists.

The aim in this chapter is to seek an answer to the fundamental problem of the existence of one kind of institutions, viz. why are there constitutions? The new economic organization theory (Williamson, 1990) may be employed to state an argument that answers puzzles about the relevance of institutions in general and constitutions in particular to government or the operations of a State. More specifically, a few models will be looked at to examine whether they shed light on the rationale of institutions in general and constitutions in particular, including the prisoners' dilemma model about the necessity of norms and a State to implement the norms as well as the principal-agent model about the necessity to structure the relationship between the rulers and those ruled in a State.

A rationale for the presence of a written constitution in so many States as well as the existence of constitutional practice in one form or another may be given by looking at the key concept in the economic theory of the State: public goods. A constitution or a constitutional practice is actually a set of institutions that operate as public goods. The special characteristics of public goods were discovered in the nineteenth century by Italian public finance scholars, but a clear presentation of their implications for politics was made by Knut Wicksell. Before we look at the economic theory of the state and Wicksell's model from a neo-institutionalist perspective, we will analyse a well-known legal model explaining tha rationale of constitutions, that of Hans Kelsen.

On key terms: 'institution' and 'constitution'

Both these words – 'institution' and 'constitution' – have the same core, as they refer to rules for human behaviour. A process of institutionalization involves that persons take rules into account when they act and that failure to follow rules meets with some type of sanction from the community. Rule orientated behaviour and collective sanction are the essence of an institution. Concrete examples of institutions include: driving a car on the left- or right-hand side of the road, the marriage and the contract, rules against public littering and so on.

One separates between various kinds of institutions depending on the sanction applied against failure to conform. Legal institutions are those rules that are backed by state sanctions of an ultimately violent nature. Such rules are laid down in statute law, created by parliament and customary law or precedents, established by judicial interpretation. Another type of institution is the convention or general agreement about social behaviour that is respected due to the reaction a break would call forth, i.e. rules that are upheld simply by means of group pressure.

The institutions that make up the legal order are particularly interesting in a State perspective. But also conventions are of great political importance, in particular constitutional conventions such as in British constitutionalism. When one gives examples of institutions one often refers to private sector institutions such as the market with its rules about voluntary exchange based upon private property schemes, but the public sector also comprises numerous institutions, such as regulatory schemes governing the operations of agencies at various levels of government.

The constitution is a special kind of institution, as it is a sort of meta-institution, or an institution for the making and interpretation of institutions. One often speaks of layers of institutions in neo-institutionalism. On the first level there is the individual person who acts by orientating his/her behaviour in terms of various institutions such as the market or the family. On the second level there are the organizations that substantiate the prevailing institutional order: the firm or the private enterprise with or without limited liability in the private sector or the bureau or the agency exercising authority in the public sector. On the third level there is the constitutional arena, where institutions are introduced, reformed and interpreted (Ostrom, 1990).

Constitutions offer rules for how institutions may be altered and how they are to be interpreted. Constitutional rules may have a different status as institutions meaning that they tend to be legal rules, either in the form of statute law, precedents or customary law, though constitutional institutions may also be conventions agreed upon sometime in the course of constitutional development and later on considered self-evident.

One may see the connections between the key words involved here: 'institution', 'constitution' and 'state' or 'government' by focusing upon their standard definitions in *The Compact Edition of The Oxford English Dictionary* (OED). Consider the following:

> Institution: An established law, custom, usage, practice, organization, or other element in the political or social life of a people; a regulative principle or convention subservient to the needs of an organized community or the general ends of civilization (OED, 1971: 354).

The OED lists this entry as its number six entry, documenting it back to Thomas Moore's *Utopia* in 1551, with the usage becoming frequent in the seventeenth century. Institutions are rules that regulate activities in a purposeful manner. Note:

> Constitution. The system or body of fundamental principles according to which a nation, state, or body politic is constituted and governed (OED, 1971: 876).

The OED has this entry as its number seven entry, dating it back to 1689 in a Declaration of the Estates of Scotland from 11 April. If institutions are regulative principles of an organized community, then constitutions comprise a special set of institutions, viz. the basic principles of the body politic.

One may note that OED lists as its third entry the following definition of 'constitution':

> A decree, ordinance, law, regulation; usually, one made by a superior authority, civil or ecclesiastical; spec. in Roman Law, an enactment

made by the emperor (*OED*, 1971: 876).

However, such a concept of a constitution would almost obliterate the dividing line between institutions and constitutions. It fails to capture what is essential in the modern concept of constitution, namely that a constitution offers rules for how decrees, ordinances, laws and regulations are to be made, implemented and adjudicated. It is no accident that the *OED* lists as its sixth entry a definition that cannot be traced further back than the seventeenth century:

> The mode in which a state is constituted or organized; especially, as to the location of the sovereign power, as a monarchical, oligarchical or democratic constitution (*OED*, 1971: 876).

Here, we have the essence of the modern usage of 'constitution'. A constitution is a set of institutions about the location of sovereign power, which implies that a constitution being a set of institutions dealing with the concept of sovereignty will bring us finally to the third concept, viz. the state or government.

Actually, there is an interesting passage in Thomas Paine's *The Rights of Man*, which makes the crucial distinction between the Roman law concept of the constitution as decree, ordinance, law, regulation and the constitutionalist interpretation of a constitution as rules for or limits upon the making of law. Paine notes succinctly:

> The Constitution of a country is not the act of its Government, but of the people constituting a Government. It is the body of elements, to which you can refer, and quote article by article; and which contains the principles on which the Government shall be organised, the powers it shall have (Paine, 1966: 48).

Paine underlines that a constitution is a thing 'antecedent' to a government, because government is the creature of a constitution. At least, that was the way it should be, if Paine's democratic constitutionalism would win the day. As is well known, Edmund Burke had in his *Reflections on the Revolution in France* (1790) argued the other way around, denying the possibility of constitutional innovation and intentional restructuring of government in accordance with rationally laid down articles. The question of the feasibility of constitutional design is just as relevant today when so many new constitutions have been enacted since 1989.

It remains to look at the role institutions play in definitions of the words 'State' and 'government'. Let us again quote from *The Compact Edition of The Oxford English Dictionary*. It lists a number of entries on the word 'State' such as: 'a particular form of polity or government', and 'a republic, non-monarchical commonwealth'. However, in these entries 'State' seems to stand for a type of government, which is not quite the sense the word receives from 1600 and onwards, namely civil government itself:

> State: the body politic as organised for supreme civil rule and government; the political organisation which is the basis of civil government; hence, the supreme civil power and government vested in a country or nation (*OED*, 1971: 852).

The dictionary traces this usage of 'State' back to 1538 in a text by Starkey but more frequently from around 1600. The connection with the meaning of 'constitution' is clear, as the State is the body politic or civil government for which the constitution handles down its institutions. 'Government' is also given a couple of entries, as the word may stand for either 'guidance in action' in general or more specifically:

> The action of ruling; continuous exercise of authority over the action of subjects or inferiors; authoritative direction or regulation; control, rule (*OED*, 1971: 320).

However, 'government' is also given an institutional definition: 'the system according to which a nation or community is governed; form or kind of polity'. Since around 1550 there is talk about political, church or ecclesiastical government or monarchical, oligarchical and republican government. Obviously, the word 'government' is more general than the 'state' and less specifically tied to only political matters. However, its institutional connotation is obvious, as it often means a form of polity to be expressed, presumably, by means of a constitution.

Thus, there is a kind of triad – institution, constitution, State or government – where the entities hang together. Why is that so? The fact that these concepts are connected by means of definitions is hardly an accident, but reflects deeper realities. Can we offer some theory that explains why in general social life needs institutions and in particular States require constitutions? Let us first probe into a well-known legal theory about the necessity of a constitution for a state. When it comes to constitutions, then legal thought is close to

political theory. In legal theory the place of constitutions is prominent. Whether constitutional law is a political science subdiscipline
or a part of jurisprudence has always been unclear. After that we
bring up economic organization theory.

A legal theory

As stated above, whenever one talks about constitutional law, then
it is impossible not to touch upon the concept of the State. One
cannot conceive of a state without the notions connected with public
law. And public law is based upon constitutional law and closely
intertwined with administrative law – see Chapter 7. But what, more
exactly, is the relationship between the State and the constitution,
generally speaking?

The legal doctrine that the State must have a system of fundamental institutions which lay down the chief rules for politics and
policy-making in the country has an almost unchallenged status
today in constitutional law. It is strongly entrenched in those countries that either are or seek to become democracies. It is widely advocated in international law. And it has been firmly defended in
political thought for a long time. The close relationship between the
State and the constitution appears as almost self-evident.

Yet, first one must remember that several States lack a true constitution, i.e. a system of rules that in reality limit the power of the
State and provide for a separation of powers either functionally –
executive, legislative and judicial functions – or territorially – decentralization, regionalization or in the form of a federation. Most
States have a constitution, but some of them are either left-wing or
right-wing dictatorships, in which often the formally written constitutional document does not correspond to the real constitutional
practices.

Secondly, we need to recall that a few democratic countries operate without a written constitution meaning that the existence of
strongly institutionalized constitutional practices is sufficient for
democratic stability or vitality. If formally designed constitutions are
phony in many States and if democracy can work without explicitly
codified institutions, then perhaps the link between the State and the
constitution is not as close as is usually assumed?

As we saw in Chapter 1 the conception of the State is an essentially contested concept. A number of characteristics have been men-

tioned as the typical features of the State: authority, legitimacy, employment of physical force or the provision of public goods, as described in a number of instructive overviews of the literature on the 'the state' (Jasay, 1985; Vincent, 1987). One may distinguish between sociological and economic models of the State, the first underlining legitimate authority and the other emphasizing public goods. If one takes a legal approach to the State and emphasizes the closeness between the legal order and the State, then one may suggest a juristic argument for the necessity of a constitution whenever there is a State. Hans Kelsen has proposed a theory about the place of the constitution in the state that has been much discussed (Kelsen, 1961, 1967).

Kelsen's model focuses upon the concept of a basic norm or a set of basic norms, i.e. a constitution. Starting from the assumption that the State and the legal order are one and the same entity, Kelsen argued that each decision by a State organ has to be validated by some rule that empowers a person or group of persons to make that decision – the legality principle. In its turn, the validity of such a rule presupposes another rule which empowers other State organs to promulgate such rules. This argument leads stepwise and backwards to a fundamental norm that initiates the whole process of law-making and decision-making, making it possible to enact laws that in turn make it possible to issue ordinances, which in turn make it possible to lay down administrative rules or make administrative decisions. Without such a fundamental norm it would be impossible to avoid an infinite regress in the legal order. The constitution of a State typically provides for just such a basic norm from which all other rules or decisions are derived step by step – the *lex superior* principle.

Kelsen complements this rational deduction of a constitution from the two premises, the principle of legality and the principle of *lex superior*, with the notion that constitutional institutions are special or require special treatment. According to the Kelsen framework constitutions are not just any kind of institution. Being a distinct set of laws they require special protection, or constitutional inertia, meaning that constitutional rules should only be changed by means of a special procedure that is different from the one used to change statute law and constitutions should be protected by means of a special court, a constitutional court.

Kelsen's model, called the pure theory of law, appears credible and reasonable, as legal reasoning often gives such an appearance of deductive clarity. Armed with these three notions – principle of legality, *lex superior* and constitutional inertia – Kelsen launched an approach that received much attention. However, it has also been much criticized, because the legal order seldom has such a strict and rationally conceived structure. The importance of customary law and judge-made law as well as the complexity of modern statute law result in legal ambiguities, if not straightforward conflicts between norms. Is there really such a thing as one clearly identifiable basic norm or set of basic norms? Does every State have one or two basic norms? What is it that confers validity upon the laws in the first place, is it the fact that they can be derived from a basic norm or is it the fact that judges make use of them when applying the law?

These are difficult questions in legal theory about the place of the State in the legal order and about the way a State functions to both create and maintain law – see Chapter 7. Being a legal positivist, to Kelsen law always implies a reference to the State, because the State guarantees the efficiency of law, i.e. the fact that the legal order is upheld and persists. Only those institutions that the State guarantees by means of the threat of or actual use of physical force belong to the legal order. According to positivism, legal institutions are sharply different from moral ones, where the criterion is that the former are somehow 'positive' in the sense that they exist being applied by the state whereas moral institutions offer ideal principles of justice.

One criterion of whether an institution or rule is part of the legal order of a country is whether it can be derived from the basic norm of the country – the validity criterion. Another criterion is whether the institution is actually upheld, backed by State activity – the efficiency criterion. Kelsen seems to accept both these criteria on what is positive law, but are they always consistent? While all the norms in the legal order can be derived from the basic law conferring upon them validity, what is it that guarantees the validity of the basic norm? Perhaps it rests simply upon efficiency, i.e. the fact that it is in operation, but what is the situation if the basic law is suspended as in a *coup d'état*? What then is valid law? When the efficiency and validity criteria conflict, what happens?

Kelsen seems to move in a circle: ultimately a constitution comprising the basic norm(s) makes a State possible. However, at the same time it is the State which, by upholding the legal order including the basic sanctions, confers validity upon the constitution. The legal model implies that a constitution is necessary for a State but also that a State is necessary for a constitution. Which, then, comes first?

Here, in order to state a rationale for constitutions two steps need to be taken. First, we must establish the necessity of institutions for a society, in particular State institutions or law; secondly, we must lay down an argument for the necessity of a special set of institutions, i.e. a constitution, in a State. For the first problem we employ the prisoners' dilemma model while for the second problem we use the principal-agent model in economic organization theory. Finally, we must find an argument for the attractiveness of a democratic constitution. Knut Wicksell, around the end of the nineteenth century, presented a model that actually provides such a statement, derived from public goods theory.

The prisoners' dilemma model

A promising approach to explaining the crucial role that institutions like a constitution play for the State is to focus upon the new economic approach to interpreting organizations. Three models are especially relevant here, one which focuses upon the constitution as offering fundamental rules for society, and two additional ones which structure the relationship between the politicians and the citizens. The first model, the prisoners' dilemma game, helps us understand the role or norms in society whereas the second model, the principal-agent framework, allows us to understand why constitutional rules handing down the institutions for the key political players are crucial in any group of human individuals. Finally, the Wicksell state model sheds light on why a number of democratic institutions are considered so important.

Perhaps the most famous of all games in the game theory literature, the prisoners' dilemma has received an attention that is extraordinary in two ways. It was discovered by scholars around 1950. First, on its own terms it appears to be mind-boggling, because it resists each and every attempt at a solution. Secondly, it seems to be capable of numerous ever new applications to real life situations which are truly interesting from a social scientist point of view (Axelrod, 1984; Taylor, 1987; Hechter *et al.*, 1990).

The dilemma involves two prisoners who have been caught, but against whom there is not enough evidence for them both to be sentenced. The prosecutor decides to make an offer to each of them, which they have to reply to independently of each other. If one confesses the crime, then he/she will receive a much lower sentence than the other. What should each prisoner do? Table 8.1 displays the standard game matrix version of the game, where the outcomes of choosing either of the two strategic alternatives – confess or not confess – are rendered as the number of years that each has to spend in prison. In this version it is question of a so-called two person game, but the prisoners' dilemma model can be formulated for an N-person game with any number of players more than two. As a matter of fact, there is also a prisoners' dilemma model in a so-called supergame format (Howard, 1971).

Table 8.1
Prisoners' dilemma

| | Player B | |
	Not confess	Confess
Player A		
Not confess	–2, –2	–10, –1
Confess	–1, –10	–5, –5

Source: Luce and Raiffa, 1957.

The game has one strict solution, viz. each player should choose to confess. This alternative is the so-called Nash-solution, but it is also a dominating strategy meaning that whatever the other player chooses to do, there is no alternative strategy that can improve the actor's outcomes. However, this solution cannot be accepted because it is not the most feasible one. Instead, if both parties choose not to confess, then both are better off. This means that the rational solution to the game results in an outcome that is inferior, or to use the economists' language, not Pareto optimal. Why would anybody engage in strategies that lead to worse outcomes, if they reason rationally? The conclusion appears unavoidable: a rational pursuit of behaviour maximizing the self-interests of persons may lead to collectively irrational results.

The prisoners' dilemma literature focuses upon two problems that the game generates: (a) is there another solution to the game that allows the persons to choose the alternatives that result in the best outcome? (b) what kinds of situations in real life does the prisoners' dilemma game portray? Here, we will focus upon the application of the game to institutions (Brams, 1975, 1994).

Concerning (a) it may be stated quite generally that the search to find a route to resolve the prisoners' dilemma has stimulated a lot of highly abstract research about rational choice and the conditions under which individuals interact in order to stabilize outcomes. According to one line of research the dilemma is virtually impossible to handle unless one admits some additional element that forces the players to choose the strategy that will result in the best outcome for both, i.e. not to confess or to collaborate under the terms of a previously made agreement not to cheat on each other. One such element could simply be a social norm obligating each individual to keep promises made or to trust other persons (Elster, 1989).

According to another line of research, the dilemma may be resolved if one assumes that the game is played repeatedly. If a person faces a successive number of the prisoners' dilemma games in relation to another person, then each player has to take the possibility of retaliation into account. This means that if one player cheats in one round, then he/she could expect the other player to cheat in the next round, and so forth – the so-called Chainstore paradox. The only way to break such a consecutive row of inferior outcomes is to start coordinating the strategies so that the superior outcome can be reached (Rapoport and Chammah, 1970).

In such a series of prisoners' dilemma games (a tournament), it is possible to show both experimentally (Axelrod, 1984) and theoretically in so-called meta-games (Howard, 1971) that one rational strategy is to play tit-for-tat, i.e. to reward cooperation with cooperation and punish defection with defection. Another possibility is the Grim strategy, whereby a player starts by cooperating but defects for ever once the other player defects (Rasmusen, 1994). What is critical in this supergame interpretation – relying on the elaboration of meta-strategies (meaning strategies for choosing a strategy) – is that the players face an infinite succession of prisoners' dilemma games, but is that a plausible assumption about human interaction?

In any case, moving to (b) the practical relevance of modelling prisoners' dilemma games becomes more obvious. By identifying the alternative 'not to confess' with cooperation and 'to confess' with defection, one arrives at Table 8.2, which may be used to model situations involving players choosing between cooperating or defecting, a frequent scenario indeed.

Table 8.2
Cooperation versus defection

	Player A	
	Cooperation	*Defection*
Player B		
Cooperation	5, 5	1, 10
Defection	10, 1	2, 2

Source: Rapoport, 1970.

Note: the outcomes have been scaled differently in order to allow for a more general analysis of any kind of interaction.

The power of the prisoners' dilemma model for social science purposes is that it captures a vital aspect of many forms of human interaction, viz. any predicament where two or more persons may benefit from collaborating but where each individual may benefit even more if he/she exploits the fact that all other persons stick to the terms of collaboration. There is an advantage to be had if one player pretends that he/she will cooperate but defects, given that the other player continues to cooperate.

A lot of interesting situations may be found where the basic interaction conditions are of the prisoners' dilemma kind: trade union membership, wage negotiation, public goods provision, taxation and economic growth, for example. A number of well-known models have been proposed to model these forms of interaction, where cooperation may bring mutually beneficial outcomes but where a single individual may benefit even more by free riding (Musgrave, 1959; Olson, 1975; Riker and Ordeshook, 1973; Olson, 1982).

A most general formulation of these interaction problems, where defection is individually rational but socially catastrophic when all players are rational, is to focus on a group of size N. As long as the group is fairly large, the individual contribution of a single player will be marginal meaning that two problems arise: (a) the N-1 problem; (b) the $1/N$ problem.

The N-1 problem implies that as long as the group is large enough to secure enough cooperation it is always rational for a single individual to defect, since he/she can enjoy the mutual benefit without sacrificing anything. And from an individual point of view it is most often the case that the group is not so small that his/her contribution is critical.

The l/N problem implies that a single individual when contributing to a group in order to bring forward some mutual benefits will have to share the benefits with all the others in the group. If the group is large, then the share of the individual person will be very small. Thus, single persons have little individual incentive to bring forward collective benefits that the entire group shares.

The N-1 problem and 1/N problem may be employed to understand a critical aspect of society, namely its strong orientation towards norms as well as its firm reliance upon the employment of coercion in order to uphold its norms, i.e. the institutionalization of social interaction. Society is a highly institutionalized phenomenon, i.e. it consists of rules or norms that are upheld by sanctions. Voluntary exchange is one of the most elementary forms of social interaction, but it cannot work unless supported by institutions like the rules for contracting.

Individual persons may be be able to solve numerous problems by means of voluntary exchange. Markets offer institutions for voluntary exchange starting from the rules concerning contracting and property rights. As long as benefits and costs may be fully internalized by the participants in voluntary exchange, markets deliver outcomes that are Pareto efficient or socially rational. There is only one problem: how to guarantee that the players in voluntary exchange respect the institutions of the market. Markets cannot solve the prisoners' dilemma situation so that it is individually rational to take advantage of the situation and not play by the rules. The market needs an external umpire that ensures that its institutions are upheld and respected. There is no other umpire than government, as Hobbes realized.

Before the market there is the state, before voluntary exchange there is government (Coleman, 1988). The State may be seen as the apex of a pyramid of institutions in society. The State guarantees the smooth operation of certain absolutely vital human institutions, such as the fulfilment of contracts, the respect for mutual obligations as well as preservation of property rights. Without these institutions markets would be impossible. Governments employ taxation to pay for the allocation of these institutions which are public goods. Without such public goods social interaction could not be institutionalized and it would decline to anarchy or anomy.

Small groups may be able to engage in collective action and provide themselves with arrangements that make voluntary interaction

schemes work (Taylor, 1987). But the severity of the *N*-1 problem
and the 1/*N* problem is such that only a State can solve the prisoners'
dilemma by forcing individuals to choose to cooperate. The State is
the organization that guarantees the critical institutions of the private sector by enforcing cooperation in prisoners' dilemma situations. When the State fails, as in anarchy or civil war, or when it
degenerates into genocide, it no longer sticks to its task of allocating
public goods and maintaining the institutions that make voluntary
exchange or contracting possible and mutually beneficial. But if we
can claim that a State is necessary in order to maintain crucial human
institutions like the market, then why must there be a constitution?

The principal-agent model

All over the world there are States. When the State fails, then the
tragic phenomena of civil war and anarchy occur. The State is an
institutional device for handling the prisoners' dilemma problem. Its
existence may be derived from a theory about the consequences of
free riding for collective action. And some kinds of collective action
are necessary for any society such as the protection of life and liberty as well as the protection of the contract. In the last resort only
a State can protect such vital institutions. But how is the State to be
run?

One may interpret the exercise of public powers as a contractual
problem of how a principal or the people are to make agreements
with agents such as politicians and bureaucrats about what the latter
should do for the former. Such contractual matters may be resolved
by means of short-term or long-term contracting. If the principal
were to give instructions to the agent on a continuous basis – short-
term governance format – then there would have to be ongoing referenda all the time. Yet, the transaction costs involved in such a
scheme would be staggering. Thus, in order to economize some form
of long-term governance scheme will be required, but which one?
And were one to settle for governance by referenda, one would still
face the monitoring problem of checking that decisions are implemented, which again is a contractual problem (Rasmusen, 1994).

Even if we can account for the omnipresence of the State by means
of the necessity of institutions, as derived from the prisoners'
dilemma model, we have not explained why we need a constitution
for the State. A constitution is necessary, because it offers the rules

in terms of which the State itself is institutionalized. Thus, any society needs a set of institutions that only the State can uphold in the long run. And a constitution is necessary to regulate the State due to the principal-agent problems that arise in the State.

Human interaction takes two modes, short-term interaction and long-term interaction. Consumer behaviour in the market place is an example of the former, whereas the hierarchical relationship between the rulers and those ruled is a case of the latter. One kind of long-term interaction is that a person hires another person to look after his/her interests against some form of remuneration, stated in a contract. The principal is the person who hires the other person, the agent. And the principal–agent relationship entails the reciprocity between the persons that stems from the interest of the principal to have the agent attempt to further his/her case as well as from the interest of the agent to further his/her own interests in the relationship with the principal. The access to information about behaviour and outcomes will be critical when principals and agents make contractual agreements as well as monitor their fulfilment.

The principal–agent model is the core framework in the new economic organization theories that have been developed in order to explain why institutions such as the firm or the market have evolved (Milgrom and Roberts, 1992). The basic idea is that the principal and the agent have both mutual and conflicting interests, as e.g. in the insurance sector where the insurance company, as the principal, attempts to identify and select various agents taking the insurance in order to protect itself against moral hazard and adverse selection. How can the person hiring an attorney as his/her agent when accused of having committed a crime monitor the efforts of the attorney to promote his/her case, when the behaviour of the agent is not observable? Or how is the population to guarantee itself of the best performance from the politicians, when there exist both hidden information and hidden actions?

The principal-agent model highlights basic governance problems that exist in any State. How is the population or how are the citizens in a country to instruct the rulers of the State about what their interests are and how they are to be protected? How are the rulers of the State to instruct and monitor the organizations of the State so that policies may be implemented? The answer is the constitution, or a set of special institutions that regulate these principal–agent relationships.

The constitution is a broad long-term contract between those ruled and the rulers that specify the conditions on which the agents may exercise power in order to enhance the interests of the principal. The rules of the constitution identify what the common objectives of the principal and the agent are, what activities the agent may never undertake, how policies are to be enacted and implemented by the principal and the agent and how conflicts about the interpretation of the constitution are to be resolved. Human rights, separation of powers, checks and balances, judicial review – all these institutions – belong to the constitutional regulation of the principal–agent relationships in the State.

Just as institutions constitute restrictions on human behaviour, so constitutions put up restrictions on the behaviour of the rulers as they frame and implement rules. Whether a constitution really binds or the extent to which it is truly effective depends upon the State and its commitment to the institutionalization of the constitution. The fact that constitutions fail and that they are reduced to mere formal documents does not reduce their significance for regulating the political principal–agent relationships. When constitutions are not upheld, then there is a substantial risk for an exploitation by the agent of the principal, as has happened in many states such as in Cambodia, Eastern Europe, West Africa and so forth.

A constitution, by offering rules for the conduct of the business of the State, always limits arbitrariness and unpredictability, but it does not necessarily habour a democratic regime. A democratic constitution is one way to institutionalize the principal–agent relationship, but it is not the only one. Many constitutions have not been democratic, but they have put restrictions on the capacity of rulers to exercise power, if they were not mere curtains for totalitarian rule. Thus, a constitutional monarchy typically has a written and effective constitution. Even authoritarian regimes may have actually operating constitutions, such as the Republic of South Africa under the apartheid regime, Spain under the Caudillo and the Soviet Union. Why, then, does a democratic constitution provide such an ideal way to institutionalize the principal–agent relationship?

Wicksell's model

Knut Wicksell gave an interesting economic interpretation of decision-making institutions when making collective choices in a short

paper entitled: 'A New Principle of Just Taxation' in 1897. It anticipated the public choice approach (Wicksell, 1967), as it focused
upon various costs involved in making decisions in the State. There
are many different types of democratic constitutions, as there exist
several alternative democratic institutions, partially described in
Chapter 6. Here we look at the advantages of a democratic regime
from an economic organization perspective. Whatever definition of
democracy one chooses, the concept implies at the very least the
institution: One Man–One Vote.

Collective decision-making or so-called social decisions in the form
of a state is a *sine qua non* for social order. A legal order is necessary for civil society and only the State can guarantee the legal order.
But how are decisions about such public goods to be made? However elementary the State may be, there must be a constitutional
choice about how these vital group decisions are to be made. Theoretically speaking, three possible alternative decision rules may be
singled out: dictatorial, majoritarian and unanimity or consensus
based rules.

A dictatorial choice principle means that one person can impose
his/her preferences upon the group whatever the group decision
should be under a rule of non-dictatorship, for example with Saddam
Hussein. This is an extremely unfortunate solution to the principal–agent problem, as it makes the principal totally dependent
upon the agent. The risks for high external decisions costs are overwhelming. There is no way for many citizens to protect themselves
against capricious decision-making on the part of the dictator. The
whole population becomes a 'dummy' in the vocabulary of the game
theorist.

A consensus rule or unanimity implies that each person has a veto
against any group decision that he/she dislikes. The external decision
costs will be minimized by the choice of such a decision rule; actually every group decision will be Pareto efficient, since it will not be
possible to reduce the position for any single individual. One may
distinguish between various institutions for arriving at consensus,
from the requirements of concurrent majorities with a two-thirds
majority or larger to schemes that comprise so-called veto players
like a president or a second chamber with special powers (Tsebelis,
1990).

However, the drawback is that the internal decision costs will
increase drastically if one adopts the veto principle, in particular in

the form of an individual veto for each group member. The time and effort needed to reach an agreement in a group where each has a veto will rise the larger the majority required for a positive decision – the so-called transaction costs. Besides the costs of negotiating an agreement all kinds of strategic behaviour will arise in order to maximize the gains from what Oliver Williamson calls 'opportunistic behaviour' (Wlliamson, 1986).

Thus, collective action or group decision-making faces two kinds of costs: external and internal costs. The first kind decrease the more people are required to say *yes* for a positive decision to result, whereas the transaction costs increase, i.e. these two cost curves move in opposite directions to each other (Figure 8.1).

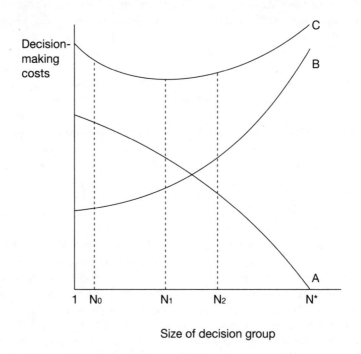

Figure 8.1 Wicksell's democracy model: external and internal decision costs

Note: A=external costs to the group participants; B=internal or transaction costs; C=A+B.

Curve A depicts the external decision costs which are at the maximum when there is a dictator; curve B identifies the transaction costs which are at the maximum when each person has a veto. Curve C is the addition of curves A and B, measuring the combined decision-making costs. They are at their minimum when the group settles for simple majority, or 51 per cent of the votes for a positive decision. Thus, if one starts from the principle One Man–One Vote, then a simple majority rule appears to be the most cost effective for any group.

The majoritarian principle of at least 50 per cent of the votes appears to be an attractive institution for the state. It minimizes the decision costs when both the costs to the citizens (external costs) and the transaction costs (internal costs) are included. It is possible to arrive at a different decision rule if the costs develop in a different manner. Thus, if the external costs are especially high in relation to some especially important types of decisons such as constitutional decisions or financial decisions, then a larger majority than the simple majority may be required, such as a qualified majority rule, or two-thirds majority (i.e. the curves in Figure 8.1 may have different slopes in relation to different issues).

Norms, constitutions and States

In this chapter we have advanced some theoretical arguments for the importance of constitutions in political life. Starting from the concepts of an institution and of a process of institutionalization one may argue that a State is necessary for the maintenance of social order in any society. The model employed to state the argument for the necessity of a State is the prisoners' dilemma game. It implies that if individuals act only on the basis of rational considerations about their own self-interests, then socially unacceptable outcomes will result. Norms, i.e. institutions, are required in order to make individuals cooperate for the achievement of acceptable outcomes. And the institutionalization of such norms of good behaviour and cooperation requires the existence of a State.

Thus, the first theoretical argument claims that society needs a system of norms which are institutionalized by the State. The second theoretical argument states that a State must have a constitution, if it wishes to avoid running into anarchy or resulting in complete personal rule which is fundamentally unstable. The model used to state this argument is the principal–agent framework. It outlines a few

crucial problems in human interaction, where it is a long-term contract between persons. The constitution sets the conditions for the
political principal–agent relationships in a State, where rulers exercise formidable powers over those ruled. Constitutionalism is the historical doctrine that recommends certain principles that should
govern the interaction between the principal and the agent in politics – such as separation of powers, accountability, predictability,
legality, checks and balances, fundamental rights and duties – with
the aim of constraining the agent in accordance with the wishes of
the principal.

The third theoretical argument suggests some reasons why a democratic constitution is often regarded as the best way to handle some of
the principal–agent problems. If the State is of such importance to
society, then how are State decisions to be made? Decision rules that
allow for less than a simple majority of votes, such as a dictatorial
decision rule, imply very high decision costs for the principal, as he/she
may be adversely affected by whatever actions a dictator may take. On
the other hand, if the State demands a larger majority than a simple
majority, such as a qualified majority, then the transaction costs will
start increasing. If a veto rule is used, such as in the infamous Polish
liberum veto institution, then transaction costs will explode.

It seems possible to put forward an argument that constitutions
are vital to the State and that the State is of crucial importance to
society. A good case may also be stated for the employment of some
kind of democratic constitution. Yet, one cannot assume that human
beings always bring about what is necessary or socially optimal.
States may fail, bringing about disaster for society. And there are
many examples of historical constitutions that have not been democratic. Chapter 6 surveyed actually existing constitutions and looked
at the variety of institutions that may be employed in a democracy.
Kelsen (1967) launched a theory about the constitution arguing that
all constitutional States need an explicitly written constitution characterized by inertia. But why would each and every State be a constitutional State?

In political thought much speculation has been devoted to finding
the essence of the State. In German political science the organism
model became widely accepted around 1900, advocated by among
others Otto Gierke (Gierke, 1958). However, is the State really a kind
of biological phenomenon, with its own life span as it were? Some
scholars argued in the sixteenth century that the State must pay

attention to its own interests – the reasons of State. The question, though, is how such interests are to be identified and how they relate to morals. Conservative or fascist scholars, such as for example, Carl Schmidt claimed that the State is basically power and that moral considerations cannot govern the State when it looks after its own interests (Neumann, 1986).

Rejecting the idea that the State is an organization that is separate from the persons who live in it and act on behalf of it, sociologists like Max Weber (1978) suggested that the State is simply the political organization that guarantees law and order in a country. However, in the twentieth century the State has grown far beyond the allocation of what economists in the public finance school call 'public goods', which are the very things Weber had in mind. The welfare state has implied the growth of the 'tax state', as Joseph Schumpeter described the process of public sector expansion that has dominated politics all over the world. Actually, very few States today limit themselves to the regulation of the legitimate employment of physical violence, in the words of Weber (1978).

Richard Rose has identified three kinds of states: the guardian state of classical liberalism in the eighteenth century, the infrastructural state of the industrialization and urbanization processes in the nineteenth century and the welfare state in the twentieth century (Rose, 1984). One may wish to add that the Communist state, which dominated civil society totally by means of the planned economy, constitutes a fourth type, albeit no longer as relevant. Given such a variety, who can tell what the essence of the State is? If the State is the allocation of public goods such as external defence and internal law and order, then the State's resources – the military and the police – may be used for other purposes than safeguarding a democratic regime or upholding the principles associated with constitutionalism, as described in Chapter 1. It is neither a contradiction nor an impossibility that the agent may dominate the principal and install a set of institutions which makes the agent a so-called dictator and the population or the citizens a so-called dummy, reversing the relationships discussed above between the major players in the constitutional game.

Conclusion

In this chapter we have taken an exclusively theoretical look at constitutions, trying to find arguments that prove how necessary they are

in society and for the State. The new economic models of organization or transaction cost theory appear to hand down a few interesting insights that really prove or at least indicate why constitutions
are such omnipresent phenomena.

First, there is the prisoners' dilemma model which shows that
norms or institutions backed by sanctions are necessary for bringing
about a society where there is reciprocal interaction or cooperation.
The state is an organization that is highly suitable for delivering
these norms – what Jon Elster (1989) refers to as the 'cement of
society'. Secondly, constitutions are necessary to structure the principal–agent relationships involved in setting up a State. Interpreting
the State with the principal-agent model directs one's attention to the
basic contract between the electorate on the one hand and the politicians and bureaucrats on the other about the rules for the exercise
of State power. Finally, the Wicksell model about two types of decision costs – external and internal – in collective choice offers a rational argument for the choice of a democratic constitution. It also
seems fair that the power to change and the power to block should
be the same for each individual or group, which democracy as plurality or simple majority entails.

This is about as far as one can come by means of deductive reasoning. It is now time to take a look at constitutions as they exist
today in space or have existed in time, looking at similarities and differences between countries. In an inductive or empirical approach to
constitutions one is interested in the range and scope of constitutional variation. In Chapter 4 we started from the first modern constitutions in the late eighteenth century and in Chapter 9 we will now
assess the claim that constitutions matter critically for social, economic and political outcomes.

9

Do constitutions matter?

Introduction

In the rapidly growing neo-institutionalist literature there is widespread agreement that institutions play a major role in social life, in politics as well as in economic life (Hechter, *et al.*, 1990; Powell and DiMaggio, 1991). Structuralism in macrosociological thought used to underline the impact of major social forces, e.g. affluence, urbanization, ethnic diversity and religious creed. The rational choice approach on the other hand focused upon individual incentives underlining the calculus of benefits versus costs in terms of a model of self-interest maximization behaviour. Both these major approaches – structure versus actor – bypass the fundamental place of institutions or rules, neo-institutionalism claims (March and Olsen, 1995).

In *Do Institutions Matter?* (1993) R.K. Weaver and B.A. Rockman collect a number of pieces of evidence that political rules have an impact upon performance and outcomes. In this chapter we assess this claim with regard to constitutional institutions as a subset of political institutions. It can only be done by means of empirical research.

In Chapter 6 we surveyed a number of constitutions around the world. Constitutions are both intrinsically and extrinsically interesting. Although one operates with simple categories when looking at country similarities and differences in the basic political institutional set up, it is fascinating to observe the institutional variation between several countries. Just keeping track of constitutional changes and portraying constitutional development is a worthwhile effort in itself, particularly now with the strong push towards constitutional reform on all the five continents. This is the *intrinsic* perspective upon constitutions.

Yet, we also ask if alternative constitutions have an impact upon societal outcomes. This is the *extrinsic* interest in basic political institutions such as those contained in the constitutional framework. The present strong focus upon constitutions involves the hypothesis that constitutions matter for political, social and economic outcomes, as Giovanni Sartori argues in *Comparative Constitutional Engineering* (1994). But how are we to substantiate such a belief?

In this chapter we first discuss methodological problems involved in testing hypotheses about the impact of constitutions on real life results. Then, on the basis of the international literature, we formulate a few models that we test on the basis of data about two sets of countries, one broad covering at most 145 countries and one narrow including 22 OECD countries. The overriding problem is this: if constitutions matter, then how, when and to what extent? When one speaks of constitutional evaluation, then it is important to remember the distinction between the formally written constitution – the constitutional document(s) – and the real constitution, i.e. the regime, as spelled out in the introductory chapter. We focus in particular upon the causes and effects of democratic institutions.

Constitutional evaluation

Constitutions are enacted by political élites with a view to promoting positive results or at least to counteracting outcomes that they consider negative. Such considerations may include broad macro phenomena, for example political stability, freedom, economic affluence and social justice. Constitutional design or the attempt to promote political, social and economic outcomes by means of engineering constitutions involves two problems, logically speaking. The first set of problems refers to the translation of a formally written constitution into real life institutions – the regime. The second set of problems deals with the impact of real life constitutions upon societal outcomes.

Step 1. It is one thing to draw up constitutional documents. One may write a huge document with many different institutions – the maxi strategy. Or one may enact a parsimonius document – the mini strategy. Yet, whichever approach one tries in a constitutional setting, constitutional realities will never match the constitutional *formalia* perfectly. The real constitution or the regime always approximates the written constitution more or less. The key question in the first step is: what is the probability that the constitution or the constitutional reforms enacted will be implemented?

During this century lots of constitutions have been written and enacted formally, but never really implemented. Moving a constitution from the document stage to the institutional stage involves lots of difficulties, which in many countries cannot be overcome. Many new constitutions or parts of constitutional reforms remain simply paperwork. The successful institutionalization of a new constitution depends upon several circumstances, which is conducive to uncertainty about whether a new constitution or a constitutional reform will be carried into effect.

The probability of moving a constitution from the document stage to the institutional stage depends not only upon environmental forces – political, economic, social. It also hinges upon the nature of the constitution itself as it is outlined in the formally written documents. Complicated constitutions with contradictory institutions such as the Weimar constitution prove more difficult to implement than a simple compact constitutional document. Constitutional documents that diverge widely from prevailing institutional practice may have been enacted without any intention to institutionalize its paragraphs – the *facade constitution.*

Step 2. Once there has been a successful institutionalization of a new constitution or of constitutional reforms, then one may ask whether desirable outcomes are promoted. The kind of outcomes that figure prominently in the debate about alternative constitutional schemes and the design of institutional mechanisms concern the most basic human values such as stability, affluence, freedom and equality. One must remember though that authoritarian constitutions may be framed and implemented in order to promote outcomes that are the very opposite of human values.

There is no clear-cut limit on the range of the outcomes that one may include in an evaluation of constitutions, but since there has to be a choice of a few outcomes to concentrate on, there is every reason to focus upon those that are of great concern to mankind. What kinds of basic political institutions could have an impact upon such eminently value related predicaments? Indeed, are constitutional mechanisms at all important for stability, affluence, freedom and equality taking into account that we know that other factors matter?

We should hasten to point out that the concepts that we employ here to talk about constitutions and outcomes are difficult to handle.

How are they to be defined? Can they be measured at all? Actually, these concepts are truly complex and one needs to be aware of several difficulties when one employs them in social science discourse. Let us exemplify four main problems.

Stability

Of the four outcomes selected here this is the most contested one, because stability may be both valuable and detestable. Instability may result in tragic consequences such as civil war, genocide or the killing of innocent people on a huge scale. However, instability may also express a possibility for change for the better, as for example when an authoritarian regime is being brought down.

The word 'stability' is not only a value-loaded concept; it is in addition ambiguous. Not only may one separate between political, economic and social stability. It is also possible to distinguish between various kinds of political instability such as political violence and government crises. To the former one counts the occurrence of revolutions, assassinations and guerrilla warfare, or the occurrence of protest phenomena such as general strikes, riots and anti-government demonstrations. The latter concept covers the premature break-up of governments, or lack of government durability. It must be explicitly pointed out that constitutional stability has an ambiguous value. An authoritarian constitution may well prove to be long lived such as in Saudi Arabia, whereas a democratic constitution such as the new Russian one could crumble after only a few years.

Affluence

A high average income or wealth in a country is clearly valuable for the population of the country, all other things being equal. Country affluence opens up possibilities and opportunities, whereas poverty drags the people down into misery and its attributes. This economic dimension may be mapped either by looking at the level of affluence or by the rate of growth in affluence.

Equality

It has been argued that affluence is not as crucial as has often been claimed, because it is only an aggregate measure. Distributional considerations have to be added, when evaluating outcomes. It is not enough that there is a high level of economic growth, because all the fruits from an increase in production may end up with the already rich. Social justice, it is argued, implies equality or at least equal opportunities. We will look at measures for the distribution of income. In addition, we also pay attention to the gender issue, as inequalities may have a strong aspect of sex discrimination.

Freedom

The concept of freedom is hardly less difficult to handle than the concept of stability, as it may mean different things. Yet, in a constitutional context there is one standard interpretation, i.e. freedom as the institutionalization of human rights. Freedom has a somewhat different status in constitutional settings from the other values mentioned above, since the concept tends to figure so prominently in constitutional documents. However, here we are not looking at how human rights are referred to in the formally written constitution, but at whether human rights are carefully protected in constitutional practice.

The successful institutionalization of human rights is one of the key characteristics on the basis of which constitutions may be evaluated. The distinction between a democratic constitution and an authoritarian one can hardly be made with regard to any other reference than human rights and their real protection in State and society. Each and every index that measures the occurrence of a real democratic constitution takes into account the institutionalization of human rights. We employ a few of these indices.

Given the centrality of freedom and the close connection between freedom, human rights and a democratic constitution, we will organize the constitutional evaluation around democracy. First, we ask whether a real democratic constitution matters in the sense that it promotes the other values discussed above: stability, affluence and equality. Secondly, we discuss whether there are major political institutions that enhance democracy. And thirdly, we evaluate the claims that have been made in the literature that certain democratic institutions operate better than others in the sense of promoting valuable outcomes, particularly in countries with an advanced economy.

Constitutional models

The logic of real constitutional evaluation suggested here implies that we begin by investigating what we call a *first order question*, i.e.

we enquire into the possibility of relationships between the four values of freedom, stability, affluence and equality. A few models focus upon whether democratic constitutions that respect and protect human rights (freedom) are accompanied by affluence, stability and equality. One may place a high value on democracy for intrinsic or extrinsic reasons. Here, we look at models that claim or deny that a democratic constitution promotes stability, affluence and equality. It may be true that a democratic constitution has few developmental implications, but it may still be considered of utmost importance, because of its intrinsic advantages such as the protection of liberty.

The first order question has been much discussed in the development literature: democracy and development or democracy *versus* development. According to the basic modernization model democracy is closely connected with economic affluence and social transformation. The modernization approach harbours a variety of models that either look upon democracy as a determinant of modernization or as determined itself by the process of modernization (Diamond, 1993).

The most discussed hypothesis in the modernization approach is the affluence model, which connects democracy with the overall level of economic development in a country. Several studies have shown that there is a clear positive although not firm association between the indices of democracy (human rights) and various measures of the level of affluence (Lipset, 1959; Cutright, 1963). Thus, affluence and democracy tend to go together when one looks at the States of the world. However, there is as yet no really satisfactory explanation of the statistical association. Is democracy a cause of affluence or is affluence a condition for democracy?

Since it is impossible to tell the direction of causation from simple correlations, much effort has been devoted to interpreting the finding that indices of democracy tend to covary with an affluence measure like GDP per capita. What speaks against the interpretation that democracy is the cause of affluence is that there is no association between democracy and economic growth. It seems to follow logically that if democracy is a cause of affluence, then it should promote sustained high rates of economic growth. But the experience from South East Asia is the opposite one, viz. that there may be long periods of rapid economic development without democracy.

It has been argued that the causal connection works the other way around, i.e. affluence is a major condition for democracy. The explanation for such a causal connection would be that a high level of affluence creates a middle class that finds a democratic constitution suitable to the style of politics that it prefers, viz. negotiations and compromise. In whatever way the statistical association between democracy and affluence is interpreted, it is still strong enough in our data to warrant attention.

In order to test models that claim that democracy promotes valuable outcomes, one needs to make sure that one looks at countries that have been democratic for a certain period of time. There is a set of countries where a democratic constitution has been institutionalized for a long period of time, in some case even from the end of the First World War, if not even earlier. There is also a set of countries where a democratic constitution has either been attempted and failed or is being tried at the moment. When one tests models that ascribe to democracy a number of crucial outcomes, then it is appropriate to focus upon the former set of countries where democracy has had a certain longevity. Our measure of democracy divides the states that have one million or more in population into those that have a long experience of democracy and those that are either dictatorships or fluctuate between a democratic and an authoritarian constitution (Appendix). The set of stable democratic countries may be identified in various ways, but in our data we count to 35 firm democracies.

Models that favour democracy claim not only that democracy promotes social and economic development, but also that democratic politics enhances equality and social stability. On the one hand, a few democracy models underline that democracy implies popular sovereignty which leads to, it is claimed, more equal outcomes. On the other hand, other democracy models argue that democratic politics by inviting contestation and strife between different groups and ideologies is conducive to bargaining. Democracies, if they are to survive, promote compromise politics, which reduces social unrest (Held, 1987; 1993).

Opposing these models, these is a set of development models that reject democracy as a tool for social and economic development, favouring a strong State that has enough social control to create equality and undo harmful opposition (Myrdal, 1968). In a developmental perspective, a democratic constitution has been regarded as an invitation to inefficiency and a lack of social control. Can we find any evidence of these opposing theories in the outcomes of democracy when it has been institutionalized in constitutional practice for some time?

Yet, even if one cannot show that democracy results in major social and economic outcomes, one must remember that a democratic constitution is intrinsically valuable. Democracy institutionalizes freedom in the form of human rights. It may not promote rapid economic growth, it may not enhance social equality and it may not resolve conflicts to such an extent that political stability prevails, but democracy still involves just that valuable phenomenon, freedom. The immense value attached to a democratic constitution leads us to ask a *second order question*: which institutions are conducive to democracy?

One may identify two kinds of institutional models in the literature on democracy. (a) One set of general models claim that major political institutions such as federalism, presidentialism or parliamentarianism promote democracy. (b) Another set of institutional models focus upon encompassing social and economic institutions, such as for example property rights regimes. Both these two sets of models pose measurement problems as it is far from obvious how these alleged determinants of democracy are to be identified. Whereas the (a) set of models may be found in both classical and modern political theory, the (b) set of models are more innovative. In economic neo-institutionalism it is argued that the way economic institutions have been framed and implemented have important consequences not only for economic life but also for politics (North, 1990). The emphasis is especially upon individualism or the institutionalization of private property rights, both of which are factors which are not easy to pin down in measures. When it is a matter of the consequences of federalism, presidentialism or parliamentarianism as well as property rights regimes, then one should cover countries with democratic and non-democratic constitutions.

Looking at how alternative democratic constitutions perform among countries with a rather similar background economically speaking, one may ask a *third order question*: which type of democratic institutions promote valuable political, social and economic outcomes? There is a set of models that focus on alternative democratic frameworks and how they perform *vis-à-vis* each other. These models deal specifically with countries that have been democracies for a long time and have an advanced economy, i.e. the OECD countries. Here there is the consociational model launched by Arend

Lijphart which argues that a specific set of democratic institutions have particularly nice economic, social and political outcomes (Lijphart, 1992). Another such model is the corporatist model which states that corporatist institutions promote stability, affluence and equality (Korpi, 1990; Streek, 1992). When one looks at the outcomes attending alternative kinds of democratic states – Westminster systems, consociational democracies, corporatist systems – then it seems appropriate to concentrate upon the democratic countries only.

The data set and the variables and indicators employed are presented in the Appendix. Let us begin the evaluation of constitutions by starting with the first order questions about how the four basic values interact, then move to second order questions about which institutions enhance the key value of freedom or democracy and finally bring up the third order problem of how alternative democratic institutions compete in relation to outcomes. However, first we shall say a few words about the problem of how a written democratic constitution may become a real democratic constitution. Before it can have an impact upon outcomes, a formally written constitution must be translated somehow into constitutional practice.

Constitutional institutionalization

It is hardly difficult for a government to have a new constitution written or an old one rewritten. The constitutional language is an international one and there are many constitutional models floating around. The formally enacted constitutions in the world are available in print should a government wish to copy what is used elsewhere.

There can be no doubt about the occurrence of constitutional copying. When constitutional laywers draw up new constitutional documents they are almost always well aware of major systems of constitutional paragraphs in other countries. What they attempt to determine is how these rules operate in practice and how a combination of rules taken from different countries may work for their own country.

There has beeń constitutional diffusion going on ever since the enactment of the first modern constitutions in the eighteenth century, the American constitution of 1787 and the French constitutions of 1791, 1793 and 1795. English constitutional practice has long been admired by both political theorists and constitution makers. There is

hardly any limit to the extent to which one state may 'steal' constitutional ideas from another state. Major crises in world politics initiate constitution making and constitutional diffusion, in which
processes a variety of institutions are considered in different mixes.

When one examines the constitutions that were enacted after the
First World War, then one receives a broad picture of what is possible in *constitutional plagiarism*. The break-up of the major empires
in Europe involved the creation of a number of new states which all
delivered new constitutions which drew upon existing documents but
added new institutions or combined the existing ones in a novel fashion. Thus, Estonia attempted to be a democracy but declined to
employ a head of State as an institution. The new Yugoslavia introduced a constitutional monarchy without parliamentarianism.
Poland vacillated between presidentialism and parliamentarianism
until a *coup d'état* finished its young democracy.

The Austrian constitution, written by Hans Kelsen, launched a
large number of institutions, none of which worked well enough to
ward off the rising threat of authoritarianism. However, the most
well-known constitution at that time, Germany's Weimar constitution, was overburdened by the attempt to combine in one document
very many institutions. In the words of one author:

> The Germans have made use of all the devices new and old by which a
> democracy can express itself, and have sought at the same time to find
> room for the application of new theories. Cabinet government has been
> borrowed from England, the idea of a strong popular president from
> America, direct legislation from Switzerland (Headlam-Morely in Haw
> good, 1939).

In such a constitutional policy the risk of contradictions is eminent:

> The President and the Reichstag are to occupy a position of equal
> importance; both are representative of the sovereign people, each is to
> act as a counterpoise to the other; in cases of dispute the decision rests
> with the people. A referendum can be brought about by the decision of
> the President, or of a minority in the Reichstag, or on the demand of a
> section of the people themselves ... . The Reichstag is the chief legisla
> tive authority, but it is not the only representative assembly; a Reich
> srat or second chamber has been established to represent the interests
> of the member-states and to serve as a check on the actions of the
> Reichstag, and an Economic Council to give expression to the needs of
> the industrial life of the nation (Headlam-Morley, in Hawgood, 1939:
> 352–3).

The constitutions enacted in the wake of the First World War proved to be extremely fragile, as several of them were swept away by the authoritarian movements that grew strong during the inter-war years. There is really no prototype fascist constitution, because in none of the fascist countries was there introduced a compact constitutional document. The Third Reich, like several authoritarian regimes today, was governed by means of emergency powers.

After the Second World War there was a new process of constitution making, first in Europe and Japan and then later in the Third World when the colonial empires broke up. Constitutional images were imported in many countries. Constitutionalist ideas were introduced in the former fascist states, the Leninist model was exported from the Soviet Union to Eastern Europe and China and Indo-China whereas many Third World states vacillated between presidentialism and parliamentarianism when new states were declared in Africa and Asia. At the same time Latin American countries have hovered between democratic and authoritarian constitutions during the postwar period.

The first constitutions to be enacted after the Second World War – the French 1946 constitution, the Italian 1947 constitution and the German 1949 constitution, had a striking constitutionalist tone, emphasizing human rights and the role of courts in protecting these. Friedrich observed:

> Perhaps the most startlingly novel aspect of these constitutions is their abandonement of the idea of national sovereignty as a central presupposition of their political theory. Here, again, the constitutional provisions are increasingly radical, as we compare the French, the Italian, and the German documents (Friedrich, 1950: 28).

However, this early constitutionalist tendency failed to materialize when many of the new independent states chose their own constitutional framework in the 1960s. Very soon after the declaration of independence the real, if not the written constitution, expressed more and more authoritarianism, either in the form of the sovereignty of the one party state or the institutionalization of a personal dictatorship or a military government. It was not until 1989 that the principles of constitutionalism – human rights and the separation of powers – again became a major force in shaping constitutional matters around the world.

The history of constitution making in the twentieth century shows

conclusively how difficult it is to translate a formally written constitutional document into steady constitutional practice. It is one thing
to devise a constitution but quite another matter to implement it.
Constitutional plagiarism is easy but constitutional translation is
hard.

All constitutions tend to be short-lived, not only democratic ones.
In whatever way constitutional longevity is measured the finding is
the same: constitutions are mortal. Table 9.1 illustrates data on constitutional longevity.

Table 9.1
Constitutional longevity

		Average year of introduction	Earliest introduction	Latest introduction
Western Europe	(15)	1943	1814	1993
Eastern Europe	(19)	1985	1922	1993
North America	(2)	1885	1789	1982
Central America	(12)	1970	1917	1987
Latin America	(10)	1967	1853	1993
Northern Africa	(7)	1980	1959	1992
Sub-Saharan Africa	(36)	1984	1960	1993
Asia Minor	(13)	1968	1921	1991
Asia Major	(26)	1977	1945	1993
Oceania	(3)	1909	1852	1975

Note: constitutional longevity is measured as the length of time of the most recently
enacted constitution.

Constitutions are in general short-lived phenomena. Most constitutions last only one or two decades or even less with the exception
of North America and Oceania. Getting a new constitution in place
meets with profound problems not just in Third World polities. Constitutions have tended to last for a short time also in Europe, especially so in Eastern Europe. Constitutional longevity is more of an
illusion than a real phenomenon, because when there is talk about
constitutions the focus is always upon those few that have lasted for
a long time. Constitutional instability reflects the fact that regime
changes are often happening in the States of the world. The average
age of constitutions in Africa is shockingly low with the States in
Asia Major not doing much better. The constitutional instability in
Central and Latin America is also high.

Getting a constitution to operate smoothly involves the translation of constitutional paragraphs into real life institutions, going from the written constitution to the living constitution. Yet, constitutional changes and constitutional reforms may be made without altering the basic regime, as for example when France moved from the Fourth Republic to the Fifth Republic while remaining a democracy. What are the conditions and effects of a real democratic constitution that has been in place for not such short a period of time?

Causes and effects of real constitutions

Once a formally written constitution is in place and operates through real life institutions, then one may enquire into its consequences for outcomes, especially if there is constitutional longevity. Given the existence of many facade constitutions in authoritarian political systems constitutional evaluation can never proceed simply from the set of documents that are designated as the 'constitution'. Constitutional practice will always diverge to a greater or lesser extent from constitutional documents.

The real constitution is the set of actually operating institutions that regulate state power and the relationship between government and citizens. We have derived three questions about real life constitutions above, first, second and third order problems as it were. Let us begin by enquiring into any connections between democracy and three outcomes, viz. affluence, equality and stability.

Outcomes of democracy

We know already that a true democratic regime scores high on one of the essential outcomes, freedom. Although one may define the concept of democracy in such a way that human rights do not play a major role, it remains the case that all the key indices on democracy include scores on how human rights are safeguarded. Thus, once a democratic regime has been institutionalized in a country, then it will score high on freedom as an outcome. However, it has been argued that a democratic regime may not be the best mechanism for enhancing stability, affluence or equality. Social and economic development require a strong state which democracy may fail to deliver. Does democratic longevity promote stability, affluence and equality? Table 9.2 has the answer.

Table 9.2
General effects of democracy (correlations)

Variable	Indicator			Number of cases
1. Affluence	GDPC90	=	.66	(N = 125)
	GNPC	=	·65	(N = 112)
2. Development	HDI92	=	·61	(N = 125)
3. Economic growth	GRO6580	=	·29	(N = 119)
	GRO8091	=	-·04	(N = 101)
4. Inflation	INF8090	=	-·06	(N = 109)
5. Stability	VIO8089	=	-·11	(N = 125)
	VIO9193	=	-·11	(N = 122)
	PRO8089	=	·06	(N = 125)
	PRO9193	=	·07	(N = 122)
	CRI8089	=	·04	(N = 125)
	CRI9193	=	·03	(N = 122)
6. Equality	LOW	=	·03	(N = 54)
	RATIO	=	-·17	(N = 54)
	WOMEN	=	·38	(N = 111)
7. Welfare effort	GOVCON	=	·17	(N = 100)
	HEALTH	=	·59	(N = 99)
	SOCEXP	=	·51	(N = 71)

Note: The indicators above are defined in the Appendix.

The findings include a confirmation of the affluence model that associates democracy with a high level of affluence. The much debated positive correlation between democratic longevity and GDP per capita recurs in our data which also shows that the human development index correlates with democracy to a considerable extent. However, it is clear that democracy is not a condition for rapid change in affluence, meaning high rates of economic growth. Finally, we note that long standing democracies tend to favour a welfare state effort and gender equality, at least to some extent. Negatively, the overall finding is that democracy does not matter for economic development, political stability or equality. The implication must be that democracy is more of an intrinsic than an extrinsic value. Democracy protects freedom in the form of human rights but is does not result in rapid economic development, at least not in the short run.

Institutional causes of democracy
We now turn to the second order question turning around the focus in order to look at the institutional factors that promote democracy.

If a democratic regime is intrinsically valuable being closely tied up with freedom as human rights, then which institutions tend to enhance the prospects of democracy? In the literature there are a few well-known models that pinpoint institutions, but one must remember also that other kinds of factors have been mentioned as conditions for democracy.

The federal model attributes an alleged impact upon democracy by the special state structure in federalism, viz. the occurrence of a dual system of administrative, legislative and judicial powers, one at the national (federal) level and the other at the provincial (state) level – see Elazar, *Federal Systems of the World* (1991). The model explains the positive contribution of federalism on democracy by the capacity of the dual framework to contain and disperse conflict (Ostrom, 1991). But, looking at the facts one may ask how many federal States are stable democracies? Table 9.3 lists this data. Among 35 firm democracies 11 have a federal constitution, while at the same time there are almost as many federal states that are not stable democracies.

Table 9.3
Federal States and firm democracy

	Democracy	Non-democracy
Federal	11	6
Unitary	24	85

Note: Pearsons' correlation amounts to: $r = .33$ ($N = 126$).

Among the States of the world with a population larger than 1 million, one quarter of them have a firm democratic regime. Here we find India with its federal system where the division of its 25 States follows the language cleavage, but almost all federal States that have been democratic for an extended period are to be found among the OECD countries. The federal States in the Third World either have an authoritarian or a quasi-democratic regime such as Pakistan and Nigeria in the former group and Argentina, Brazil, Mexico and Malaysia in the latter group. An interesting exception is the United Arab Emirates, which is super-rich, federal and authoritarian. It is difficult to tell whether Russian federalism will promote democracy in this country, as the connection between federalism and a democratic regime is more complex than is claimed by those who advocate the federal model. Several, but certainly not all, unitary States are firm democracies.

Republicanism has been a constitutionalist doctrine directed against monarchism and other forms of absolutism in the history of political thought, but is a republican state structure a certain remedy against authoritarianism? The answer is no, as Table 9.4 shows.

Table 9.4
Republics and firm democracy

	Democracy	Non-democracy
Republics	22	79
Non-republics	13	12

Note: Pearsons' correlation amounts to: $r = -.27$ ($N = 126$).

Actually, most republics are not firm democracies. Surprisingly, more than half of the non-republics which are mostly monarchies have democratic longevity. The explanation is that authoritarian regimes seldom employ the institutions of a king or emperor (czar), as most dictatorships involve either a military junta or a president. The decline in the attraction of monarchies is evident in the fact that few kings and emperors exercise real political power with the exception of Thailand, Morocco, Jordan and Saudi Arabia. In several countries a monarchical head of State has been retained on the condition that parliamentarianism is practised – a trade-off that was accepted in Nepal in the early 1990s. In Bhutan there is probably more of an absolute monarchy than a constitutional monarchy, although the rhetoric is the opposite one. In the Arabic world there is the Emir instititution which is non-democratic in effect.

When one enquires into the impact of presidentialism upon democracy, then one must pay attention to the distinction between formal and real presidentialism (Linz, 1992). A president may only be a figure-head, the nominal head of State in a country where the executive power rests with the premier. Or a president may not only be the head of State but also the head of the government, dispensing with the need for a premier. When we enquire into any link between presidentialism and democracy, then we focus upon the latter type, or real presidentialism. A few scholars, among them Juan Linz, argue that real presidentialism is counterproductive to a democratic regime (Linz and Valenzuela, 1994).

Formal presidentialism is practised in several countries which tend to have a parliamentary system of government. Thus, one basic constitutional choice is often depicted as real presidentialism versus parliamentarianism. Tables 9.5 and 9.6 have data about the relationships of these two institutions with democratic longevity. Let us begin with Table 9.5.a where the classification of countries with a presidential regime is based upon *Encyclopedia Britannica*.

Table 9.5a
Presidentialism and firm democracy (Encyclopedia Britannica)

	Democracy	Non-democracy
Presidentialism	10	38
Non-presidentialism	25	53

Note: Pearsons' correlation amounts to: $r = -.12$ $(N = 126)$.

Most countries that practise real presidentialism fall outside of the set of firm democracies. In the debate about the pros and cons of presidentialism it has been argued that this type of regime implies a danger or the temptation for the head of State to augment his/her powers beyond the constitution when facing difficulties. The data in Table 9.5 weakly confirms this negative theory of real presidentialism, as there are few countries with such institutions that have experienced democratic longevity, such as for example the USA, France, Finland, Costa Rica and Botswana. At the same time there have been many non-presidential regimes which are not stable democracies, such as for instance Communist dictatorships like China.

It is not entirely clear which countries are to be classified as presidential states, as one may employ various criteria. It has been argued that real presidentialism implies a popular election of the president, but this is not always the case. There exist hybrid forms as, for instance, in the new Republic of South Africa where the president has much executive power but is politically responsible to the legislature who appoints him/her. Another classification of presidential regimes is presented in Table 9.5.b, based upon Stepan and Skach (1993), Mainwaring (1993) and Shugart and Carey (1992).

Table 9.5b
Presidentialism and Firm Democracy (Stepan and Skach, Mainwaring, Shugart and Carey)

	Democracy	Non-democracy
Presidentialism	8	27
Non-presidentialism	27	64

Note: Pearsons' correlation amounts to: r = -.07 (N = 126).

This more restricted concept of presidentialism does not change the finding above that presidentialism is hardly an institution that provides a safe guarantee against non-democratic forces.

Among the non-presidential systems we find both the parliamentary systems and military governments in which a junta rules. Looking at the distinction between parliamentary and non-parliamentary systems in Table 9.6 we receive further strong confirmation of the theory that parliamentarianism is conducive to firm democracy.

Table 9.6
Parliamentarianism and firm democracy

	Democracy	Non-democracy
Parliamentarianism	25	21
Non-parliamentarianism	10	70

Note: Pearsons' correlations amount to: r = .45 (N = 126).

More than half of the countries which practise parliamentarianism have been democracies for a number of years, whereas most non-parliamentary systems of government are either authoritarian regimes or quasi-democracies, i.e. they hover between democracy and dictatorship. Among the countries which adhere to parliamentarianism but which cannot be designated as stable democracies we find not only countries that have experienced a profound regime transformation recently, such as for example the Czech and Slovak Republics but also a few Third World countries including Bangladesh, the Lebanon, Lesotho and Singapore.

The overall finding thus far is that the institutional links are not very strong; positively there is the finding that a parliamentary regime tends to go together with democracy and negatively that a republican system tends to be associated with dictatorship or quasi-democracy. This sounds astonishing given the fact that the United States of America has both a real presidential regime and forms a republic, although it has the oldest existing constitution with a strong bent towards firm democracy, at least so since the 13th Amendment from 1865 which prohibited slavery. Let us here also look at the structure of the legislature. Table 9.7 has the data.

Table 9.7
Bicameralism and firm democracy

	Democracy	Non-democracy
Bicameralism	23	26
Unicameralism	12	65

Note: Pearsons' correlation amounts to: r = .34 (*N* = 126).

Interestingly, almost half of the countries that employ a two-chamber system are firm democracies. At the same time a small fraction of the countries with unicameralism belong to the same set, most of these countries being dictatorships or quasi-democracies. Bicameralism may enhance the prestige of the legislature which could enhance the prospects of democracy.

One may continue the analysis by looking at other institutional characteristics, but the problem is that few institutional traits are as omnipresent as the ones mentioned above. To cover additional institutions it is necessary to move on to a third order question. What the findings concerning our second order question show is that there is not really a single close connection between macropolitical institutions and democracy. Indeed, if there could be any such connection, then the obvious candidate is an institutional mix which combines parliamentarianism and bicameralism.

Besides political institutions, one may look at possible effects from other kinds of institutions. Here we come to the theory that states that economic institutions are of profound importance, in particular the structure of property rights in a country (Table 9.8). One way to measure the relevance of private property in a society is to focus on the extent of economic concentration, i.e. the degree to which economic resources are owned or controlled by the State. In some societies the means of production are basically in private hands

whereas in other societies public ownership or control plays a major
role (Wright, 1992).

Table 9.8
Property rights and firm democracy

	Democracy	Non-democracy
Market Regime	32	11
Non-market regime	4	84

Note: Pearsons' correlation amounts to = .74 (*N* = 131).

The finding in Table 9.8 indicates that market institutions are a
necessary but not sufficient condition for democracy. Few non-market
regimes qualify as democracies, whereas most market regimes tend
towards democracy. Almost all non-market regimes, whether left-
wing or right-wing ones, belong in the category of dictatorships.

From investigating the importance of economic institutions one
may broaden the analysis to include cultural institutions. One index
measures the extent of diversity, conflict and compromise in the cultural institutions as against the degree of hierarchical relationships in
the country culture (Pourgerami, 1988). Table 9.9 shows its relationship to democracy.

Table 9.9
Culture and firm democracy

	Democracy	Non-democracy
Liberal culture	21	2
Non-liberal culture	12	58

Note: Pearsons' correlation amounts to: r = .67 (*N* = 93).

The association is clearly strong, as most liberal cultures have a
democratic regime, at the same time as most societies where hierar-
chy dominates social interaction tend to be non-democratic.

Another interesting way of mapping cultural institutions is to look
at the structure of the family system in a country. One classification
focuses on the place of a nuclear family pattern, i.e. a family where
individualism is strongly entrenched versus a family pattern where
collectivism looms large (Todd, 1983).

Table 9.10
Family institutions and firm democracy

	Democracy	Non-democracy
Individualist family pattern	21	16
Collectivist family pattern	15	80

Note: Pearsons' correlations amount to: r = .41 (*N* = 132).

The connection here is not as straightforward as with regard to culture and regime, but very few countries with a collectivist family structure have had a stable democratic regime.

The finding in this part of the analysis concerning institutional conditions for democracy is that non-political institutions are more powerful than political ones. Democratic stability depends less upon the erection of macropolitical institutions such as a federal state or a republic, but is more dependent upon general cultural conditions, especially those that foster individualism, diversity and private property rights.

Effects of various democratic institutions
A number of less broad constitutional models have been put forward, focusing upon the outcomes connected with different kinds of democratic regimes. Such narrow models do not refer to all States in the world, but to a specific subset, viz. those countries that have been democratic for some time and share a similar economic background, i.e. a rather high level of affluence. In this research the focus is upon the OECD countries, as one bypasses the few countries that are both democratic and poor or the few affluent countries that are not members of the OECD. This third order problem concerns the competition between alternative democratic institutions.

The key question here is whether alternative democratic models perform differently. It has been claimed that consensus democracies meet with better outcomes than democracies that adhere to the Westminster model (Lijphart, 1994b). It has also been argued that corporatist states have better outcomes than democracies where there is more of a market regime. Those that reject the Westminster model of democracy, which emphasizes plurality elections, often underline the crucial contribution of a proportional election system to making

democracy responsive to citizen needs, thus enhancing its performance.

By 'better' performance one is in this research thinking about a
variety of outcomes: economic growth, unemployment, inflation,
gender issues, cabinet stability, state deficits, and so on. Actually, the
literature on the variation in policies and outcomes among the rich
countries of the world is very extensive nowadays. And it is not difficult to find institutional hypotheses. Table 9.11 may help answer
some of the questions about the impact of constitutions on political,
economic and social outcomes, although it only presents data on distribution.

Table 9.11
Impact of democratic institutions (OECD countries)

Institutions				Outcomes				
	FED	PRES	PRESO	PARL	BICAM	PROP	CORP	CSOC	WEST
GDPC91	·52	·44	·31	−·44	·52	−·26	·28	·27	·10
GNPC	·35	·42	·11	−·42	·32	·05	·39	·34	−·18
HDI92	·33	·19	·11	−·19	·42	−·28	·29	·21	·20
VIO8089	−·32	−·15	−·08	·15	·17	−·00	−·34	−·26	−·07
PRO8089	−·19	−·05	·05	·05	·34	−·42	−·22	−·23	·18
CRI8089	−·11	−·21	−·18	·21	·13	·40	−·07	·16	−·31
GRO6580	−·25	−·46	−·29	·46	−·09	·42	−·04	−·09	−·51
GRO8091	−·28	−·23	−·15	·24	·11	·38	−·10	−·23	−·16
UNEM7579	−·07	−·14	·15	·14	·05	−·04	−·22	−·25	·16
UNEM8290	−·18	−·30	−·04	·30	·30	−·03	−·27	−·18	·18
UNEM9193	−·25	−·33	−·11	·33	·05	−·09	−·18	−·35	·23
INF8090	−·31	−·15	−·10	·15	−·51	·15	−·32	−·26	−·14
INF92	−·22	−·11	−·08	·11	−·29	·23	−·27	−·14	−·12
LOW	−·28	−·42	−·37	·42	·04	·68	·48	·25	−·71
RATIO	·40	·51	·38	−·51	·04	−·65	−·51	−·10	·69
WOMEN	−·10	−·10	−·13	·10	−·40	·29	·78	·05	−·24
SOCSEC	−·12	−·23	−·17	·23	·03	·17	·67	·20	−·26
HEALTH	·52	·47	·64	−·47	·41	−·41	·20	·10	·35
GOVCON	−·14	−·19	−·02	·19	−·58	−·11	·38	−·38	·05

Note: The indicators are explained in the Appendix. Iceland and Luxembourg have
been excluded from the OECD set employed here.

The belief in constitutional engineering is hardly confirmed in the
correlations reported in Table 9.8. Major political, social and eco-

nomic outcomes in the OECD countries do not have strong sources in specific institutional factors with one major exception, viz. corporatist institutions. Corporatist regimes are accompanied by a special outcome profile scoring high on income and gender equality as well as promoting an ambitious welfare state effort, especially with regard to income transfers.

The claims on behalf of the set of consociational institutions are not corroborated. Comparing consociationalist institutions with Westminster model institutions in terms of these outcomes it is hardly possible to claim that the first outperforms the other. Typical of the performance of the Westminster model is that it is weak with regard to economic growth and that it tends to result in income inequality. However, neither the consociational model nor the corporatist model result in high levels of economic growth.

One may note a few other relationships, although they are not strong ones. Federalism tends to go together with a high level of affluence and social inequality, whereas the opposite is true of parliamentarianism. Proportionality promotes equality and reduced social instability but at the cost of government instability. Bicameralism seems to keep government expenditure down at the same time as it goes together with affluence.

Gøsta Esping-Andersen has launched a welfare state theory which claims that different institutional combinations of public and private sector mechanisms result in specific outcomes (Esping-Andersen, 1990). In *The Three Worlds of Welfare Capitalism* he distinguishes between three welfare regimes – liberal, conservative and socialist. However, his classification of countries has met with criticism. Esping-Andersen's argument ties in with the corporatist model, which argues that countries with an extensive and general welfare regime outperform countries that are orientated towards the market economy.

Let us look at the data on performance in Table 9.12 where we have classified the OECD countries with regard to how they mix the public and private sectors in various welfare regime constellations around 1980. Selective regimes are to be found in the welfare societies, which emphasize means-tested programmes targeting particular groups. The universal regime entails a comprehensive approach based on general criteria equally applicable to all social groups. The mixed regime combines features from both these two fundamental types of welfare regimes.

Table 9.12
Performance profile of welfare regimes (average scores)

	Selective	Mixed	Universal	Mean
GDPC91	17,211	14,630	16,576	15,982
GNPC	20,750	16,658	22,263	19,489
HDI92	0·90	0·90	0·92	0·90
VIO8089	4·1	5·1	0·0	3·4
PRO8089	16·6	15·1	2·3	12·0
CRI8089	1·1	3·8	1·3	2·3
GRO6580	2·8	3·8	2·6	3·1
GRO8091	2·3	2·3	1·8	2·2
UNEM7579	5·6	5·1	3·6	4·9
UNEM8290	6·9	10·2	5·7	7·9
UNEM9193	7·8	10·2	8·8	9·1
INF8090	10·2	8·4	6·1	8·3
INF92	10·5	7·9	1·2	6·9
LOW	17·5	19·5	18·7	18·5
RATIO	7·6	5·7	6·3	6·6
WOMEN	9·9	12·0	30·7	16·4
SOCSEC	12·2	18·7	24·1	18·1
HEALTH	8·2	7·6	8·3	8·0
GOVCON	17·0	17·3	21·3	18·3

Note: The classification of the 22 OECD countries is given in the Appendix.

It is hardly the case that the universal welfare regime results in higher rates of economic growth than the selective regime. Actually, the overall level of affluence is higher in the selective welfare regimes than in the universal welfare regimes. Surprisingly, the inflation figures are lower in the universal regimes than in the selective. What is not surprising is that the universal regimes score higher on equality and public expenditure than the selective ones.

Conclusion

The constitutional arena becomes relevant when new States are founded as well as when old States attempt major institutional reform. Given the focus upon constitutional questions at such special occasions, there can be no doubt that constitutions are important. But, how important?

Well, it depends. Merely framing a constitution will not in itself be of decisive importance. Constitutional engineering faces a number of obstacles before it is successful. First, a formally written constitution has to be translated into constitutional practice which is a difficult task involving lots of problems of institutional design and judicial interpretation. Secondly, an implemented constitution will not automatically produce attractive outcomes. Actually, the link between constitutional institutions and political, social and economic outcomes is not a very strong one.

First and foremost, constitutions matter insofar as they safeguard human rights. A democratic constitution that is successfully institutionalized is intrinsically valuable, because it safeguards freedom. A democratic regime will not necessarily bring about economic and social development, but it does institutionalize human rights. Although it tends to be associated with a high level of affluence, it does not result in high rates of economic growth. Several developmental regimes such as those in South East Asia do not cherish a real democratic constitution. Development but not democracy is the overriding concern among the so-called 'Baby Tigers' in South East Asia.

Given the preference for democracy, which major political institutions promote a democratic regime? Well, for the purposes of constitutional design it must be admitted that there is no single institutional mechanism that automatically leads to democracy. It seems as if parliamentarianism is the best bet. Nor do the findings support any of the models that claim that one democratic framework is superior to another. When constitutional evaluation is narrowed down to the OECD countries, then the constitutional performance by the competitive models – consociationalism, corporatism, federalism, parliamentarianism, proportionality – is actually rather meagre. Constitutions are important – yes, but they do not determine outcomes.

In the literature there has been an extensive debate about the pros and cons of alternative democractic models from a constitutional starting point – see for instance *Constitutionalism and Democracy: transitions in the contemporary world* (Greenberg *et al.*, 1993). It actually deals with the comparative evaluation of basic democratic institutions, taking the economic background for given thus limiting the observations about performance to the OECD countries. The data hardly corroborate the claims made on behalf of the adherents of the consociational model, the Westminster model and the corporatist model. Neither one of these three models results in excellent economic outcomes such as a high rate of economic growth, low inflation and little unemployment. Also the theory that alternative welfare institutions play a major role in shaping outcomes is not confirmed. It is true, though, that corporatism results in both social equality and a large welfare state effort. And federalism and bicameralism tend to go together with a high level of affluence and less public expenditure.

There is constitutional politics and ordinary politics. Countries enter the constitutional setting on special occasions, when they deliberate on the fundamental institutions that they wish to adhere to. From the perspective of ongoing politics on a day to day basis, constitutional politics is the exception. It implies the making and implementation of policies in relation to the institutions of the rule of law – the Rechtstaat. It has been argued that the rule of law implies that government be subordinated not only to the legal order but also to moral principles or ideas of fundamental principles of justice. What more precisely is involved in such notions?

Appendix

Data and variables

DEMO: democratic stability: democracies from 1976 – according to the rankings of Freedom House.

GDPC90: real GDP/capita 1990 in US$ as reported in UNDP (1993) Human development report 1993.

GDPC91: real GDP/capita 1991 in US$ as reported in UNDP (1994) Human development report 1994.

GNPC: GNP/capita 1992 in US$ as reported in World Bank (1994) World development report.

HDI92: Human development index 1992 as reported in UNDP (1994) Human development report 1994.

GRO6580: GNP/capita annual growth 1965–80 as reported in UNDP (1994) Human development report 1994.

GRO8091: GNP annual growth 1980–91 as reported in UNDP (1994) Human development report 1994.

UNEM7579: Unemployment rate 1975–79; based upon OECD (1994) OECD economic outlook, June 1994.

UNEM8290: Unemployment rate 1982–90; based upon OECD (1993) OECD employment outlook, July 1993.

UNEM9193: Unemployment rate 1991–93; based upon OECD (1994)

OECD economic outlook, June 1994.

INF8090: average annual rate of inflation 1980–90 as reported in UNDP (1994) Human development report 1994.

VIO8089: occurrence of assassinations, guerrilla warfare and revolutions 1980–89 as reported in the Banks political events data.

VIO9193: occurrence of assassinations, guerrilla warfare and revolutions 1991–93 as reported in the Banks political events data.

PRO8089: occurrence of general strikes, riots and anti-government demonstrations 1980–89 as reported in the Banks political events data.

PRO9193: occurrence of general strikes, riots and anti-government demonstrations 1991–93 as reported in the Banks political events data.

CRI8089: occurrence of government crises and purges 1980–89 as reported in the Banks political events data.

CRI9193: occurrence of government crises and purges 1991–93 as reported in the Banks political events data.

LOW: income share of lowest 40 per cent of households 1980–91 as reported in UNDP (1994) Human development report.

RATIO: ration of income share of highest 20 per cent to income share of lowest 20 per cent 1980–91 as reported in UNDP (1994) Human development report 1994.

WOMEN: percentage of seats in parliament occupied by women 1992 as reported in UNDP (1994) Human development report 1994.

GOVCON: central government consumption as a percentage of GDP 1991 as reported in UNDP (1994) Human development report 1994.

HEALTH: total expenditure on health as a percentage of GDP 1991 as reported in UNDP (1994) Human development report 1994.

SOCSEC: social security benefits expenditure as a percentage of GDP 1985–90 as reported in UNDP (1994) Human development report 1994.

FED: federalism; 1 = federalism; 0 = non-federalism.

REP: republic; 1 = republic; 0 = non-republic.

PRES: presidentialism; 1 = presidentialism (criteria: the same person occupies the position of chief of State and head of government); 0 = non-presidentialism.

PRES0: modified measure of presidentialism where dubious cases are classified as non-presidential.

PARL: parliamentarianism; 1 = parliamentarian; 0 = non-parliamentarian.

BICAM: bicamerialism; 1 = bicameral legislatures; 0 = unicameral legislatures.

ECFREE: economic freedom; 0 = freedom high; 1 = freedom low. based upon Wright (1982) in *Freedom in the World.*

CULT: cultural traditions; 1 = tradition of diversity; 0 = hierarchical relationships; based upon Pourgerami (1988).

TODD1: family systems; 1 = relying on liberal traditions; 0 = relying on non-liberal traditions; based upon Todd (1983).

CORP: corporatism; 1 = corporatism; 0 = non-corporatism.

CSOC: consociationalism; 1 = consociationalism; 0 = non-consociationalism.

WEST: Westminster; 1 = Westminster model; 0 = non-Westminster model.

Welfare regimes around 1980
Universal: Scandinavian Countries, Finland, the Netherlands, New Zealand.
Mixed: Germany, France, Italy, Ireland, Greece, Belgium, Austria.
Selective: USA, UK, Switzerland, Turkey, Australia, Japan, Canada.

Part V

Justice and democracy

10

Is there a 'best' constitution?

Introduction

Questions about the **is** and the **ought** permeate constitutional research. Looking at descriptive problems about existing constitutions and their impact upon outcomes is as relevant as enquiring into topics about what a constitution should look like. A constitution reflects the dominating values in a society, but since these values may change one is entitled to pose the difficult question about the criteria that a 'good' constitution should satisfy. Actually, this problem is highly relevant in present day debates in political theory and moral discourse, as it enters the intense debate about justice.

This chapter discusses the criteria one could employ in arguments about whether one constitution is better than another. One could include formal criteria such as compactness and coherence, clarity of exposition, interpretative accessibility, implementability and longevity. However, here we will focus upon material criteria, in particular justice. If a constitution reflects in a crucial way basic political values, then surely it must be vital to discuss what a just constitution would amount to. Perhaps the best constitution is exactly that, i.e. a just constitution. But what does a just constitution amount to?

In constitutional debate there are lots of references to justice. However, the concept of justice is truly an essentially contested one, as ethics is replete with different theories about justice. The purpose in this chapter is to discuss the concept of justice in relation to the constitutional agenda.

'Just' and 'justice'

'Justice' is no doubt a key word in modern normative political theory as well as in moral philosophy (Pettit, 1980; Kymlicka, 1990;

Reiman, 1990; Miller and Walzer, 1995; Ryan, 1995). Some argue
that it is the key concept when it comes to politics and morals,
whereas others claim that it is one of the most relevant concepts
when evaluating political practice. Justice seems to be linked somehow to other values such as freedom and equality, which figure
prominently in constitutional discourse. Surely, then, justice must be
a relevant concern when constitutions are made or remade?

First, let us issue a small warning. From the fact that justice is considered of the utmost importance in social life, it does not follow that
it should loom large in constitutional deliberations. It may be the
case that justice can be promoted outside of the constitutional arena,
for example by means of ordinary legislative action or through
public policy-making. However, a short look at democratic constitutions indicate that justice has in fact entered the constitutional
arena. Justice in a constitutional setting is often referred to by means
of terms like 'rule of law', 'equal treatment', 'due process of law' and
'fairness'.

The concept of justice displays all the difficulties that so-called
essentially contested concepts are characterized by (Gallie, 1955-56).
There is the word 'justice' in English or 'Gerechtigkeit' in German,
but then the agreement stops. There is wide disagreement about how
to define the term, reflecting the existence of various theories of justice – see Brian Barry *Theories of Justice* (1989) and *Justice as Impartiality* (1995). Barry argues that there are two main traditions in how
the concept of justice has been approached since David Hume's classical text *A Treatise of Human Nature* (1739–40): justice as mutual
advantage versus justice as impartiality, the former emphasizing self-
interest and the latter underlining reasonable principles that anyone
would accept as the basis for the derivation of a concept of justice
(Barry, 1989: 257–92).

In *Justice* (1988) Tom Campell outlines two approaches to the
analysis of the idea of justice. One approach is to list the different
conceptions of justice and then try to find some common core on
these justice conceptions that could form the universal concept of
justice. Another approach is to start from a concept of justice and
then examine to what extent other suggested definitions come more
or less close to that concept.

Yet one may first mention the so-called meta-ethical approach,
which comprises theories about the use of the term 'justice'. According to one such meta-ethical framework the term 'justice' stands less

for an idea than it functions as a recommendation or expresses an emotion. Calling something 'just' is to make a certain kind of speech act in order to achieve certain practical ends like making an impact upon other persons. Calling a constitution 'just' is more to express likings (Edwards, 1965) or commands and imperatives (Hare, 1967), than to establish some fact about the constitution. To use the words 'just' or 'justice', especially in the context of a court, is to employ utterances known as performatives in semantic terminology (Austin, 1962), meaning that it is not a matter of a statement that can be true or false but the performing of an action such as putting down what, for example the law, is.

The difficulty with this so-called emotive theory of moral terms or the non-cognitivist approach to ethics is that it only partially captures the use of language (Urmson, 1968). When a constitution is called 'just', then there appears to be more involved than simply a recommendation. Asked why it is so designated, one would look for reasons, which may very well include deliberations about an idea of justice. In any case, the fact that words such as 'good', 'just' and 'best' are used to direct behaviour do not imply that they cannot have additional functions, like referring to certain properties that form the basis for the recommendation. But which exactly these properties are that make for a just constitution is the critical question.

A meta-ethical approach does not really help when it comes to sorting out the various meanings of words such as 'good', 'best' or 'just' (Kerner, 1966; Brandt, 1979). There is more to the semantics of the word 'justice' than what the logical positivist analysis implies. However, given the fact that the word is ambiguous, how do we choose between alternative definitions? Is there really one concept of justice that pins down what is the core or ought to be the core in all the various theories of justice (Alexy, 1994)?

What is justice?

The debate about justice typically starts out from the well-known definition of Aristotle in the *Nicomachean Ethics* that justice requires treating equals equally and unequals unequally in proportion to their relative differences. Aristotelian ethics required that each and everyone be given his due, but here we encounter the problems that beset theories of justice: what is due to a person? Who are equals and unequals in terms of what? And what are the proportions involved in treating people according to their relative differences? Typical of the concept of justice has always been the fact that it is opaque (according to what criteria) and elliptic (in terms of what).

Michael Walzer has suggested one solution to the ambiguity of the word 'justice' in his *Spheres of Justice* (1983), which implies that ambiguity is less of a drawback than what could be expected, because it is a fact that 'justice' is employed in different circumstances. In the various sectors of society for example politics, economics, religion, education, the concept of justice has different implications to such an extent that there is really no core meaning covering all these spheres, according to Walzer. Thus, justice would imply one principle in sports for example, but another principle in economic interactions and probably yet another one in religious practice. Walzer's approach makes the concept of justice context dependent.

Still another approach to the analysis of justice underlines the choice of values. It argues first that justice involves the choice of values and secondly that there is a finite set of candidates to choose between. The choice of one value like equality as the principle of justice instead of another value like freedom is a matter for the resolution of fundamental moral convictions. Since justice principles may collide, there must be a choice of ultimate values. The ultimate values approach makes the concept of justice values dependent – see Arnold Brecht's *Political Theory* (1959).

One may wish to distinguish between ultimate, absolute and intrinsic values in ethics and justice discourse. If justice is an intrinsic value, then it has a value independent of whether it promotes or is instrumental for another value. If justice is an absolute value, then it overrides other values whenever there is a conflict, meaning that it is not a conditional value. Finally, if justice is an ultimate value, then there is no other value which can be adduced to support it. In a constitutional context, a 'just' constitution would have to satisfy certain criteria, some of which may be ultimate or absolute or intrinsic values, but not all.

The present debate about a communitarian approach to justice is an attempt to come to grips with the opaqueness and ellipticity of the justice concept. The communitarians such as Michael Sandel in *Liberalism and the Limits of Justice* (1982), Alisdair MacIntyre in

After Virtue (1981) and Charles Taylor in *Sources of the Self* (1990) claim that questions about justice are to be decided by reference to the community. It would be impossible to take an individualistic or atomistic approach to the problem of defining the concept of justice, because each and every notion of justice is constituted by the values of the community in which each person is always a member.

Communitarians argue that individuals derive their moral ideals from their constitutive attachment to the communities of which they are a member and not the other way around (Kymlicka, 1991; Bell, 1994). Communitarians claim that communal membership is essential to any possibility of defining what is right and wrong or good or bad. More precisely, they assert that community precedes moral agency. Moreover, communitarians take the position that since justice is based on social meanings any conception of justice is enclosed in communal frameworks. The new communitarian approach to justice seems to imply a radically relativistic stand on meta-ethical questions, as it underlines that questions about what is just and unjust always have to be resolved in relation to some community. However, can one not ask, whenever someone states what is justice in a community, Yes, but is it really just?

Communitarianism is perhaps first and foremost a new ethical theory about the good and the right. It tends to reject individualism and favour some form of collectivism. It has been much preoccupied with analysing how ethical conceptions originate in the interaction between individuals in a social context as well as with how different social contexts tend to develop alternative conceptions of justice (Walzer, 1983). However, does it really illuminate the basic problem in theories of justice, namely the criteria of justice? Friedrich states:

> The famous triad Honeste vivere, neminem laedere, suum cuique tribuere is not only the broad formula of natural law on which the Corpus Juris Civilis is supposed to rest, but also the ground on which philosophers, notably Leibniz and Kant, have built their theories of justice (Friedrich, 1963: 24–5).

Justice would thus imply 'suum cuique tribuere' or to give to each man/woman what is due to him/her. The basic problem of justice is to specify what this means more concretely whether it is a matter of one community or another.

David Miller has suggested in *Social Justice* (1976) that there are three criteria of justice that resolve the problem of what is due to each and everyone, viz. needs, rights and deserts. However, if justice is to give to each man/woman according to his/her needs or rights or deserts, then we need to know what the needs, rights and deserts are as well as how these entities are to be handled when they collide. Miller's intention was to show that the concept of justice could be given three different interpretations, depending on what justice concerned.

The prevailing approach to justice in the present literature looks upon the task of handling the concept of justice as one of explication. Justice is one thing, although it happens to be the case that so far our theories of justice have not thus far been able to identify the necessary and sufficient properties of justice. Although there is a set of definitions in political and moral theory, the problem remains to sort them out, eliminating those that are not on target and expanding those that come close to the essence of the concept.

Rawls' *A Theory of Justice* from 1971 restarted the debate about what the concept of justice implies. It launched a full scale theory stating several principles of justice derived from rational considerations based upon an ethical approach to justice. Rawls is not concerned with a semantical analysis of the various meanings of 'justice'. Typical of Rawls' approach is the Kantian starting point, by which is meant the contractarian approach, the claim to moral autonomy and the emphasis upon rational deliberations.

In Kant's ethical system outlined in the *Metaphysics of Morals* it is not enough that principles express ultimate values, because they may differ with various persons, nor that they maximize positive consequences like the total happiness or average utility. First, the concept of justice with Kant implies generalizability in the sense that each and everyone would rationally agree to the idea that the rules of justice be applied equally onto all persons, themselves included. This notion has been restated by means of such a concept as universalizability in R.M. Hare's *Freedom and Reason* from 1963. Secondly, the concept of justice is based upon the notion of a moral personality, i.e. one which possesses moral autonomy meaning having the capacity to transcend the peculiar self-interests of a single individual and realizing what it is in the duty of a person to do. Finally, the just constitution is the one constitution that citizens will assent to by rational choice (Ross, 1965; Aune, 1979).

Against the contractarian approach today stands another major framework for the derivation of principles of social justice, the utilitarian approach. There are several versions of utilitarianism, from the old Benthamite formulation to modern versions by J.J.C. Smart, J.C. Harsanyi and D.H. Regan (Smart and Williams, 1973; Regan, 1980; Sen and Williams, 1984). The basic idea in the utilitarian approaches to social justice is that of maximizing total or average utility in society. Thus, utilitarianism is not a rights based theory or a duty based theory of justice but a goal based theory, as it is a consequentialist ethics. At the same time it is aggregative, i.e. it employs no distributive criteria for determining justice. The criterion on justice is the aggregate score of such things as happiness, utility or welfare and it is to be measured by looking at the consequences of actions.

The idea of maximizing utility may be developed in various ways, the two basic versions being act-utilitarianism and rule-utilitarianism (Lyons, 1965). The latter version of utilitarianism allows for the elaboration of institutions, which are just only if they score high on the aggregate measure of the Greatest Happiness Principle (Smart, 1973). A lot of discussion has focused upon the problems involved in measuring happiness or comparing the utility of different persons. However, a basic difficulty with utilitarianism is that it may constitute an argument not only for real but also for formal inequalities, if such inequalities would maximize total or average utility in society. Thus, it is argued that it is at odds with an individualist approach to justice underlining rights (Williams, 1973) or what an individual would reasonably consent to or accept voluntarily (Scanlon, 1982). At a more basic level, utilitarianism's consequentialism has been questioned as to whether the moral value of an action consists solely in the good consequences it brings about – the teleological approach, or whether ethics must take into account the right or wrong principles that an agent follows when acting – the deontological approach (Scheffler, 1987).

This is not the place to discuss the concept of justice in ethical theory involving key philosophical problems (Broad, 1967; Mayo, 1986). The focus here is on the constitutional setting and the implications of justice for the notion of a just constitution. One way to get a perspective on the relevance of the concept of justice for the constitutional agenda is to separate between legal justice on the one hand and redistributive justice on the other hand. It will be argued that the ambiguity of 'justice' stems to a considerable extent from the fact that the word stands for two different concepts: legal justice and social justice. It will be shown below that these two concepts of justice – legal and social justice – have their own difficulties, but making the distinction between them is conducive to conceptual clarity because legal and social justice are rather different kinds of things, especially in a constitutional context.

Legal justice

Impartiality is essential to justice. Justice reigns where there is no partiality meaning that persons are treated differently without cause. Favouritism is a typical example of partiality. To be impartial is to treat people as equals in certain ways. Institutions claim impartiality, as to govern by means of rules implies that each and everyone be treated alike under the rules. Thus, it is impossible to judge whether there is partiality except with an explicit reference to a set of rules.

With regard to legal systems impartiality requires justice under the laws. The same goes for any institutions or set of rules. Thus, market institutions are based upon impartiality in the sense that anyone may enter into contractual relationships as long as that person is qualified to do so, for example by fulfilling the requirements for short-term or long-term contracting with regard to, for instance, property rights or employment opportunities. The institutions of games such as sports or chess also exemplify impartiality, in that players who obey the rules expect to be treated alike.

Impartiality is not the same as equality. Distinctions may be made between various persons on a number of grounds. Institutions may separate between groups of people according to a number of criteria. The demand for impartiality requires that these distinctions be made in a consistent pattern. Thus, persons have different purchasing power in the market and athletes have different capacities when competing. Impartiality does not imply that such differences be bypassed. On the contrary, they are relevant for the operation of the rules and should be taken into account. What impartiality forbids is that persons be treated differently in ways that are irrelevant to the operation of the rules. Impartiality holds the same requirements with regard to how people are treated in the various branches of law, from private law to public law including also criminal law.

Equality of treatement is basic in the notion of legal justice. The rules of the legal order are to be applied in the same way to all persons independently of their status, power or wealth. The requirement for impartiality under the laws is often expressed by notions such as fairness, due process, natural justice or equity. A central issue in theories of justice is the extent to which such principles are recognized in law and implemented by special legal institutions. It has implications for the question of legal review and the setting up of special constitutional courts.

Legal justice is an integral part of such notions as *Rechtsstaat* (German), *état de droit* (French), *estado de derecho* (Spanish) and *stato di diritto* (Italian). The institutionalization of legal justice may require a written constitution that sanctions a human rights catalogue. It is claimed that legal justice in a constitutional state implies a set of institutions through which the rights in the constitutions are protected or guaranteed:

> the basic element of the état de droit is the existence of a system of judicial review ... .The two fundamental objectives of this system of judicial review are obviously: one, to ensure that all those acts of the state are adopted or issued in accordance with the law of said state; two, to ensure that state acts respect the fundamental rights and liberties of citizens (Brewer-Carias, 1989: 81).

However, things are more complicated with regard to legal review than in relation to the notion of legal justice. Firstly, it should be pointed out, as explained in Chapter 7, that legal review can be done by means of different institutions, which it is not easy to choose between. Secondly, it must be explicitly underlined that legal review is contested to a much higher extent than the equation of legal justice as impartiality. Here, we enter an area where democracy and constitutionalism may come into conflict, as institutions for judicial review may result in a transfer of political power from the democratically elected bodies to the appointed judges or the self-employed lawyers in the court room – see the concluding chapter.

Legal justice may be promoted by means of different institutions. A thick set of institutions for enhancing legal justice would include not only a written constitution with a large human rights catalogue, but also strong judicial review by means of the general courts or a separate constitutional court. However, legal justice may also be institutionalized by means of constitutional practice and weak legal review. Many countries that tried the former alternative failed to implement civil and political rights.

It should be pointed out that the concept of legal justice may be given either a thin or thick content. Here, we have focused upon the thin version, legal justice as equality under the law. The thick concept of legal justice would comprise the whole plethora of human rights, covering both the classical negative liberties and several positive liberties. The thin version may be considered inadequate, because if the law is wrong then what good is the application of the principle of equality under the law? At the same time, the thick version could be made very large indeed comprising besides civil and political rights also social and economic rights of various kinds. A very thick definition of legal justice as involving any conceivable individual right would be difficult to implement through public administration and the legal system, which is a drawback.

Sometimes in the literature on legal justice one finds a tendency to focus on the so-called Habeas Corpus rights, which refer to the protection of the individual against arbitrary seizure, detention and trial as well as penalties. The Iraqi constitution mentions various such rights in its Fundamental Rights and Duties. First, we have the rules about a fair trial:

> Art. 20. (a) An accused is presumed to be innocent, until proved guilty at a legal trial. (b) The right of defense is sacred, in all stages of proceedings and prosecution. (c) Court sessions are public, unless it becomes secret by a court's decision.

Then, there are the rules about punishments:

> Art. 21. (a) Penalty is personal. (b) There can be no crime, nor punishment, except in conformity with the law. No penalty shall be imposed, except for acts criminalized by the law, while they are committed. A severer penalty than that prescribed by the law, when the act was committed, cannot be inflicted.

Finally, we have the rules about arrest:

> Art. 22. (a) The dignity of man is safeguarded. It is inadmissible to cause any physical or psychological harm. (b) It is inadmissible to arrest a person, to stop him, to imprison him or to search him, except in accordance with the rules of the law. (c) Homes have their sanctity. It is inadmissible to enter or search them, except in accordance with the rules of the law.

These Habeas Corpus rights would naturally be included in the concept of a constitutional State, if they are fully implemented that is to say. Many would still argue that the core of the conception of legal justice does not consist of these rights, however much importance must be attached to them. They would instead read the first line in the Iraqi list:

Art 19. (a) Citizens are equal before the law, without discrimination because of sex, blood, language, social origin or religion. (b) Equal opportunities are guaranteed to all citizens, according to the law.

Here, we have the core meaning of 'legal justice', i.e. equality before the law, which of course also demands full implementation. Since the concept of equality has such a prominent place in legal justice, it is necessary to take a close look at it. Could it be the case that equality is the common core of all meanings of 'justice'? Perhaps justice involves more than just legal justice as equality under the law means equality also in other respects?

The concept of legal justice implies a host of such notions that have been analysed above, such as due process, equal protection, equity, natural justice and individual liberties. They are relevant to any legal system, whether of the Romano-Germanic family or the common law family, as they are crucial in a constitutional democracy. Yet one of the fundamental tenets in the post-war debate on justice is that legal justice is either not enough or not the essence of justice. Besides, there is social justice or as it is sometimes called redistributive justice. If justice is interpreted as fairness or impartiality, is there also a clear concept of social justice besides that of legal justice?

Social justice

As we move away from the terrain of legal justice towards the domains of social justice, the amount of contestation between alternative approaches rises sharply (Kymlicka, 1990; Mulhall and Swift, 1993). On the one hand, there is the position that social justice is marginally different from legal justice. This would be the position of scholars adhering to the economic analysis of law approach, such as Posner. On the other hand, there is the Rawlsian position that social justice interpreted as fairness implies a preference for equal outcomes and a demand for the implementation of the difference principle, meaning that inequalities are only acceptable if they favour the least advantaged, which indeed goes much further than the requirement of legal justice.

Issues about social justice are heavily policy relevant, as they refer to the distinctions between state and market, the public and the private sectors as well individual and collective responsibilities. They are also strongly connected with redistributive questions, as they involve if and how rewards and benefits are to be redistributed by the state from one group to another. Even in a society where the principles of legal justice are implemented, it would still be an open question whether or not redistribution should be accomplished. The debate about social justice focuses upon the interpretations of freedom and equality as well as how they relate to each other. Let us look at the Rawlsian approach.

Rawls' theory of justice comprises a formulation of two valid principles of social justice and an argument that attempts to derive these two principles from the notion of a moral personality choosing under a veil of ignorance. Here we are interested in the two principles of justice, as the first one comes close to what we have referred to as legal justice whereas the second one would be a definition of social justice. Rawls says that his principles 'apply to the basic structure of society' and that 'they are to govern the assignment of rights and duties and to regulate the distribution of social and economic advantages' (Rawls, 1971: 61). He goes on to state:

> As their formulation suggests, these principles presuppose that the social structure can be divided into two more or less distinct parts, the first principle applying to the one, the second to the other. They distinguish between those aspects of the social system that define and secure the equal liberties of citizenship and those that specify and establish social and economic inequalities (Rawls, 1971: 61).

The concept of legal justice seems to cover well the first part of the social system in Rawls' interpretation. Here he mentions the basic individual liberties: freedom of speech and assembly, liberty of conscience and freedom of thought, freedom of the person and personal property, freedom from arbitrary arrest and seizure as well as political liberty such as the right to vote and to hold political office.

What is controversial in Rawls' framework is not his version of the concept of legal justice: 'each person is to have an equal right to the most extensive basic liberty compatible with a similar liberty for others' (Rawls, 1971: 60). What was truly original in Rawls' approach, and what caused much debate, is the second principle of justice which applies to the distribution of income and wealth, i.e. what we refer to as social justice.

Rawls presents alternative formulations of his second principle of justice. One states that the distribution of wealth and income must be to everyone's advantage and that positions of authority in organizations must be accessible to all. However, the most often quoted version of the second principle is the so-called difference principle. Let us quote from Rawls:

> Social and economic inequalities are to be arranged so that they are both: (a) to the greatest benefit of the least advantaged, consistent with the just savings principle, and (b) attached to offices and positions open to all under conditions of fair equality and opportunity (Rawls, 1971: 302).

Whereas Rawls' first principle of justice is a little controversial, coming rather close to conventional approaches to legal justice, his second principle of justice is radical. One need not accept both. Legal justice is one thing and social justice another matter. The difference principle calls for extensive public policies redistributing income and wealth up until such policies disadvantage those that the redistribution is targeting. The only deviation from strict numerical equality in distributional matters that is allowed from the standpoint of justice is that too much equalization of income and wealth would lower the size of redistribution going to the least advantaged.

Rawls lumps both principles together calling them 'social justice' or 'fairness', but it is clarifying to keep them separate. Legal justice is a separate conception from that of social justice. The difficulty lies with the interpretation of social justice. What is social justice, once we recognize and implement legal justice? Rawls claims that equality is crucial in any notion of social justice. What, then, is meant by 'equality', if equality is more than equality under the law?

Equality has always been an essentially contested concept in political theory. Often the contest about equality is framed in terms of either/or, for example either equality or freedom, either equality or merit, and so forth. As Amartya Sen points out in *Inequality Reexamined* (1992), the entire debate about equality may be phrased into the simple question: equality in terms of what? Take your pick from political discourse: happiness (utilitarians), income and wealth (egalitarians), liberties (liberitarians), opportunity (meritocrats), and so on. The debate about equality is concerned with specifying the qualities human beings are to be considered equal with regard to. Yet, there is a second crucial question in the debate about equality, viz. can and should government do anything in order to enhance equality. The conceptual problem is somewhat different from the policy question. Even if one can define what is meant by 'equality', it does not necessarily follow that governments can or should act on equality in terms of public policies.

Equality

Egalitarians often point out that they do not seek a society where each and everyone is equal in all respects (Rees, 1972; Plant, 1991). R. H. Tawney suggested in his well-known *Equality* from 1931 that what matters in a society is 'equality of consideration for all its members' (Tawney, 1964: 50). This did not imply equal treatment of all in every respect, argued Tawney, but would be consonant with 'differentiation of treatment' in accordance with 'special needs of different groups and individuals among them' (Tawney, 1964: 50). Such an approach to the concept of equality will, however, not do, as it is incomplete or elliptic. In the debate about the concept of social justice there is a search for a principle or a set of principles for how persons are to be treated. Equal consideration as a solution to this question cannot work if one does not specify what this means.

One interpretation of 'equal consideration' is the so-called conditional equality conception. It does not require numerical equality but may allow for proportional equality or that persons are treated differently in proportion to their differences. Aristotle in *Politics*, stated the distinction between numerical or strict equality and proportional equality. The principle of conditional equality may be stated in the following way:

> all persons are to be treated equally (in the same way) save when there are reasons for treating them differently (Rees, 1972: 108).

Sometimes the idea of equality as conditional equality is expressed as a general presumption for equality, where the burden of proof rests with those who argue for inequality. However, again there is a concept of equality that is elliptic. We need to know the reasons that are considered valid for unequal treatment. If, as it is sometimes stated, such reasons have to be morally acceptable or reasonable, then we are simply moving in a circle: just treatment requires a concept of equality which requires a theory about just reasons for unequal treatment.

Now, the contention about equality does not focus upon equality under the law. What creates strong dissent is another interpretation of the concept. The concept of equality has two aspects, as in for instance the Rawlsian framework where equality plays a major role in relation to both his principles of justice. Each person has to have an equal right to the mentioned individual liberties, and income and wealth are to be distributed to everyone's advantage meaning that the distribution must be to the advantage of the least advantaged. One may call the first kind of equality formal equality and the second kind real equality, as the first refers to equality under the law whereas the second deals with income equality.

Typical of legal justice is the requirement of impartiality, but does impartiality entail real equality? Thomas Nagel argues in *Equality and Partiality* (1991) that such is the case. He states: 'The impartial attitude is, I believe, strongly egalitarian both in itself and in its implications' (Nagel, 1991: 64). Yet this is not so, as one needs to distinguish between various kinds of equality (Table 10.1).

Table 10.1
Various types of equality

	Real equality	*Real inequality*
Formal equality	I	II
Formal inequality	III	IV

Rawls' theory of justice involves category I in Table 10.1, because it combines formal equality with real equality. However, if one rejects categories III and IV as irrelevant in modern day democratic societies with their strong endorsement of legal justice, then there remains category II, or the combination of formal equality with real inequality. Category II is not necessarily unjust, as it accepts one kind of equality but rejects the other type. If the presumption in moral theory is equality between men/women, then do we speak of formal equality or real equality?

A theory of social justice may end up in category II. Such a theory would reject the second of Rawls' principles of justice, the require-ment of equality in the distribution of income and wealth. It could

accept formal equality but reject real equality, but it would have to
deliver an argument why social justice does not imply real equality.
What principles could be employed when rejecting the idea that
social justice means real equality?

A theory of social justice cannot bypass market institutions and
the way they distribute benefits and costs. A significant part of the
question of redistribution concerns whether the state should take
steps to enhance an equitable distribution of income and wealth in
relation to actual market outcomes. If social justice means real equality in income distribution, then the government must engage in
extensive public policy-making to correct market outcomes, com-
pensating the least advantaged by taxing the most advantaged. This
is, of course, Rawls' position, although he states that there are limits
to what government can accomplish in searching for equality in
income distribution.

However, it is not impossible to consider alternative approaches
to social justice which argue that social justice does not imply real
equality or equality in the distribution of income and wealth. These
approaches to social justice would tend to accept market outcomes,
not simply because they tend to be efficient under certain circumstances but also because they would be just, at least some of the time.
Key notions in such approaches to social justice could be entitle-
ments, freedom and desert. A rights based approach to social justice
need not imply such a willingness, partial or total, to accept market
outcomes, because it is an open question how citizen rights are to be
identified. To some 'rights' stand mainly for formal equality, but
others count as real equality among citizen 'rights'. Thus, for
example L.A. Jacobs in *Rights and Deprivation* (1993) include among
basic rights education, health care, adequate housing and income
support. The debate about rights is almost as confusing as the debate
about social justice in general, as there is sharp disagreement about
how rights are to be identified (Waldron, 1985; Frey, 1985).

Attracta Ingram in *A Political Theory of Rights* (1994) distinguishes between two approaches to the delimitation of citizen rights,
the libertarian approach based upon self-ownership notions versus
the welfare approach stemming from a self-government conception.
The former covers mainly what is usually designated as the negative
liberties whereas the latter includes what is called the positive liberties. Rights as emerging from self-ownership were propagated by for
example Locke and Madison and were expressed in the early human

rights declarations whereas welfare rights are contained in the human rights catalogues laid down after the Second World War. The main adherents of the self-ownership approach to rights in the present debate is Hayek and Nozick (Ingram, 1994).

Robert Nozick outlined an entitlement theory of social justice in *Anarchy, State and Utopia* (1974). Justice in redistribution implies an impractical attempt to derive a final pattern for society or end state, but the only relevant approach to justice is to identify just social procedures. Procedural justice involves principles (a) for the transfer of possessions or resources as well as (b) the initial acquisition of possessions or resources plus principles for the rectification of acts that are not in agreement with principles (a) and (b). Nozick counts the rules for market transactions among the set of principles (a) or (b), at least the ideal rules for competitive markets.

Bruce Ackerman in his *Social Justice in the Liberal State* (1980) also emphasizes just procedures. Social justice is connected with transactions or interactions between individuals under the condition of undominated equality. However, Ackerman requires that the starting-point of free exchange under a flexible transactional network, i.e. markets, must be material equality. Thus, income redistribution by the state may be necessary to rectify inequalities in material resources and educational opportunities. Nozick rejects such a notion of a just starting-point as involving material equality.

The problem of social justice boils down to what is a just distribution of income and wealth. Formal equality is not enough when it comes to social justice. What matters is whether the State should do something to correct market outcomes, increasing real equality. Government could either enhance real equality *ex ante* market operations, i.e. promote equality of opportunity, or government could seek to achieve real equality *ex post* market operations, i.e. it may enhance equal outcomes. One may favour an *ex ante* approach, redistributing wealth by means of inheritance taxes or one may go for an *ex post* approach, redistributing income from the most advantaged to the least advantaged by means of progressive taxes.

Income equality – the trade-offs

If social justice is equality in the distribution of income and wealth, or if social justice is enhanced when the degree of income inequality is reduced, then shall government take action by means of various

public policies? In the debate about equality there is another problem, which does not concern the definition of the concept but relates
to practical considerations about what is possible, given the circumstances. If a theory of social justice delivers what is desirable, then
such a theory must also present what is feasible. Here, we face
another major difficulty with the interpretation of social justice as
equality, in particular distributive equality.

In 'The Idea of Equality' Bernard Williams in 1962 pointed out
that equality among men and women can be increased more easily
in relation to certain objects than with regard to others. While it is
almost impossible to eradicate inequalities in power and prestige,
access to goods like health and education can be made more equal.
Whether governments can reduce income inequalities is a contested
issue in public policy and economic theory. A policy to increase
equality in the distribution of income and wealth will result in certain costs to society which will necessitate balancing increased equality against other values, where there are two such trade-off problems
that are endemic in government policies to promote income equality.

First, there is the equality-efficiency trade-off, which Arthur M.
Okun called 'the big tradeoff':

> The society that stresses equality and mutual respect in the domain of
> rights must face up to the implications of these principles in the domain
> of dollars (Okun, 1975: 118).

An efficient economy needs the institutions of the market economy
which emphasize private incentives and reward mechanisms. Redistributive policies interfere with markets redistributing income from
some groups to other groups. According to Okun, the more ambitious the redistributive policies become, the less efficiently markets
will operate, reducing overall production and thus total income.
Okun states:

> More important, the prizes in the marketplace provide the incentives for
> work effort and productive contribution. In their absence, society
> would thrash about for alternative incentives – some unreliable, like
> altruism; some perilous, like collective loyalty; some intolerable, like
> coercion or oppression. Conceivably, the nation might instead stop
> caring about achievement itself and hence about incentives for effort; in
> that event, the living standard of the lowly would fall along with those
> of the mighty (Okun, 1975: 119).

The crux of the matter is that a most ambitious redistributive set of policies would hurt those that it is aimed at helping, the lower income groups, because its negative impact upon total income would also reduce the part that ends up with this group. Thus, income equality and economic output cannot be maximized at the same time. Which is most important? To decide that one requires a stronger concept of social justice than simply the presumption for equality.

The second big trade-off comes in the form of a confrontation between the two core values in political theory, equality and freedom. Increasing income equality for some groups may require policies that reduce the liberties of other groups. One case of such a collision between freedom and equality is progressive taxation. Another case, although entirely different, is positive discrimination schemes like affirmative action.

Individualists tend to focus upon the trade-off between equality and freedom, when they reject the interpretation of social justice as real equality. Individualists accept only formal equality or equality under the law in their conception of social justice. It is possible to occupy the middle ground between these two positions, but it is not feasible to have a policy that maximizes both equality and liberty at the same time. How to make that trade-off requires, again, a more elaborate theory of social justice.

Distributive justice

Can constitutions improve upon justice or can the concept of justice deliver constitutional principles? One position taken in relation to this double-edged question is to place the constitution outside of the domain of social justice. Constitutions deal only with procedural or formal justice and never with substantive justice. Thus, whether income inequality is to be decreased or not is a task for ordinary statute law, and not for the constitutional arena.

The making and implementation of constitutional law and constitutional policies cannot bypass the concept of justice. Legal justice is no doubt at the heart of a constitutional state. But what to do with social justice? The main theories of social justice today reveal a number of difficulties that are unlikely to be resolved in the short run. These difficulties may be identified by focusing upon social justice as involving the specification of criteria for just treatment of men and women. Below, the open statement 'X is a just treatment of A and B' will be used, where 'A' and 'B' stand for any person or set of persons. How can we translate it into another statement not using the word 'just', which is the concept to be defined?

First, the meta-ethical difficulties suggest that there is no agreement as to how to go about resolving conflicts in moral discourse, for instance in relation to social justice. The new communitarian ethics argues that the difficulty in completing the proposition:

(1) X is a just treatment of A and B if and only if X results in JP for A and B,

where 'JP' in (1) stands for the justice making or enhancing property that theories of social justice hunt, can be remedied by making a reference to a community C. Thus, we get:

(2) X is a just treatment of A and B if and only if C thinks so where A and B enter C.

However, (2) immediately raises a *petitio principii*: why is the fact that one community and not another considers something just a criterion on social justice? What if two communities have different standards on what is social justice? Are both concepts of social justice equally valid?

The prevailing approach to social justice in the literature favours reason as the tool or faculty for finding the justice enhancing property P (Scanlon, 1982). Thus, we get:

(3) X is just treatment of A and B if and only if X is reasonable to A and B,

which is of little help though, as we still need to know which P a reasonable argument will deliver. Why rule out the use of an empirical approach to determining JP?

There is still the utilitarian approach to social justice, despite all its difficulties with measuring and comparing utility. It favours another faculty, viz. the observation of the consequences of actions:

(4) X is a just treatment of A and B if and only if X maximizes good consequences for a society consisting of A and B.

Yet, (4) presents new problems as it is not easy for a government to observe all the consequences of actions as well as to calculate their impact upon pleasure or pain or some such measure of welfare. Since a teleological approach to justice is cumbersome, perhaps a deontological framework is more workable, underlining the selection of right principles. Let us try Kant's version:

(5) X is a just treatment of A and B if and only if X implies that A and B are treated as ends and not as means.

However, Kant's moral law can host many different principles of treating people. It is not vacuous, but it does not give guidance when alternative principles such as strict equality or proportional equality compete.

Secondly, there is the problem of opaqueness, or the difficulty in determining what it is that is to be taken into account when a treatment is just. There are several possible reference terms:

(6) X is a just treatment of A and B if and only if X takes A's and B's merits into account, or

(7) X is a just treatment of A and B if and only if X takes A's and B's needs into account, or

(8) X is a just treatment of A and B if and only if X takes A's and B's rights into account, or

(9) X is a just treatment of A and B if and only if X takes A's and B's capabilities into account, and so on.

It has been argued that the different implications of these principles for treating people can be accommodated within one conception of justice, justice as equality (Vlastos, 1985). However, the concept of equality is an essentially contested one.

Thirdly, there is the difficulty with ellipticity, or incomplete specification of criteria for just treatment. The classical definitions of justice as either equality or impartiality suffer from the fact that they do not specify with regard to what people are to be treated equally or impartially: rewards, consideration, respect, attention or rules. Try the proposal by Nagel (1991) and Barry (1995):

(10) X is a just treatment of A and B if and only if X handles A and B impartially.

Such a formulation is certainly both opaque and elliptic as long as there is no clarification of what aspects of A and B are to be treated as well as of what the treatment is all about. Notice that (10) is much too open ended to allow for a specific interpretation such as:

(11)   X is a just treatment of A and B if and only if X results in A
       and B having the same income.

It is possible to treat people impartially by rewarding their different
achievements differently, as long as A and B are treated according to
the same criteria.

Justice as ultimate values

Given the difficulties inherent in the concept of justice one may
remind the reader of one approach that has not been given much
recent attention, the ultimate values approach listed above. It looks
upon social justice as involving necessarily a choice between conflicting fundamental principles or a commitment to one set of values
while rejecting another set. What is typical of the concept of justice
when it is a matter of distributive justice is the inherently conflictual
nature of the values that may be considered to be just. Interpreting
justice as impartiality (Barry, 1995) amounts to an incomplete definition, because the specification of what it is that is to be treated in
an impartial manner is crucial.

Distributive justice involves two political questions that cannot be
decided without the employment of values. The first problem is the
identification of inequalities, i.e. the assessment of how people are to
be ranked according to various distributive criteria such as income
and wealth. Income distinctions may be generated by values connected with performance, separating between persons according to
how unequal they are in relation to performance criteria. Different
values may be employed in ranking persons, which leads to conflict
between values, as when some favour stark income differentials
where others see the relevance of more equality.

The second problem concerns what governments should do in
relation to social inequalities. It may either accept these inequalities
as just or it may take action to decrease them, if this is feasible. Governments may take the trade-off between equality and efficiency into
account when they deliberate about what to do with inequalities in
income and wealth. However, fundamentally they have to resolve the
question with regard to values. What is the relevance of strict equality? How much inefficiency is a certain reduction in inequality
worth?

In distributive justice impartiality no doubt plays a certain role just as do considerations about the trade-off between degrees of equality in the distribution of income and wealth on the one hand and total production on the other hand. However, the critical question is the evaluation of inequalities in the market and by the State: (a) How much difference in income and wealth is justifiable in markets? (b) How far should governments go in reducing the inequalities in the markets? There is in the last resort no way to decide those two questions but by making up one's mind whether one is an egalitarian or libertarian.

Conclusion

A just constitution is a constitution that satisfies certain normative criteria. A key problem in constitutionalist theory is to pin down those criteria. Here, we have focused upon two different conceptions of justice, legal justice and social justice. While it seems obvious that a just constitution must include the precepts of legal justice, it is not equally evident that principles of social justice should also enter the 'best' constitution.

The most influential theory of justice in the post-war debate states that principles of social justice belong to a just constitution. Rawls argues not only that legal justice must be entrenched in the constitution but also that the difference principle enters a just constitution. However, there is serious disagreement about the nature of social justice, as it raises basic problems about the extent to which the state should promote real equality in the distribution of income and wealth. Actually, outside of a legal context, the concept of equality is elliptic – equality, yes, but in terms of what?

It may seem obvious that a good constitution must be a democratic one. Evidently, democratic constitutions could look very different in terms of institutions. The more attention one pays to the requirement of justice, the more institutions one would want to include in the State. Is there, then, a risk that a constitutional State, taking into recognition the various requirements of justice, legal or social, by means of elaborate institutions, may become overburdened in relation to the democratic state? Are democracy and constitutionalism compatible?

The old discipline of normative political theory has been rejuvenated largely as a response to the attempts to identify justice. The

debate during the past twenty years has resulted in a number of definitions of 'justice', but there is little agreement among scholars
about necessary or sufficient properties of the concept, if indeed an
unambiguous single concept exists.

The problem of defining 'justice' is to come up with a set of criteria that, if present in institutions, enhance justice in social life. One
may wish to make a distinction between a set of rules on the one
hand and their application in concrete cases on the other hand. One
can discuss whether the basic rules of the game are reasonable as well
as raise the question whether they are implemented in a just manner
in a tournament. The same distinction is important when one eval-
uates any kind of social institution: (1) Are the rules in themselves
just? (2) Are the rules being applied in a just manner? The second
question has a legal ring, whereas the first question raises the ethical
question.

Is the choice of just institutions an arbitrary one? Can the view
that one set of institutions is more just than another set be challenged
on rational grounds? The so-called 'Scanlonian approach', after a
proposal by T.M. Scanlon about how matters pertaining to right and
wrong are to be decided in an ethical argument, underlines reason.
Scanlon says:

> An act is wrong if its performance under the circumstances would be
> disallowed by any system of rules for the general regulation of
> behaviour which no one could reasonably reject as a basis for informed,
> unforced general agreement (Scanlon, 1982: 110).

Yet it should be pointed out that the 'Scanlonian approach' in no
way solves the problem of identifying the criteria of justice. Which
criteria would reasonable men/women not reject? Impartiality?
Equality? Liberty?

It may be claimed that justice entails fairness. Such an approach is
close to the ethical connotations of the concept of justice, because
any argument about fairness seems to belong to ethical moral discourse. To ask whether an institution is fair, is asking for criteria
that would sort out fairness from unfairness.

The fairness concept is important when it comes to evaluating
institutions, focusing upon the actions or outcomes that the institutions in question result in. Fairness is to be fair towards someone.
Thus, fairness seems to be incomplete without a reference to who
should be treated fairly. Fairness refers to how people are treated

under a set of institutions. To treat someone fairly implies that the actions taken under the institutions or the outcomes that a set of institutions result in for people are reasonable. Since no one could reasonably reject what is fair, it would seen that the fairness criteria must be the same as the justice criteria or constitute some subset of the criteria of justice.

Thus, we have to discuss the concept of fairness in relation to institutions. What is at stake is not whether the institutions are being applied in a fair manner but whether the institutions themselves are fair. It has been suggested that the criteria for fair treatment are conceived of in a different way from one sphere of human interaction to another (Walzer, 1983). However, we may always ask whether the criteria actually employed are really fair or truly just. Fairness requires not only that a single individual be treated fairly, but also that each and every one be treated in the same way. Fairness implies universalizability as Kant emphasized. Surely fairness must involve something that is general across various spheres of justice.

Looking at the different criteria that are used for treating people one may ask whether there are any criteria that would occur constantly across different forms of human interaction. Impartial treatment seems to meet the Scanlonian test. In many circumstances no one would reasonably reject that in a group of people of A and B each person is treated in a just manner if they are treated in an impartial way. However, impartial treatment is not the same as equal treatment. What impartiality prohibits is that individuals be treated differently without any reason.

Yet justice also contains a distributional conception as there is a search for a theory of justice that is relevant for the problem of distribution of income and wealth in any society. Such a theory would have profound implications for basic questions in public policy concerning what the state should do in relation to markets and market outcomes.

The economy is to a considerable extent like a game. Various players interact under more or less clearly specified institutions governing the interaction in various markets for labour, capital, equity, goods and services. Justice requires that the interaction is fair. What is important to emphasize is that markets do have institutions which operate under a requirement for impartiality which is policed in various ways (Williamson, 1985).

Whether the institutions of the market economy can be improved upon is certainly a very important matter of public policy-making, as one may wish to argue the case that state intervention could be expanded in quantity or strengthened in quality. A quite different matter of justice concerns whether the outcomes of market operations are acceptable. The institutions of real life, like various games, separate between winners and losers. No one would reasonably reject these institutions as long as they are impartial in themselves and have been implemented in an impartial manner. But once the game is over and one person has been declared the winner and received the prize, what should be done with the person who lost the game and received nil?

Justice as fairness in human interaction is one thing, whereas justice in income compensation or maintenance is another. Scoring the right winner requires certain institutions, but the amelioration of the predicament of the losers calls for other kinds of institutions. The maintenance of income or compensation against losses in the face of adversity, poor performance or merely bad luck is an entirely different matter. Such demands may be just even if the operation of the institutions has been fair. The critical question for the welfare state is this: how much security or compensation should government provide? What levels of income maintenance would no one reasonably reject?

The distributional criteria that no one could reasonably reject include: need, desert, aggregate utility, liberty, endowments and equality. But which is the one that no one can reasonably reject when these criteria have different implications? Resolving distributional conflict entails specifying a social welfare function. If one cannot derive a social welfare function by rational deliberations about ultimate values, then maybe democratic voting can resolve matters?

11

Democracy and constitutionalism

Introduction

Having looked at constitutions from many sides including both the **is** and the **ought**, one difficult problem remains to be discussed, viz. the risk for a conflict between democracy and constitutionalism. This question was raised in the introductory chapter, where we noted that it has recently been argued that too many constitutional rules may restrict democracy or the sovereignty of the people.

The purpose in this concluding chapter is to discuss the relationship between the institutions of a constitutional state and the various institutions of democracy in order to pin down how it may be difficult to reconcile one with the other. One must be aware of the fact that there are two problems involved here: (a) is a constitutional state always compatible with democracy? and (b) is there some trade-off between constitutionalism and democracy that may actually be preferred instead of choosing either one or the other? Let us start by looking at the requirements of a democratic State.

First one may point out that the problem of reconciling the democratic state with the constitutional state belongs to the **ought** or the normative problems in constitutional theory. It is fundamentally a problem of defining proper institutions. Actually it is about what just institutions involve, or, following Rawls' suggestion that 'justice' be seen 'only as a virtue of social institutions', the arrival at just practices (Rawls, 1958: 164). How can democracy and constitutionalism collide when it comes to the specification of just institutions?

What is democracy?

A succinct statement of the collision between the doctrine of constitutionalism and populist democracy was made by Robert A. Dahl in his *A Preface to Democratic Theory* from 1956. There Dahl not only formulated in a precise way how constitutionalism may run into conflict with democracy as the sovereignty of the people, but he also launched his own model of democracy, that of polyarchy.

Thus, constitutional provisions that protect private property at times considered vital elements in constitutionalism, may at the same time set limits on the proper exercise of the sovereignty of the people. Although it seems obvious that democracy implies simple majority rule on the basis of the One Man–One Vote principle, it may collide with numerous constitutionalist ideas about minority or group rights as well as about separation of powers or checks and balances. Thus, strong judicial review provides judges who are not accountable to the electorate with a veto against legislation by a directly elected legislature.

How much conflict one preceives between constitutionalism and democracy depends upon how the key concepts are defined. If for example a democratic State is modelled on the basis of a concept of democracy defined in such a way as to include a constitutional State, then the problem simply goes away. Then, however, it will reappear elsewhere as a question about possible internal contradictions within the democratic model.

The concept of democracy is certainly an essentially contested one. Semantic investigations into the use of the word 'democracy' reveal different usages (Lively, 1985; Sartori, 1987). Some have called attention to distinctions between political democracy and economic democracy, between democracy in political institutions and democracy in economic life as well as between democracy in political parties and democracy in organizational life. Others have focused upon the techniques of democracy such as participation, representation and trust. David Held shows in his *Models of Democracy* (1987) that it is possible to identify almost ten different models of democracy in the history of political thought and modern political theory. Is there one single model that may be singled out as the 'true' one?

Democracy theorists have underlined different properties of democracy: participation (Rousseau), representation (Mill), checks and balances (Madison), élite competition (Schumpeter), contestation (Dahl), decentralization (Tocqueville), equality (Marx) and freedom (Hayek). Perhaps the well-known Lincoln definition captures the various dimensions in the concept of democracy: government by the people of the people for the people. Who can tell which one of these aspects of democracy is the most important one: government of the people or representation, government by the people or participation, government for the people or freedom and/or equality? Actually the French 1958 constitution's Article 2 states that French democracy is all these three mechanisms.

The relationship between democracy and constitutionalism is basically an institutional problem. Can one design a set of fundamental political institutions that satisfy the requirements of a constitutional state without infrigements upon democracy? Well, that depends upon the design of democratic institutions. The new institutionalism in political science has called attention to the immense importance in political life of institutions. Which, then, are the typical institutions of a democratic state?

Democracy affords a set of institutions for arriving at a social decision. By a 'social' decision is meant a mechanism that somehow aggregates the preferences of individuals into a group decision (Kelly, 1986). The minimum set of democratic institutions involve the following two basic principles: (a) one man–one vote; (b) simple majority decision-making. Democracy does not allow a person to vote with more than one vote and democracy implies a so-called plurality winner, or the choice rule that the candidate or the alternative having most votes is declared the winner. Democracy is alien to quantitative voting or the possibility that a voter may place more than one vote on an alternative such as in cardinal utility voting (Riker, 1982: 36–7). Nor does democracy accept a dictator or the possibility than one person may decide the outcome of a choice process in accordance with his/her preferences against the will of a majority in the group (the non-dictatorship criterion). Finally, democracy requires that any alternative that becomes the social decision must result from the aggregation of citizen preferences, i.e. no alternative can become the social decision simply on the basis of its own merits (citizen sovereignty criterion).

A set of minimalist democratic institutions

The minimalist institutional requisite for democracy is the set of institutions that can accomplish simple majority voting where each person has one vote. A referendum with two alternatives is such an institution or a presidential election with two candidates or a parliamentary election where two parties compete. Such a minimal insti-

tutional set up for achieving democracy has a few attractive properties for a social decision, identified by Kenneth May (1952). In a
group consisting of more than two persons and where these persons
have rational preferences, i.e. preferences over the choice alternatives
or candidates that are connected and transitive (the rationality criterion), simple majority voting will result in a determinate outcome or
social decision. Thus, we have:

(1) *First theorem*: A democratic decision with at least three voters
    and two alternatives x and y results in a social decision that dis-
    plays neutrality, monotonicity and anonymity.

These technical terms within the literature called 'social choice' stand
for a few attractive properties that one may wish aggregation rules
to satisfy in order to count as acceptable institutions for the arrival
at a social decision based upon the preferences of individuals. By
'neutrality' is meant that no alternative has a favoured position but
that all alternatives are handled in the same way. Qualified majority
institutions do not satisfy the neutrality criterion, because there is a
requirement for more votes for an alternative x to defeat an alternative y than for y to defeat x, if for example x stands for a change or
amendment proposal and y for the *status quo* or the original proposal. 'Monotonicity' stands for the property that the social decision
faithfully represents the preferences of the individuals in the sense
that if one persons changes his first preference from y to x when the
group is indecisive between x and y, then the social decision will be
x. Finally, by 'anonymity' in relation to social decisions is meant that
the identity of the voters has no impact upon the outcome.

That a minimalist set of democratic institutions satisfy the plausible requirements for neutrality, monotonicity and anononymity creates a strong case for democracy, because these properties
approximate the notion of equality in a political context. Actually,
only the minimalist set of democratic institutions satisfy these three
normative criteria on social decisions.

The case for a democratic state seems quite straightforward according to May's theorem. If we want political decisions to be taken in a
manner that satisfies the requirements for neutrality, monotonicity
and anonymity, then we cannot accept qualified majority voting,
unanimity or individual veto, dictatorship or various quorum rules.
Since neutrality, monotonicity and anonymity seem fair requirements,
simple majority rule or democracy is also intuitively fair.

However, when one admits more than two alternatives, then the problems in justifying the simple majority rule begin. The basic difficulty is that once there are three alternatives from which a social decision is to be made, then the minimalist democratic institutions are not enough to derive determinate outcomes (Moulin, 1983). Additional institutions have to be introduced in a democratic State, but which ones? – that is the critical problem (Fishburn, 1973).

Suppose there are three individuals or groups of individuals, (A), (B) and (C) in society and that they have the following preferences over these three alternatives, x, y and z, which could be motions, candidates or parties:

(A) x, y, z
(B) y, z, x
(C) z, x, y.

What is now the meaning of democracy? An additional institution besides the one man–one vote rule and the simple majority rule must be introduced, because how are the alternatives to be compared? One mechanism is to interpret the simple majority rule as involving an overall comparison of all the alternatives simultaneously. Another mechanism is to interpret the simple majority rule as involving piecemeal comparisons between the alternatives taking two alternatives at a time.

The problem in relation to three or more alternatives of an overall comparison versus a piecemeal comparison hits the democratic state whether it is a matter of referenda, presidential elections or voting in legislative assemblies. When representative assemblies have been recruited by means of proportional schemes, allocating the mandates in accordance with the relative number of votes in the electorate, the same problem with simple majority rule reoccurs when the assembly is going to derive a social decision from the preferences of the parliamentarians.

A number of different voting mechanisms have been constructed, either based on an overall comparison, as in plurality voting or approval voting on the one hand, or based upon a piecemeal comparison or pairwise comparison such as in the successive procedure or the amendment procedure. The French second ballot voting or run-off election is a blend of the two types of mechanisms for making a social decision from three or more alternatives, starting out with an overall comparison and then ending up with a choice between the alternatives that have received the largest number of votes, if no one alternative can get a simple majority in the first round of voting (Murakami, 1968).

The social choice literature has shown that each of these additional institutions for aggregating individual preferences into a social decision presents difficulties. One problem for a larger set of democratic institutions comprising not only the one man–one vote principle and the simple majority rule but also for example the plurality rule, the second ballot rule or the pairwise comparison schemes such as the successive, amendment and elimination methods is that they do not always result in a so-called Condorcet winner (Riker, 1982; Nurmi, 1987). The Condorcet winner criterion means that the alternative that becomes the social decision would defeat all the other possible alternatives in pairwise comparisons. Thus, we have:

(2) *Second theorem*: A set of democratic institutions that is larger than the minimalist one does not always identify the Condorcet winner, when there exists a Condorcet winner.

However, another problem for a large set of democratic institutions is that when there exists no Condorcet winner as in the example above, then there is no determinate outcome at all. This was proved by Kenneth Arrow in 1951 in *Social Choice and Individual Values*, showing that when there is no Condorcet winner, then social decisions will be either irrational or dictatorial. Starting from five plausible requirements on institutions for the making of social decisions: universal admissibility of preferences, monotonicity or positive responsiveness, independence of irrelevant alternatives, citizen sovereignty and non-dictatorship, Arrow derived an impossibility finding, i.e. every method of aggregating preferences that satisfy these five requirements will result in decisions or outcomes that do not satisfy the requirement of rationality, i.e. connectivity and transitivity. Or stated the other way around, any set of institutions that satisfy the first three of the requirements and produces a rational decision will be either imposed from the outside or dictatorial (Arrow, 1963). Thus, we have:

(3) *Third theorem*: When there exists no Condorcet winner, then a larger set of democratic institutions result in either irrational social decisions or in imposed or dictatorial decisons.

In the example above, there is a so-called paradox of voting, meaning that alternative x beats y which beats z which beats x and so forth in pairwise comparisons. This leads to cycling, meaning that society cannot arrive at a decision that is transitive or rational. In order to break the cycle, the voting process must be stopped somewhere and one of the alternatives be declared the winner. However, whichever alternative is declared the winner, it will be a dictatorial decision, since there is a majority against either x, y or z (Riker and Ordeshook, 1973). Thus, we have:

(4) *Fourth theorem*: A set of minimalist democratic institutions can only deliver rational social decisions where there are two alternatives.

In order to bypass these difficulties when the set of alternatives are enlarged, the set of democratic institutions may be strengthened by adding other voting mechanisms such as the Borda technique, the Copeland rule, the Schwartz technique, the Kemeny rule, the Dodgson rule, the Nansen technique, the Hare rule and the Coombs method (Nurmi, 1987). However, these more complicated methods present more or less equally large difficulties. If one allows for methods of aggregating preferences that take into account the intensity of the voters' preferences, then the difficulties go away. However, voting in accordance with such schemes as, for example, utilities, violates the requirement of anonymity.

The difficulties with a larger set of democratic institutions than the minimalist ones is the lack of stability. When there is a paradox of voting, then there are unstable outcomes or social decisions that may be defeated in a new round of voting. The requirement of single-peaked preferences is an attempt to create stable outcomes by demanding some kind of consensus among the voters. There is a variety of such consensus criteria (Sen, 1970: 166–72), but they are not easily harmonized with democratic notions, which imply that all kinds of citizen preferences are admissible.

The problem with a democratic state is thus that its minimalist institutions, one man–one vote and simple majority rule, are not enough to handle all relevant types of social choices. Actually, the minimalist institutions of a democracy can only handle a choice situation with two alternatives. A democratic state suffers from institutional indeterminacy, which, once there are three or more alternatives involved, leads to instability. These difficulties are aggravated when one allows for the possibility of insincere voting and vote trad-

ing (Riker, 1982). Independently of each other, Gibbard and Sat-
terthwaite in 1973 and 1975 showed that there is no aggregation
method that is strategy proof, i.e. cannot be manipulated (Riker,
1982; Nurmi, 1987). Here, we have the weakness of the democratic
state:

(5) *Fifth theorem*: When there are more than two alternatives
involved, then a set of minimalist institutions result in social decisions that are unstable, whenever there is more than one dimension involved in the ordering of the alternatives.

The lack of stability for social decisions made in accordance with a
minimalist set of democratic institutions has drastic effects (Mueller,
1989). McKelvey's so-called chaos theorem showing that the paradox
of voting may easily arise meaning that any alternative could win
means that there is no social decision that cannot be defeated by
some other decision (McKelvey, 1976; 1979). But perhaps there are
outcomes that many agree should be stable? One way to improve
upon the stability of social decisions is to enact a constitutional state,
which enhances stability by either changing the institutions of
making certain kinds of decisions or by removing certain outcomes
from future decision-making.

If instability is such a prominent feature of decision-making in
terms of a set of minimalist democratic institutions, then perhaps a
set of institutions may enhance stability, as argued by Kenneth Shepsle in 1979 (Shepsle, 1979; 1986; 1989)? The possible conflict between
constitutionalism and democracy may be analysed against this background of a profound lack of stability in outcomes of democratic
decision-making. If a constitutional state could provide for more stability, then perhaps that would benefit democracy. Or maybe it
would result in too much stability, i.e. protection of the *status quo*?

Stability in social choice and political stability

But perhaps the paradox of voting is not really such a great problem
for the democratic state, as it may not occur that often. Duncan
Black showed in *Theory of Committes and Elections* (1958) that the
paradox of voting cannot occur when the preferences of the voters
are single-peaked or order the alternatives consistently along one
dimension such as, for example, the right–left continuum. The typical feature of the paradox of voting is that there is no consensus

among the voters about which alternative is placed in the first, second and third positions. However, instability in democratic outcomes is frequent, which becomes obvious as one moves to multidimensional models of voting.

The word 'stability' as it is used in the social choice literature requires a small comment here with regard to the problem of marrying democracy with the constitutional state. When one speaks of a fundamental problem of 'stability' in a simple set of democratic institutions, then the word has a technical sense which in no way implies the general notion of political stability as involving high levels of conflict expressed in different forms such as armed resistance, protests and constitutional struggle.

One of the most powerful results in social choice theory is that a set of minimalist democratic institutions will not be able to aggregate the citizens' preferences into a determinate social decision. What matters for outcomes of voting procedures, besides the raw materials of politics and the preferences of the citizens, is tactical and strategic manoeuvres by the choice participants. It matters who sets the agenda, who decides on the alternatives and who chooses the voting procedure in a democracy. As a matter of fact, given the same preferences any alternative could win and thus be the social outcome. If all kinds of preferences are allowed, the issues involved have two or more dimensions inherent in them and strategic behaviour or insincere voting takes place. Political games in this sense – the lack of stability when preferences are aggregated into a voting outcome – are very different from market games – see Ordeshook (1992).

Political games may be either of the two-person or N-person format, depending on whether the interaction involves two persons, groups or organizations or more than two persons, groups and organizations. Political games may be either zero-sum games or non-zero-sum games depending on whether the outcome of the interaction is of the type that one person's gain is the other person's loss or both may benefit from the interaction. Some political games are zero-sum games whereas others are non-zero-sum games. Game theory is the set of models that show if and how these various games have solutions, or determinate outcomes (Rapoport, 1966; 1970).

Two-person zero-sum games are stable in the sense that there are determinate solutions or outcomes. Each player has a so-called dominating strategy, i.e. a strategy that is the best one whatever the opponent does, which is the famous so-called minimax strategy of minimizing one's maximum losses. Two person non-zero-sum games may have one determinate outcome, a so-called Nash equilibrium meaning that the outcome is the best each player could do on his/her own terms. However, many two person non-zero-sum games have more than one solution meaning that they are indeterminate. What is worse, however, is that a Nash equilibrium need not be Pareto optimal, i.e. such a game may have a different solution which is strictly better than the Nash-equilibrium or the solution that follows from the rational choice of strategies. This is the conflict between Pareto optimality and rational choice that we met in Chapter 8 discussing the prisoners' dilemma.

Negotiations or bargaining in politics is seen as a two-person non-zero-sum game. The typical game is called 'Battle of the Sexes' (Table 11.1).

Table 11.1
Battle of the sexes

	Player A	
	A1	A2
Player B		
B1	3, 2	0, 0
B2	0, 0	2, 3

Two players can, if they coordinate their activities, reach a positive outcome for both, but only if they coordinate their strategies. At the same there are two ways of doing that – two Nash equilibria – which benefit them differently. By cooperation the set of feasible outcomes would be as in Figure 11.1.

By cooperation the set of outcomes has been expanded to include the set of Pareto optimal outcomes along the line A3B2–A2B3. A Pareto optimal solution is an outcome where is it impossible to increase the benefit for one player without decreasing the benefit for another player. The cooperative Battle of the Sexes is indeterminate, as there are many solutions to the bargaining problem of choosing one of the several Pareto optimal outcomes. One way to increase the stability in solving the bargaining problem is to employ an institution that requires fairness. Thus, institutions may enhance stability by limiting the set of possible outcomes. In the Battle of the Sexes fairness could be interpreted as equality, immediately resulting in one determinate solution of the game (Riker and Ordeshook, 1973: 220–39). Solutions to the bargaining problem may also be derived by the employment of criteria such as threat capacity, resources or each player's discount factor (Rubinstein, 1982).

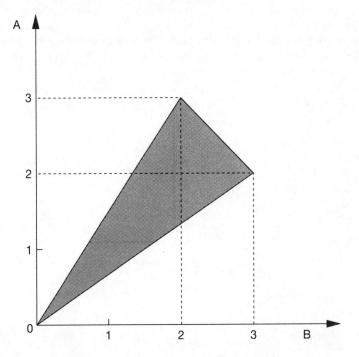

Figure 11.1 Cooperative battle of the sexes

N-person games may also either be zero-sum games or non-zero-sum games. One may ask in relation to N-person games whether they have a core in relation to the set of possible coalitions between the players. A core is a solution concept that focuses on whether there is any outcome for the players that is such that it is better than all other conceivable outcomes from the point of view of any coalition. N-person zero-sum games have no core meaning, they are fundamentally unstable. Any game involving more than two players where a certain pay is to be divided among the players is an N-person zero-sum game and it lacks a determinate solution as the pay can be divided in lots of ways depending upon which coalitions form.

One method for achieving more stability is to insert institutions governing the making of coalitions. Again, we find the theoretical conclusion that institutions enhance stability in social choice by limiting the number of outcomes. N-person non-zero-sum games may have a core. If it has such a solution, then it is Pareto optimal. However, it does not hold that all Pareto optimal outcomes are in the core. However, there is not always a unique core containing one determinate solution. When the core comprises numerous solutions, then there is again instability (Shubik, 1987).

Many political games concern the distribution of gains between various players. Consider the so-called fundamental triangle (Figure 11.2).

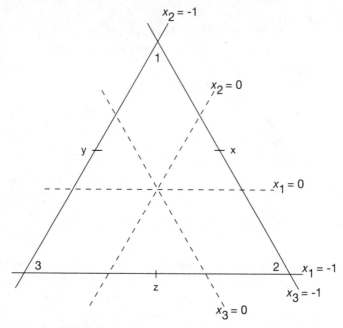

Figure 11.2 The fundamental triangle

In political games, for instance in legislatures or in government coalition formation, there may be three players or groups of players involved who are going to divide up a cake between them in accordance with the rule that a coalition of two players wins. Thus, in Figure 11.2, the vertex 3 stands for player C's best outcome (−1, −1,

2), which is also the worst outcome for player A and player B. The vertex 2 stands for B's best solution (−1, 2, −1) and so on.

How unstable any outcome in these N-person games is appears when one considers that any point within the fundamental triangle is a solution to the game. The outcomes x, z and y have the special quality that they divide the gain equally between the two players in the coalition that defeats the third player, or:

$x = (1/2, 1/2, -1)$
$y = (1/2, -1, 1/2)$
$z = (-1, 1/2, 1/2).$

How is it, then, that legislative behaviour or the formation of government coalitions tends to be much less unstable? It is difficult not to point at institutions as the mechanism that reduces the set of possible outcomes. Thus, coalitions formed in legislatures or in governments tend to prevail due to implicit norms that structure politics or explicit institutions that make certain outcomes more likely than others.

The same kind of instability may arise when the issue at stake involves policy alternatives that express more than one so-called dimension. A dimension in space is the underlying measure along which the policy alternatives may be ranked, as for instance with the left–right scale. When the alternatives can be placed in a one-dimensional space, then there is a core, the so-called median solution, M, as discovered by Black. A solution is in the core when it is undominated. However, when two or more dimensions are involved, then there may exist no core (Figure 11.3).

In Figure 11.3 the best combinations of alternatives along the two dimensions involved, depicted by all combinations along the two axes expresing the two dimensions x and y, for the three players are denoted 'A', 'B' and 'C', around which one may draw circular indifference contours, denoted by 'U'. Here, there is an infinite number of solutions, as there is no median. The set of Pareto optimal solutions lie on or within the triangle formed by connecting A, B and C. However, within the set of Pareto optimal solutions there is no core, i.e. a solution that cannot be defeated by some other solution. What may be conducive to stability in such predicaments is the agenda setting power of one player. Actually, the agenda setter may lead the voting process to any outcome from the starting point s including a point f outside of the Pareto set, if the voting process is finite.

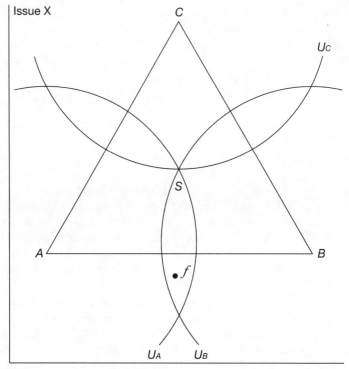

Figure 11.3   Two dimensions and three players

It is possible to formulate both necessary and sufficient conditions for there to be a determinate solution when there is majority voting on issues that involve two dimensions (Plott, 1967; 1973; Feld and Grofman, 1987). If there exists an ideal point M such that every line passing through it has exactly as many voters' ideal points to the left of that point as to the right of that point, then the alternative M is the majority winner. And if an alternative M is the majority winner, then there exists a voter's ideal point M, corresponding to that alternative, such that M is the median voter ideal point on every line passing through it. Figure 11.4 shows such an ideal point which is the median in a two dimensional space *x* and *y*.

Given the scope for so much instability in majority voting outcomes, how can there exist some degree of stability in ongoing democratic decision-making? The neo-institutionalist literature points at political institutions that restrict the possibility of cycling. Such institutions involve restrictions on how issues are voted upon as well as institutions that give certain players agenda power or veto power (Tsebelis, 1990). One rule may require that alternatives which have been defeated once may not be entered again, another rule may demand that each issue be voted upon by taking each dimension separately or there may be a rule that provides certain players or one player a special position, for example in the form of either absolute or suspensive veto power. The structure of the American constitution may be interpreted as a set of institutions that enhance stability (Hammond and Miller, 1987).

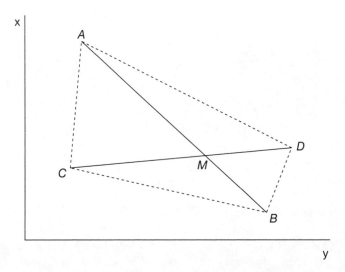

Figure 11.4 Median outcome in two dimensional space

Institutions enhance stability, claims the new institutionalism in political science. By restricting the number of possible outcomes from voting processes based upon the minimalist set of democratic institutions, institutions support certain outcomes at the expense of others meaning that the implications of the chaos theorem are limited. 'Veto players enhance political stability by making political equilibria more probable in social choice processes', states Tsebelis (1995), 'stability' then referring to determinate outcomes or transitive outcomes whatever the social decision may be. A similar argument for agency power enhancing stability in budgetary outcomes has been suggested (Steunenberg, 1994). Figure 11.5 displays the idea that a veto player V enhance stability in social choice processes in a democracy by undoing the cycling process between players A, B and C and focusing the outcome to somewhere in the core between V and Z.

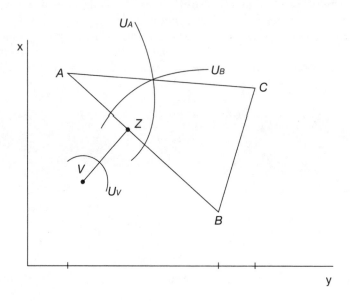

Figure 11.5   Veto players and the core

However, by constraining outcomes institutions may come into conflict with democracy. It is true that various veto institutions narrow down the set of feasible outcomes, but at the same time the more there is of veto institutions, the less scope there is for the majority principle of a democratic regime. One may wish to remind the reader of the fact that the formal reason for the outbreak of the American Civil War was the denial of the North of the interpretation of the constitution among the Southern states, which demanded veto mechanisms in the form of concurrent majorities and the right of nullification (Calhoun, 1953).

If the president is given an absolute veto in legislative matters, then there is a violation of the non-dictatorship criterion of democracy. Too many institutions may result in another kind of political instability, where various rules give too much power to certain players to constrain the operation of the minimalist institutions of democracy.

The constitutional state must walk on a tightrope allowing on the one hand for institutions that bring about stability but not providing too many institutions that constrain democracy, which eventually may result in political instability. Too many institutions may constrain democracy to such an extent that there occur deadlocks, which in turn cause political instability, though in another sense than the use of 'stability' above. Before we discuss the constitutional state we should mention that the market economy provides a set of institutions that result in determinate outcomes.

The market economy

The institutions of the market economy afford mechanisms for the arrival at determinate outcomes of human interaction. The key solution concept in economic games is the notion of Pareto optimality. An outcome is Pareto optimal or efficient if and only if it is impossible to make an improvement for one player without at the same time making things worse for the other players. At stake is the search for first-best solutions to allocation problems, i.e. Pareto optimal outcomes in consumption and production. If markets can be trusted with solving allocation problems, then the burden on democracy eases.

The conditions under which a competitive market results in stable equilibrium outcomes have been researched extensively from Leon Walras in the nineteenth century to Arrow and Debreu in the twentieth century (Eatwell *et al.*, 1989, 1990). General equilibrium analysis has proved that there exist equilibria and that they enter the core, i.e. a set of outcomes that cannot be improved upon. The equilibrium results require a competitive economy where certain conditions are satisfied. Non-competitive markets do not result in so-called first-best solutions, or Pareto optimal solutions that enter the core.

The core in an economic game is the set of Pareto optimal outcomes resulting from a cooperative game where the players make deals which are kept later on. It has been shown in equilibrium analysis that as the number of participants in an exchange economy grows the set of equilibrium prices (the core) becomes smaller. When the number of players becomes very high, then there will exist a unique equilibrium or determinate solution. One distinguishes between, on the one hand, partial equilibrium analysis, which deals with one market only such as the market for goods, capital or labour, and, on the other hand, general equilibrium analysis, which investigates the conditions under which all markets tend to clear.

The existence of determinate solutions to games involving inter-action on fully competitive markets with no externalities, economies of scale and perfect information offer relief to the troublesome con-cept of stability in political games based upon the minimalist set of institutions. If social decisions are not made by the political author-ities but are given over to the market economy, then there will be not only determinate outcomes but also Pareto efficient outcomes.

The critical question in relation to the market economy is not whether there is a core or a set of determinate solutions, because eco-nomic games often have a core. Instead the problem is whether the conditions for the operation of competitive markets are satisfied. The institutions of the market economy – private property rights, joint stock companies and bourses (Williamson, 1985) – function not only in fully competitive markets, but may also handle non-competitive markets such as monopoly. Thus, there is an institutional problem in economic interactions as well.

The traditional theory of market failure used to state the limits of the results of equilibrium analysis, showing that there will not be Pareto optimal outcomes in a market where there occur externalities or economies of scale. The remedy used to be public policy, solving market failure by either public resource allocation or regulation. However, the neo-institutionalist revolution in economic theory has shown that there may be institutional remedies. Coase's theorem implies that creating property rights may be the best way of handling externalities and economies of scale can be taken care of by the market, if there is a tendering process for short-term or long-term contracts to hire infrastructure.

The connection between a specific set of institutions, the compet-itive market institutions, and efficiency in resource allocation is a strong one. Not only is it the case that markets that operate under perfect competition result in Pareto optimal allocation, but it also holds that every Pareto optimal allocation is a perfectly competitive one. It is both a necessary and sufficient condition for an efficient allocation of resources that all markets be perfectly competitive (Henderson and Quandt, 1958).

Yet decisions about the structure of private property as well as other decisions about the preconditions for the market economy have to be taken by the State. Getting the institutions right is an enormously difficult problem for the State not only with regard to the economy but also in relation to its own domain, the public sector. Institutional problems are typically handled at the political level, where a set of minimalist democratic institutions are afflicted by much instability, or lack of determinate outcomes. A constitution, being a set of meta-institutions, may help by restricting the set of feasible outcomes.

The constitutional state

A constitutional State would enhance stability in social decisions by several of its mechanisms. First, by identifying certain civil and political rights as unalterable it would promote stability by removing certain alternatives from ever being included for possible social decisions. Secondly, by asking for separation of powers it would make certain kinds of decision-making more difficult by entering at various points veto options by various bodies or persons, again enhancing stability. Finally, by focusing upon a written constitution and enshrining it with a special status thereby making it more difficult to change than ordinary law and meaning that certain decisions would require special majorities, which would also be conducive to stability.

Thus, a constitutional State affords two kinds of mechanisms that enhance stability in social decisions, one creating so-called immunities or rights that cannot be changed and the other introducing inertia in the decision-making processes. Immunities and inertia would reduce the consequences of cycling, strategic voting and log-rolling. The critical question in relation to the constitutional State is not whether immunities and inertia *per se* are acceptable, but how much of these two entities are recommendable?

Given the extent to which a State entrenches immunities and inertia, one may distinguish between weak constitutionalism versus strong constitutionalism. In a strong constitutional State there would be many immunities, surrounding in particular private property. In addition, there would be a constitution institutionalized as a *lex superior*, which would be difficult to change and which would be protected by strong judicial review either by a supreme court or a special constitutional court. Would not such a strong constitutional state set up too many barriers for democracy?

In a weak constitutional State, there would be less of immunities and not much of constitutional inertia in combination with only weak judicial review. Such a weak constitutional State would safe-guard the classical negative liberties by designating them freedom of thought, religion and association with the possible exception of pri-vate property, which would only be regulated by ordinary statute law. There would be constitutional inertia, but not in the form of qualified majority rules and the legal control of public administration would be important, but judicial review would not take the form of a power of a court to invalidate legislation.

The problem with a strong constitutional State is that it may bol-ster the *status quo* to such an extent that democracy is hurt. These mechanisms that strong constitutionalism involve – immunities, qualified majorities, judicial review – all come into conflict with the desirable properties that were identified above in relation to the making of social decisions: neutrality, anonymity and monotonicity or positive responsiveness. Ultimately, strong constitutionalism runs into conflict with the egalitarian stand in the concept of democracy, viz. that any alternative should be relevant for social decision, that each and every person should have the same say and that when the support for one alternative increases among the voters, then the probability of its acceptance as the social decision should increase.

One may contrast British constitutionalism with American consti-tutionalism in this respect, the former being an example of a weak constitutional state whereas the latter represents a strong constitu-tional State. Which one is to be preferred? Or perhaps there is a middle ground in between these two models, such as German or French constitutionalism? In any case, British constitutionalism com-prises only practice and not a *lex superior*, stems from the sovereignty of Parliament not the supremacy of the constitution, and does not accept constitutional review by the courts as in American constitu-tionalism (Brazier, 1994). Evidently, few commentators on the British constitution have claimed that it presents a threat to democracy, whereas many have raised objections in relation to the United States' constitutions as involving a lack of accountability to the people.

A strong constitutional State may be difficult to bring into agree-ment with notions about democracy. There would simply be too many immunities and too much inertia for democracy to be able to rule. However, it is difficult to see how a weak constitutional State could present a threat to democratic institutions. On the contrary, the institutions of a weak constitutional State could complement the institutions of a democratic State by making social decisions more stable.

A constitutional State may be erected by means of a minimum set of institutions or a maximum set. In the minimum set there would have to be institutions that safeguard the following: (a) legality; (b) separation of powers; (c) formal equality; (d) control of the use of public competencies and the possibility of remedies. It is difficult to understand that such a minimum set of institutions would threaten democracy. When there is a maximum set of institutions in a constitutional state involving numerous checks and balances as well as veto players, then there is no doubt a potential collision.

A democratic constitutional State

It should be possible to unite constitutionalism and democracy. Besides the set of minimalist institutions of one man–one vote and simple majority rule democracy needs additional institutions. A weak version of a constitutional State affords such institutions, creating certain immunities such as human rights and introducing a certain degree of inertia in the making of social decisions by means of institutions for the separation of powers and territorial decentralization.

Some would argue that the values connected with a strong constitutional State are so large that they compensate for the fact that there will be a reduction in democracy – see J.A. Rohr's *To Run a Constitution* (1986). Others look upon the trade-off between strong constitutionalism and democracy the other way, regretting that strong constitutionalism may bring about a decline in democracy – see S.S. Wolin's *The Presence of the Past* (1990).

A democracy needs the institutions of a constitutional State with its emphasis upon procedural stability, accountability, the autonomy of the judiciary, multi-level government and civil and political rights. The isssue is how strong the institutions of the constitutional State should be framed at the peril of maximizing the rule of law while harming democracy by creating too many immunities and too much inertia. A moderate form of constitutionalism promotes the viability of the democratic State (Holmes, 1988; Nedelski, 1988).

Conclusion

Historically, the constitutional State emerged before the democratic State. It is true that there existed constitutional monarchies in Europe as well as constitutional republican States before democratic institutions were introduced in a complete fashion. Yet, today a constitutional State must be a democratic State, as the implementation of a set of civil and political rights is an essential part of modern constitutionalism. How comprehensive the set of human rights should be is a matter of contention, which also applies to the question of whether its overall orientation should be towards negative or positive freedom in Berlin's distinction (Berlin, 1969).

It is true that there is a tension between strong constitutionalist notions and democratic institutions. A constitutional State may appear attractive, because it would promote the ideals of a *Rechtsstaat*. At the same time, a set of minimalist democratic institutions such as the one man–one vote principle and the simple majority rule have an unquestionable position today. Only to a certain degree can the constitutional State be harmonized with the democratic State.

A State that implements weak constitutionalism would have little difficulty in accommodating democratic institutions. Actually, weak constitutionalism would complement democracy by bringing to it more stability in social decisions. Strong constitutionalism may run into conflict with democracy, because there could be too many immunities and too much inertia for social decisions to simply reflect the preferences of the citizens according to the requirements of anonymity, neutrality and positive responsiveness.

Democracy, defined by the minimum institutions for group decision-making of one man (woman)-one vote and plurality, entails two difficulties. First, the majority may oppress the minority ('le despotisme de la liberté') and second, the outcomes may not be stable. Both weaknesses were realized in the wake of the French Revolution when democratic decision-making was put to practice, the first by Tocqueville – equality threatening liberty, and the second by Condorcet – the risk of cycling in preference aggregation. A constitutional framework may help in both respects, safeguarding immunities and providing inertia in decision-making.

Bibliography

Ackerman, B. (1980) *Social Justice in the Liberal State*. New Haven: Yale University Press.

Ahmad, Z. H. (1989) 'Malaysia: Quasi Democracy in a Divided Society' in Diamond, Linz and Lipset, *Democracy in Developing Countries*, Vol.3, pp. 347–82.

Alexy, R. (1994) *Theorie der Grundrechte*. Frankfurt am Main: Suhrkamp Taschenbuch Verlag.

Allen, J. W. (1964) *A History of Political Thought in the Sixteenth Century*. London: Methuen & Co. Ltd..

Allen, T.R.S. (1993) *Law, Liberty, and Justice. The Legal Foundations of British Constitutionalism*. Oxford: Clarendon Press.

Althusius, J. (1964) *The Politics of Johannes Althusius*. London: Eyre and Spottiswode.

Aquinas, T. (1960) *The Political Ideas of St. Thomas Aquinas*. New York: Hafner.

Archer, C. (1992) *International Organizations*. London and New York: Routledge.

Aristotle (1961) *Politics and the Athenian Constitution*. London: Everyman's Library.

Arrow, K. J. (1963) *Social Choice and Individual Values*. New York: Wiley.

Aune, B. (1979) *Kant's Theory of Morals*. Princeton, New Jersey: Princeton University Press.

Austin, J. (1972) *Lectures on Jurisprudence*. Glashytten im Taanus: Auvermann.

Austin, J. L. (1962) *How to do things with Words*. Oxford: Clarendon Press.

Axelrod, R. (1984) *The Evolution of Cooperation*. New York: Basic Books.

Bagehot, W. (1993) *The English Constitution*. London: Fontana Press.

Banks Data (1994) (Computer file). Binghamton, NY: Computer Solutions Unlimited.

Barnum, D.G. (1993) *The Supreme Court and American Democracy*. New

York: St. Martin's Press.

Barry, B. (1989) *Theories of Justice*. London: Harvester Wheatsheaf.

Barry, B. (1995) *Justice as Impartiality*. Oxford: Oxford University Press.

Baylor, M.G. (1991) (ed.) *The Radical Reformation*. Cambridge: Cambridge University Press.

Becker, C. (1942) *The Declaration of Independence*. New York: Knopf.

Bell, D. (1993) *Communitarianism and Its Critics*. Oxford: Clarendon Press.

Bentham, J. (1988) *A Fragment on Government*. Cambridge: Cambridge University Press.

Berlin, I. (1969) *Four Essays on Liberty*. Oxford: Oxford University Press.

Berman, H.J. (1983) *Law and Revolution. The formation of the western legal tradition*. Harvard: Harvard University Press.

Berntzen, E. (1993) 'Democratic consolidation in Central America: a qualitative comparative approach' *Third World Quarterly*, Vol.14, No.3.

Black, A. (1991) 'The conciliar movement' in Burns, *The Cambridge History of Medieval Political Thought*, pp. 573–87.

Black, D. (1958) *The Theory of Committees and Elections*. Cambridge: Cambridge University Press.

Blaustein, A. P. and Flanz, G. H. (1972–) *Constitutions of the Countries of the World: a series of updated texts*. New York: Dobbs Ferry.

Bleicken, J. (1993) *Die Verfassung der Römischen Republik*. Zürich: Schöningh.

Bloch, M. (1965) *Feudal Society. (1) The Growth of Ties of Independence*. London: Routledge & Kegan Paul Ltd.

Bloch, M. (1965) *Feudal Society. (2) Social Classes and Political Organization*. London: Routledge & Kegan Paul Ltd.

Bobbitt, P. (1991) *Constitutional Interpretation*. Oxford: Basil Blackwell.

Bock, G., Skinner, Q. and Viroli, M. (eds.) (1993) *Machiavelli and Republicanism*. New York: Cambridge University Press.

Bodin, J. (1955) *Six Books of the Commonwealth*. Oxford: Blackwell.

Bodin, J. (1994) *On Sovereignty*. Cambridge: Cambridge University Press.

Bogdanor, V. (ed.) (1988) *Constitutions in Democratic Politics*. Aldershot: Gower Publishing Company Limited.

Bogdanor, V. (1994) 'Britain and the European Community', in Jowell and Oliver, *The Changing Constitution*, 3–31.

Booth, J. A. (1989) 'Costa Rica: The Roots of Democratic Stability' in Diamond, Linz and Lipset, Vol.4, *Democracy in Developing Countries*, pp. 387–422.

Botzenhart, M. (1993) *Deutsche Verfassungsgeschichte 1806–1949*. Stuttgart: Verlag W. Kohlhammer.

Bovens, M. (1995) 'The Integrity of the Managerial State: A case of Institutional Instability'. (University of Leiden, forthcoming).

Bradley, A.W. (1994) 'The Sovereignty of Parliament – in Perpetuity?', in Jowell and Oliver, *The Changing Constitution*, 79–107.

Bradley, A.W. and Ewing, K. (eds) (1993) *Wade and Bradley: Constitutional and Administrative Law*. Harlow, Essex: Longman.

Brams, S.J. (1975) *Game Theory and Politics*. New York: Free Press.

Brams, S.J. (1994) *Theory of Moves*. Cambridge: Cambridge University Press.

Brandt, R. B. (1979) *A Theory of the Good and the Right*. Oxford: Clarendon Press.

Brazier, R. (1990) *Constitutional Texts. Material on Government and the Constitution*. Oxford: Clarendon Press.

Brazier, R. (1994) *Constitutional Practice*. Oxford: Clarendon Press.

Brecht, A. (1959) *Political Theory. The Foundations of Twentieth–century Political Thought*. Princeton, NJ: Princeton University Press.

Brennan, G. and Buchanan, J.M. (1985) *The Reason of Rules. Constitutional Political Economy*. Cambridge: Cambridge University Press.

Brewer–Carías, A. R. (1989) *Judicial Review in Comparative Law*. New York: Cambridge University Press.

Brown, L. N. and Bell, J. S. (1993) *French Administrative Law*. Oxford: Clarendon.

Broad, C. D. (1967) *Five Types of Ethical Theory*. London: Routledge & Kegan Paul Ltd..

Brownlie, I. (1993) *Principles of Public International Law*. Oxford: Clarendon Press.

Brunner, O. (1965) *Land und Herrschaft*. Wien: Rohrer.

Bryce, J. (1905) *Constitutions*. New York: Oxford University Press.

Buchanan, J.M. (1991) *Constitutional Economics*. Oxford: Basil Blackwell.

Burgess, M. and Gagnon, A.G. (eds.) (1993) *Comparative Federalism and Federation*. New York: Harvester Wheatsheaf.

Burke, E. (1967) *Reflections on the Revolution in France*. London: Everyman's Library.

Burke, P. (1991) 'Tacitism, scepticism, and reason of state' in Burns and Goldie, *The Cambridge History of Political Thought*, pp. 479–98.

Burns, J. H. (ed.) (1991) *The Cambridge History of Medieval Political Thought. c. 350–c. 1450*. New York: Cambridge University Press.

Burns, J. H. and Goldie, M. (eds.) (1991) *The Cambridge History of Political Thought. 1450–1700*. New York: Cambridge University Press.

Burns, J. H. (1991) 'Scholasticism: survival and revival' in Burns and Goldie, *The Cambridge History of Political Thought*, pp.132–58.

Butler, D. and Ranney, A. (eds) (1994) *Referendums around the World*. Basingstoke: Macmillan.

Butt, R. (1989) *A History of Parliament. The Middle Ages*. London: Constable and Company Ltd.

Caenegem, R. van (1991) 'Government, law and society' in Burns, *The Cambridge History of Medieval Political Thought*, pp. 174–210.

Calhoun, J. C. (1953) *A Disquisition on Government*. Indianapolis: Bobbs-Merrill.

Campell, T. (1988) *Justice*. London: Macmillan.

Cane, P. (1987) *An Introduction to Administrative Law*. Oxford: Clarendon Press.

Canning, J. P. (1991) 'Law, sovereignty and corporation theory, 1300–1450' in Burns *The Cambridge History of Medieval Political Thought*, pp. 454–76.

Cappelletti, M. (1971) *Judicial Process in the Contemporary World*. New York: Bobbs–Merrill.

Chevalier, I. I. (1993) *Histoire de la pensée politique*. Paris: Payot et Rivages.

Cicero, M.T. (1951) *De Republica*. London: Heineman.

Cicero, M.T. (1993) *On Duties*. Cambridge: Cambridge University Press.

Clapham, C. (1993) 'Democratisation in Africa: obstacles and prospects' in *Third World Quarterly*, Vol.14, No.3.

Coase, R.H. (1988) *The Firm, the Market and the Law*. Chicago: University of Chicago Press.

Cohen, C. (1971) *Democracy*. New York: Free Press.

Coleman, J.L. (1988) *Markets, Morals and the Law*. Cambridge: Cambridge University Press.

Constant, B. (1988) *Political Writings*. New York: Cambridge University Press.

Craven, J. (1992) *Social Choice*. Cambridge: Cambridge University Press.

Cusa, N. de (1990) *Catholic Concordance*. Cambridge: Cambridge University Press.

Cutright, P. (1963) 'National Political Development: measurement and analysis', *American Sociological Review*, vol. 32: 562–78.

Dahl, R. A. (1964) *A Preface to Democratic Theory*. Chicago: The University of Chicago Press.

Damaska, M. (1986) *The Faces of State Authority and Power*. New Haven, CT: Yale University Press.

Daniels, N. (ed.) (1985) *Reading Rawls*. Oxford: Basil Blackwell.

David, R. and Brierley, J.E.C. (1985) *Major Legal Systems in the World Today*. London: Stevens and Sons.

Denning, L.J. (1979) *The Discipline of Law*. London: Butterworth.

d'Entreves, A.P. (1951) *Natural Law*. London: Hutchinson.

Derbyshire, J.D. and Derbyshire, I. (1991) *World Political Systems: an introduction to comparative government*. Edinburgh: Chalmers.

Diamond, L. (1992) 'Economic development and democracy reconsidered', in Marks, G. and Diamond, L. (eds.) *Reexamning Democracy*. Newbury Park: Sage, pp. 93–139.

Diamond, L, Linz, J.J. and Lipset, S.M. (eds.) (1988) *Democracy in Developing Countries. Vol. 2, Africa*. Boulder, CO: Lynne Rienner Publishers.

Diamond, L, Linz, J.J. and Lipset, S.M. (eds.) (1989) *Democracy in Developing Countries. Vol. 3, Asia*. Boulder, CO: Lynne Rienner Publishers.

Diamond, L, Linz, J.J. and Lipset, S.M. (eds.) (1989) *Democracy in Developing Countries. Vol.4, Latin America*. Boulder, CO: Lynne Rienner Publishers.

Dicey, A.V. (1959) *Introduction to the Study of the Law of the Constitution*. London: Macmillan.

Donnelly, J. (1993) *International Human Rights*. Boulder, CO: Westview Press.

Döring, H. (ed.) (1995) *Parliaments and Majority Rule in Western Europe*. Frankfurt: Campus.

Duchacek, I. (1987) *Comparative Federalism*. Lanham: University Press of America.

Duchhardt, H. (1991) *Deutsche Verfassungsgeschichte 1495–1806*. Stuttgart: Verlag W. Kohlhammer.

Dufour, A. (1991) 'Pufendorf' in Burns and Goldie, *The Cambridge History of Political Thought*, pp.561–88.

Dunbabin, J. (1991) 'Government' in Burns, *The Cambridge History of Medieval Political Thought*, pp. 477–519.

Dunleavy, P. and O'Leary, B. (1987) *Theories of the State. The Politics of Liberal Democracy*. London: Macmillan.

Dworkin, R. (1986) *Law's Empire*. Cambridge, MA: Harvard University Press.

Dworkin, R. (1987) *Taking Rights Seriously*. London: Duckworth.

Eatwell, J., Milgate, M. and Newman, P. (eds.) (1989) *Allocation, Information and Markets*. London: Macmillan.

Eatwell, J., Milgate, M. and Newman, P. (eds.) (1990) *General Equilibrium*. London: Macmillan.

Edwards, P. (1965) *The Logic of Moral Discourse*. New York: The Free Press.

Elazar, D.J. (1987) *Exploring Federalism*. Tuscaloosa: University of Alabama Press.

Elazar, D.J (1991) (ed.) *Federal Systems of the World*. Harlow, Essex: Longman.

Elster, J. (1989) *The Cement of Society: a study of social order*. Cambridge: Cambridge University Press.

Elster, J. and Hylland, A. (1987) *Foundations of Social Choice Theory*. New York: Cambridge University Press.

Elster, J. and Slagstad. R. (eds.) (1988) *Constitutionalism and Democracy*. New York: Cambridge University Press.

Esping–Andersen, G. (1990) *The Three Worlds of Welfare Capitalism*. Cambridge: Polity Press.

Feld, S.L. and Grofman, B. (1987) 'Necessary and sufficient conditions for a majority winner in n–dimensional spatial voting games: an intuitive geometric approach', *American Journal of Political Science*, vol. 31: 709–28.

Figgis, J.N. (1960) *Political Thought. From Gerson to Grotius: 114–1625.* New York: Harper and Row.

Finer, S.E., Bogdanor, V. and Rudden, B. (1995) *Comparing Constitutions.* Oxford: Clarendon Press.

Finnis, J.M. (1980) *Natural Law and Natural Rights.* Oxford: Clarendon Press.

Fishburn, P.C. (1973) *The Theory of Social Choice.* Princeton, NJ: Princeton University Press.

Fisher, L. (1990) *Vol.1 Constitutional Structures: Separated Powers and Federalism. American Constitutional Law.* New York: McGraw–Hill Publishing Company.

Fisher, L. (1990) *Vol. 2 Constitutional Rights: Civil Rights and Civil Liberties. American Constitutional Law.* New York: McGraw–Hill Publishing Company.

Forsyth, M. (1989) *Federalism and Nationalism.* Leicester and London: Leicester University Press.

Foulkes, D. (1990) *Administrative Law.* London: Butterworth.

Franklin, J. H. (1991) 'Sovereignty and the mixed constitution: Bodin and his critics' in Burns and Goldie, *The Cambridge History of Political Thought*, pp. 298–328.

Freedom House (1992) *Freedom in the World.* New York: Freedom House.

Frey, R. G. (ed.) (1985) *Utility and Rights.* Oxford: Basil Blackwell.

Friedmann, W. (1967) *Legal Theory.* London: Stevens and Sons Limited.

Friedrich, C.J. (1950) *Constitutional Government and Democracy: theory and practice in Europe and America.* Boston, MA: Ginn.

Friedrich, C. J. (1963) 'Justice: The Just Political Act', in Friedrich and Chapman (eds), pp. 24–43.

Friedrich, C.J. (1968) 'Constitutions and constitutionalism', in *International Encyclopedia of the Social Sciences*, Vol 3: pp. 318–26.

Friedrich, C.J. (1973) *The Philosophy of Law in Historical Perspective.* Chicago: The University of Chicago Press.

Friedrich, C.J. and Chapman, J.W. (eds.) (1963) *Justice.* New York: Atherton Press.

Gallie, W. B. (1955–56) 'Essentially contested concepts', *Proceedings of the Aristotelian Society*, vol. 56.

Ganshof, F.L. (1966) *Feudalism.* London: Longmans, Green and Co. Ltd.

Gastil, R.D. (1987) *Freedom in the World.* New York: Greenwood Press.

Gauthier, D. (1990) *Moral Dealing: Contract, Ethics and Reason.* Ithaca: Cornell University Press.

George, R.P. (1994) (ed.) *Natural Law Theory.* Oxford: Clarendon Press.

Gewirth, A. (1951–56) *Marsilius of Padua and Medieval Political Philosophy (Vol. 1). The Defensor Pacis* (Vol. 2). New York: Columbia University

Press.

Gierke, O. (1958) *Natural Law and the Theory of Society*. New York: Cambridge University Press.

Gillespie, C. G. and Gonzalez, L. E. (1989) 'Uruguay: The survival of old and autonomous institutions' in Diamond, Linz and Lipset, Vol.4, *Democracy in Developing Countries*, pp. 207–46.

Goldie, M. (1991) 'The reception of Hobbes' in Burns and Goldie, *The Cambridge History of Political Thought*, pp. 589–615.

Grafton, A. (1991) 'Humanism and political theory' in Burns and Goldie, *The Cambridge History of Political Thought*, pp. 9–29.

Greenberg, D., Katz, S.N., Oliviero, M.B. and Wheatley, S.C. (eds.) (1993) *Constitutionalism and Democracy. Transitions in the contemporary world*. Oxford: Oxford University Press.

Grotius, H. (1957) *Prolegomena to the Law of War and Peace*. Indianapolis: Bobbs-Merrill.

Grotius, H. (1979) *The Rights of War and Peace: including the law of nature and of nations*. Westport, Conn: Hyperion Press.

Gupta, J. Das (1989) 'India: Democratic becoming and combined development' in Diamond, Linz and Lipset, Vol.3, *Democracy in Developing Countries*, pp. 53–104.

Hamilton, A., Madison, J. and Jay, J. (1961) *The Federalist Papers*. New York: Mentor.

Hammond, T.H. and Miller, G.J. (1987) 'The core of the constitution', *American Political Science Review*, Vol. 81: 1155–74.

Han, S. (1989) 'South Korea: Politics in transition' in Diamond, Linz and Lipset, Vol. 3, *Democracy in Developing Countries*, pp. 267–304.

Hare, R.M. (1963) *Freedom and Reason*. Oxford: Clarendon Press.

Hare, R.M. (1967) *The Language of Morals*. New York: Oxford University Press.

Harrington, J. (1977) *The Political Works of James Harrington*. Cambridge: Cambridge University Press.

Harris, J.W. (1979) *Law and Legal Science*. Oxford: Clarendon Press.

Harris, J.W. (1992) *Legal Philosophies*. London: Butterworth.

Harsanyi, J. (1977) *Rational Behavior and Bargaining Equilibrium in Games and Social Situations*. Cambridge: Cambridge University Press.

Hart, H.L.A. (1970) *The Concept of Law*. Oxford: Clarendon Press.

Hartley, T.C. (1989) *The Foundations of European Community Law*. Oxford: Clarendon Press.

Hartlyn, J. (1989) 'Colombia: The politics of violence and accomodation' in Diamond, Linz and Lipset, Vol.4, *Democracy in Developing Countries*, pp. 291–334.

Hawgood, J.A. (1939) *Modern Constitutions since 1787*. London: Macmillan.

Hayek, F.A. (1944) *The Road to Serfdom*. London: Routledge.

Hayek, F.A. (1982) *Law, Legislation and Liberty. Vol. 1–3*. London: Routledge & Kegan Paul.

Hayek, F.A. (1990) *The Constitution of Liberty*. London: Routledge.

Haynes, J. (1993) 'Sustainable democracy in Ghana? Problems and prospects', *Third World Quarterly*, Vol.14, No.3.

Headlam–Morley, A. (1928) *The New Democratic Constitutions of Europe*. London: Oxford University Press.

Hechter, M., Opp, K–D. and Wippler, R. (eds.) (1990) *Social Institutions. Their emergence, maintenance and effects*. New York: Aldine de Gruyter.

Hegel, G.W F. (1967) *Hegel's Philosophy of Right*. London: Oxford University Press.

Held, D. (1987) *Models of Democracy*. Oxford: Polity Press.

Held, D. (ed.) (1991) *Political Theory Today*. Cambridge: Polity Press.

Held, D. (ed.) (1993) *Prospects for Democracy*. Cambridge: Polity Press.

Henderson, J.M. and Quandt, R.E. (1958) *Microeconomic Theory*. New York: McGraw–Hill.

Hesse, J.J. and Ellwein, T. (1992) *Das Regierungssystem der Bundesrepublik Deutschland*. Opladen: Westdeutcher Verlag.

Hesse, J.J. and Johnson, N. (eds.) (1995) *Constitutional Policy and Change in Europe*. Oxford: Oxford University Press.

Heywood, P. (1995) *The Government and Politics of Spain*. London: Macmillan.

Hinsley, F.H. (1986) *Sovereignty*. Cambridge: Cambridge University Press.

Hobbes, T. (1965) *Leviathan*. London: Everyman's Library.

Hohfeld, W.N. (1946) *Fundamental Legal Conceptions: as applied in juridical reasoning*. New Haven: Yale University Press

Holmes, S. (1988) 'Gag rules or the politics of omission' in Elster and Slagstad (eds.) *Constitutionalism and Democracy*, pp. 19–58.

Holt, J. C. (1992) *Magna Carta*. New York: Cambridge University Press.

Höpfl, H. (1991) *Luther and Calvin on Secular Authority*. Cambridge: Cambridge University Press.

Howard, D. (1990) *The Birth of American Political Thought, 1763–87*. London: Macmillan.

Howard, N. (1971) *Paradoxes of Rationality: Theory of Metagames and Political Behaviour*. Cambridge, MA: MIT Press.

Hume, D. (1966) *A Treatise of Human Nature*. Vol. 1–2 London: Everyman's Library.

Huntington, S.P. (1991) *The Third Wave: democratization in the late twentieth century*. Norman, Okla.: University of Oklahoma Press.

Ingram, A. (1994) *A Political Theory of Rights*. Oxford: Clarendon Press.

Jackson, D.W. and Tate, C.N. (eds.) (1992) *Comparative Judicial Review and Public Policy*. Westport, CT: Greenwood Press.

Jackson, K. D. (1989) 'The Philippines: The search for a suitable democratic solution, 1946–1986' in Diamond, Linz and Lipset, Vol.3, *Democracy in Developing Countries*, pp. 231–66.

Jacobs, L.A. (1993) *Rights and Deprivation*. Oxford: Clarendon Press.

Jasay, A. de (1985) *The State*. Oxford: Basil Blackwell.

Jellinek, G. (1966) *Allgemeine Staatslehre*. Bad Homburg: Verlag Max Gehlen.

Jennings, I. (1967) *The Law and the Constitution*. London: University of London Press.

Jillson, C.C. (1988) *Constitution Making: Conflict and Consensus in the Federal Convention of 1787*. New York: Agathon Press, Inc.

John of Salisbury, (1995) *Policraticus*. Cambridge: Cambridge University Press.

Jouvenel, B. de (1957) *Sovereignty*. Chicago: Chicago University Press.

Jowell, J. (1994) 'The rule of law today' in Jowell and Oliver, *The Changing Constitution*, 57–78.

Jowell, J. and Oliver, D. (eds.) (1994) *The Changing Constitution*. Oxford: Clarendon Press.

Kant, I. (1965) *The Metaphysics of Morals*. Indianapolis: Bobbs-Merrill.

Kant, I. (1974) *The Philosphy of Law*. Clifton: Augustus M. Kelley.

Kantorowicz, E.H. (1981) *The King's Two Bodies. A Study in Medieval Political Theology*. Princeton, NJ: Princeton University Press.

Kelley, D. R. (1991) 'Law' in Burns and Goldie, *The Cambridge History of Political Thought*, pp. 66–94.

Kelly, J.M. (1992) *A Short History of Western Legal Theory*. Oxford: Oxford University Press.

Kelly, J.S. (1986) *Social Choice Theory*. Berlin: Springer–Verlag.

Kelsen, H. (1925) *Allgemeine Staatslehre*. Berlin: Springer.

Kelsen, H. (1928) 'La Garantie juridictionelle de la Constitution (la justice constitutionelle)', *Revue du droit public et de la science politique en France et à l'étranger*, pp. 197–257.

Kelsen, H. (1961) *General Theory of Law and State*. New York: Russell & Russell.

Kelsen, H. (1967) *Pure Theory of Law*. Berkeley: University of California Press.

Kelsen, H. (1991) *General Theory of Norms*. Oxford: Clarendon Press.

Keohane, N.O. (1980) *Philosophy and the State in France: The Renaissance to the Enlightenment*. Princeton: Princeton University Press.

Kern, F. (1939) *Kingship and Law in the Middle Ages*. Oxford: Oxford University Press.

Kern, F. (1953) *Recht und Verfassung im Mittelalter*. Tübingen: Wissenschaftliche Buchgemeinschaft.

Kerner, G.C. (1966) *The Revolution in Ethical Theory*. Oxford: Clarendon Press.

Ketcham, R. (ed.) (1986) *The Anti–Federalist Papers and the Constitutional Convention Debates*. New York: Mentor.

King, P. (1982) *Federalism and Federation*. London: Croom Helm.

King, P. D. (1991) 'The Barbarian Kingdoms' in Burns, *The Cambridge History of Medieval Political Thought*, pp.123–56.

Kingdon, R. M. (1991) 'Calvinism and resistance theory, 1550–1580' in Burns and Goldie, *The Cambridge History of Political Thought*, pp. 193–218.

Korpi, W. (1989) 'Power, politics and State autonomy in the development of social citizenship: social rights during sickness in 18 OECD countries since 1930', *American Sociological Review*, Vol. 54: 308–28.

Kunkel, W. (1990) *Römische Rechts Geschichte*. Köln: Böhlau Verlag.

Kymlicka, W. (1990) *Contemporary Political Philosophy: An Introduction*. Oxford: Clarendon Press.

Kymlicka, W. (1991) *Liberalism, Community and Culture*. Oxford: Clarendon Press.

Kymlicka, W. (1995a) *Multicultural Citizenship*. Oxford: Oxford University Press.

Kymlicka, W. (1995b) (ed.) *The Rights of Minority Cultures*. Oxford: Oxford University Press.

Lagerroth, F. (1947) *Den svenska landslagens författning i historisk och komparativ belysning*. Lund: Fahlbeckska stiftelsen.

Lamounier, B. (1989) 'Brazil: Inequality against democracy' in Diamond, Linz and Lipset, Vol.4, *Democracy in Developing Countries*, pp. 111–58.

Laski, H. (1967) *A Grammar of Politics*. London: Allen and Unwin.

Laver, M. and Schoefield, N. (1990) *Multiparty Government: The Politics of Coalition in Europe*. New York: Oxford University Press.

Leibniz, G.W. (1992) *Political Writings*. Cambridge: Cambridge University Press.

Levine, D.H. (1989) 'Venezuela: The nature, sources, and future prospects of democracy' in Diamond, Linz and Lipset, Vol.4, *Democracy in Developing Countries*, pp. 247–90.

Levy, D. C. (1989) 'Mexico: Sustained civilian rule without democracy' in Diamond, Linz and Lipset, Vol.4, *Democracy in Developing Countries*, pp. 459–97.

Lijphart, A. (1977) *Democracy in Plural Societies: a comparative exploration*. New Haven: Yale University Press.

Lijphart, A. (1984) *Democracies*. New Haven: Yale University Press.

Lijphart, A. (ed.) (1992) *Parliamentary versus Presidential Government*. New York: Oxford University Press.

Lijphart, A. (1994a) *Electoral Systems and Party Systems: a study of 27 democracies 1945–1990*. Oxford: Oxford University Press.

Lijphart, A. (1994b) 'Democracies: forms, performance and constitutional engineering, *European Journal of Political Research*, 25: 1–17.

Linz, J.J. (1992) 'The virtues of parliamentarianism', in Lijphart, A. (1992), pp. 212–16.

Linz, J.J. and Valenzuela, A. (eds) (1994) *The Failure of Presidential Democracy*, Vol 1. Baltimore: John Hopkins University Press.

Lipset, S.M. (1959) *Political Man*. New York: Doubleday–Anchor.

Lipset, S.M. (1994) 'The social requisites of democracy revisited', *American Sociological Review*, Vol. 59: 1–22.

Lively, J. (1985) *Democracy*. Oxford: Blackwell.

Lloyd, D. (1991) *The Idea of Law*. London: Penguin Books.

Lloyd, H.A. (1991) 'Constitutionalism' in Burns and Goldie, *The Cambridge History of Political Thought*, pp. 254–97.

Locke, J. (1962) *Two Treatises of Civil Government*. London: Everyman's Library.

Loughlin, M. (1992) *Public Law and Political Theory*. New York: Oxford University Press.

Luce, R.D. and Raiffa, H. (1957) *Games and Decisions*. New York: Wiley.

Lucy, R. (1993) *The Australian Form of Government. Models in Dispute.* South Melbourne: Macmillan Education.

Luscombe, D.E. (1991) 'Introduction: the formation of political thought in the west' in Burns, *The Cambridge History of Medieval Political Thought*, pp.157–73.

Luscombe, D.E. and G.R. Evans (1991) 'The twelfth–century renaissance' in Burns, *The Cambridge History of Medieval Political Thought*, pp. 306–40.

Lyons, D. (1965) *The Forms and Limits of Utilitarianism*. Oxford: Oxford University Press.

MacCormick, N. (1994) *Legal Reasoning and Legal Theory*. Oxford: Clarendon Press.

Machiavelli, N. (1940) *The Prince and the Discourses*. New York: The Modern Library.

MacIver, R.M. (1927) *The Modern State*. Oxford: Oxford University Press.

MacIntyre, A. (1981) *After Virtue: a study of moral theory*. London: Duckworth.

Madgwick, P. and Woodhouse, D. (1995) *The Law and Politics of the Constitution of the United Kingdom*. London: Harvester Wheatsheaf.

Mainwaring, S. (1993) 'Presidentialism, multipartism and democracy: the difficult combination', *Comparative Political Studies*, Vol. 26: 198–228.

Malcolm, N. (1991) 'Hobbes and Spinoza' in Burns and Goldie, *The Cambridge History of Political Thought*, pp. 530–60.

March, J. and Olsen, J.P. (1984) 'The new institutionalism: Organizational factors in political life', *American Political Science Review*, Vol. 78: 734–49.

March, J.G. and Olsen, J.P. (1989) *Rediscovering Institutions. The Organi-*

zational Basis of Politics. New York: The Free Press.

March, J.G. and Olsen, J.P. (1995) *Democratic Governance*. New York: The Free Press.

Marmor, A. (1995) *Interpretation and Legal Theory*. Oxford: Clarendon Press.

Marshall, G. (1971) *Constitutional Theory*. Oxford: Clarendon Press.

Marsiglio of Padua (1991) *Defensor Minor and De Translatione Imperii*. Cambridge: Cambridge University Press.

May, K.O. (1952) 'A set of independent, necessary and sufficient conditions for simple majority decisions', *Econometrica* Vol. 20: 680–84.

Mayo, B. (1986) *The Philosophy of Right and Wrong*. London: Routledge & Kegan Paul.

McClintock, C. (1989) 'Peru: Precarious regimes, authoritarian and democratic' in Diamond, Linz and Lipset, Vol.4, *Democracy in Developing Countries*, pp. 335–86.

McIlwain, C.H. (1958) *Constitutionalism, Ancient and Modern*. Ithaca, NY: Cornell University Press.

McKelvey, R.D. (1976) 'Intransitivities in multidimensional voting models and some implications for agenda control', *Journal of Economic Theory*, Vol. 12: 472–82.

McKelvey, R.D. (1979) 'General conditions for global intransitivities on formal models', *Econometrica*, Vol. 47: 1085–112.

McKelvey, R.D. (1986) 'Covering, dominance, and institution–free properties of social choice', *American Journal of Political Science*, Vol. 30: 283–314.

Meinecke, F. (1984) *Machiavellism: the doctrine of raison d'état and its place in modern history*. Boulder, CO: Westview.

Milgrom, P. and Roberts, J. (1992) *Economics, Organizations and Management*. Englewood Cliffs, NY: Prentice–Hall.

Mill, J.S. and Bentham, J. (1987) *Utilitarianism and Other Essays*. Harmondsworth: Penguin.

Miller, D. (1976) *Social Justice*. Oxford: Clarendon Press.

Miller, D. and Walzer, M. (1995) *Pluralism, Justice and Equality*. Oxford: Oxford University Press.

Miller, N.R., Grofman, B. and Scott, L.F. (1989) 'The geometry of majority rule', *Journal of Theoretical Politics*, Vol. 1: 379–406.

Miller, W. L. (1992) *The Business of May Next: James Madison and the Founding*. Charlottesville: University of Virginia Press.

Mitteis, H. (1975) *The State in the Middle Ages. A comparative constitutional history of feudal Europe*. Amsterdam: North–Holland.

Montesquieu C. de S. (1989) *The Spirit of the Laws*. New York: Cambridge University Press.

Moulin, H. (1983) *The Strategy of Social Choice*. Amsterdam: Elsevier.

Mueller, D.C. (1989) *Public Choice II*. New York: Cambridge University Press.

Mulhall, S. and Swift, A. (1993) *Liberals and Communitarians*. Oxford: Basil Blackwell.

Munro, W.B. (1926) *The Governments of Europe*. New York: Macmillan.

Murakami, Y. (1968) *Logic and Social Choice*. London: Routledge & Kegan Paul Ltd.

Myrdal, G. (1968) *Asian Drama*. New York: Pantheon.

Nagel, T. (1991) *Equality and Partiality*. Oxford: Oxford University Press.

Nedelski, J. (1988) 'American constitutionalism and the paradox of private property', in Elster and Slagstad (eds.), *Constitutionalism and Democracy*, pp. 241–73.

Nelson, J. (1991) 'Kingship and Empire' in Burns, *The Cambridge History of Medieval Political Thought*, pp. 211–51.

Nelson, W. N. (1980) *On Justifying Democracy*. London: Routledge & Kegan Paul.

Neumann, F.L. (1986) *The Rule of Law: political theory and the legal system in modern society*. Leamington Spa: Berg.

Nicholas, B. (1975) *An Introduction to Roman Law*. Oxford: Clarendon Press.

North, D.C. (1990) *Institutions, Institutional Change and Economic Performance*. Cambridge: Cambridge University Press.

Nozick, R. (1974) *Anarchy, State and Utopia*. Oxford: Basil Blackwell.

Nurmi, H. (1987) *Comparing Voting Systems*. Dordrecht, Holland: D. Reidel Publishing Company.

Oakeshott, M. (1975) *On Human Conduct*. Oxford: Clarendon.

Oakly, F. (1991) 'Christian obedience and authority, 1520–1550' in Burns and Goldie, *The Cambridge History of Political Thought*, pp. 159–92.

Ockham, W. of (1992) *A Short Discourse on Tyrannical Government*. Cambridge: Cambridge University Press.

Ockham, W. of (1995) *A Letter to the Friars Minor and Other Writings*. Cambridge: Cambridge University Press.

OECD (1994) *OECD Economic Outlook, 1994*. Paris: OECD.

OECD (1992) *National Accounts*, Vol. 2. Paris: OECD.

OECD (1993) *OECD Employment Outlook*. Paris: OECD.

Okun, A.M. (1975) *Equality and Efficiency. The Big Tradeoff*. Washington DC: The Brookings Institution.

Olivercrona, K. (1971) *Law as Fact*. London: Stevens and Sons.

Olson, M. (1975) *The Logic of Collective Action. Public Goods and the Theory of Groups*. Cambridge: Harvard University Press.

Olson, M. (1982) *The Rise and Decline of Nations*. New Haven: Yale University Press.

Ordeshook, P. C. (1992) *A Political Theory Primer*. New York: Routledge.

Ostrom, E. (1990) *Governing the Commons*. Cambridge: Cambridge University Press.

Ostrom, V. (1987) *The Political Theory of a Compound Republic*. Lincoln: University of Nebraska Press.

Ostrom, V. (1991) *The Meaning of American Federalism: constituting a self–governing society*. San Francisco: ICS Press.

Owen, R. (1992) *State, Power and Politics in the Making of The Modern Middle East*. London: Routledge.

Özbudun, E. (1989) 'Turkey: Crisis, interruptions, and reequilibrations' in Diamond, Linz and Lipset, Vol.3, *Democracy in Developing Countries*, pp. 187–230.

Paine, T. (1966) *The Rights of Man*. London: Everyman's Library.

Parfit, D. (1987) *Reasons and Persons*. Oxford: Oxford University Press.

Pennington, K. (1991) 'Law, legislative authority and theories of government, 1150–1300' in Burns, *The Cambridge History of Medieval Political Thought*, pp. 424–53.

Pennock, J. R. and Chapman, J.W. (eds.) (1979) *Constitutionalism*. New York: New York University Press.

Pettit, P. (1980) *Judging Justice. An Introduction to Contemporary Political Philosophy*. London: Routledge & Kegan Paul.

Phadnis, U. (1989) 'Sri Lanka: Crisis of legitimacy and integration' in Diamond, Linz and Lipset, Vol.3, *Democracy in Developing Countries*, pp. 143–86.

Plamenatz, J. (1967) *Man and Society. Vol 1*. London: Longmans, Green and Co. Ltd..

Plamenatz, J. (1968) *Man and Society. Vol. 2*. London: Longmans, Green and Co. Ltd..

Plant, R. (1991) *Modern Political Thought*. Oxford: Basil Blackwell.

Plott, C.R. (1967) 'A notion of equilibrium and its possibility under majority rule', *American Economic Review*, Vol. 57: 458–73.

Plott, C. (1973) 'Path, independence, rationality, and social choice' *Econometrica* Vol. 41: 1075–91.

Pocock, J.G.A. (1975) *The Machiavellian Moment. Florentine Political Thought and the Atlantic Republican Tradition*. Princeton, NJ: Princeton University Press.

Pocock, J.G.A. (1987) *The Ancient Constitution and the Feudal Law. A Study of English Historical Thought in the Seventeenth Century*. New York: Cambridge University Press.

Posner, R. (1992) *The Economic Analysis of Law*. Boston: Little, Brown and Co.

Pourgerami, A. (1988) 'The political economy of development: a cross–national causality test of the development–democracy–growth hypothesis', *Public Choice*, Vol. 45: 123–41.

Powell, W.W. and DiMaggio, P.J. (1991) *The New Institutionalism in Orga-*

nizational Analysis. Chicago: University of Chicago Press.

Pufendorf, S. (1991) *On the Duty of Man and Citizen according to Natural Law*. Cambridge: Cambridge University Press.

Qadir, S., Clapham, C. and Gills, B. (1993) 'Democratisation in the Third World: an introduction' *Third World Quarterly*, Vol.14, No.3.

Rapoport, A. (1966) *Two–Person Game Theory*. Ann Arbor: University of Michigan Press.

Rapoport, A. (1970) *N–Person Game Theory*. Ann Arbor: University of Michigan Press.

Rapoport, A. and Chammah, A.M. (1970) *Prisoner's Dilemma*. Ann Arbor: University of Michigan Press.

Rasmusen, E. (1994) *Games and Information. An introduction to game theory*. Oxford: Basil Blackwell.

Rawls, J. (1958) 'Justice as fairness', *The Philosophical Review*, Vol. 68: 164–94.

Rawls, J. (1971) *A Theory of Justice*. Cambridge, MA: The Belknap Press of Harvard University Press.

Raz, J. (1980) *The Concept of a Legal System*. Oxford: Clarendon Press.

Raz, J. (1988) *The Morality of Freedom*. Oxford: Clarendon Press.

Rees, J. (1972) *Equality*. London and Basingstoke: Macmillan.

Regan, D. H. (1980) *Utilitarianism and Co–operation*. Oxford: Clarendon Press.

Reiman. J. (1990) *Justice and Modern Moral Philosophy*. New Haven: Yale University Press.

Reiss, H. (ed.) (1970) *Kant's Political Writings*. Cambridge: Cambridge University Press.

Rijnierse, E. (1993) 'Democratisation in sub–Saharan Africa? Literature overview' *Third World Quarterly*, Vol. 14, No.3.

Riker, W.H. (1964) *Federalism: origin, operation, significance*. Boston: Little, Brown and Co.

Riker, W.H. (1982) *Liberalism against Populism*. San Francisco: W. H. Freeman and Company.

Riker, W.H. and Ordeshook, P.C. (1973) *An Introduction to Positive Political Theory*. Princeton, NJ: Prentice–Hall Inc.

Riley, P. (1983) *Kant's Political Philosophy*. Rowman & Allanheld Publishers.

Robinson, I. S. (1991) 'Church and papacy' in Burns, *The Cambridge History of Medieval Political Thought*, pp. 252–305.

Rohr, J.A. (1986) *To Run a Constitution. The Legitimacy of the Administrative State*. Lawrence, Kansas: University Press of Kansas

Rose, L. E. (1989) 'Pakistan: Experiments with democracy' in Diamond, Linz and Lipset, Vol.3, *Democracy in Developing Countries*, pp. 105–42.

Rose, R. (1984) *Understanding Big Government*. London: Sage.

Ross, A. (1974) *On Law and Justice*. Berkeley: University of California Press.

Ross, D. (1965) *Kant's Ethical Theory. A Commentary on the Grundlegung zur Metaphysik der Sitten.* Oxford: Clarendon Press.

Ross, D. (1966) *The Nichomacean Ethics of Aristotle.* London: Oxford University Press.

Rousseau, J.J. (1993) *The Social Contract and Discourses.* London: Everyman.

Rubenstein, A. (1982) 'Perfect Equilibrium in a Bargaining Model', *Econometrica*, Vol. 50: 97–109.

Rubinstein, N. (1991) 'Italian political thought, 1450–1530' in Burns and Goldie, *The Cambridge History of Political Thought*, pp. 30–65.

Ryan, A. (1995) (ed.) *Justice.* Oxford: Oxford University Press.

Sabine, G.H. and Thorsen, T.L. (1973) *A History of Polical Thought.* Hinsdale, IL: Dryden Press.

Salmon, J.H.M. (1991) 'Catholic resistance theory, Ultramontanism, and the royalist response, 1580–1620' in Burns and Goldie, *The Cambridge History of Political Thought*, pp. 219–53.

Samudavanija, C. (1989) 'Thailand: a stable semi–democracy' in Diamond, Linz and Lipset, Vol.3, *Democracy in Developing Countries*, pp. 305–46.

Sandel, M. (1982) *Liberalism and the Limits of Justice.* Cambridge: Cambridge University Press.

Sartori, G. (1987) *The Theory of Democracy Revisited. Part One: The Contemporary Debate.* Chatham, New Jersey: Chatham House Publishers, Inc.

Sartori, G. (1987) *The Theory of Democracy Revisited. Part Two: The Classical Issues.* Chatham, New Jersey: Chatham House Publishers, Inc.

Sartori, G. (1994) *Comparative Constitutional Engineering. An Inquiry into Structures, Incentives and Outcomes.* London: Macmillan.

Scanlon, T.M. (1982) 'Contractualism and Utilitarianism' in Sen and Williams, 1982. pp. 103–28.

Scheffler. S. (1987) *The Rejection of Consequentialism. A Philosophical Investigation of the Considerations Underlying Rival Moral Conceptions.* New York: Oxford University Press.

Schmidhauser, J.R. (ed.) (1987) *Comparative Judicial Systems.* London: Butterworth.

Schulze, H.K. (1990) *Grundstrukturen der Verfassung im Mittelalter. Band I.* Stuttgart: Verlag W. Kohlhammer.

Schulze, H.K. (1992) *Grundstrukturen der Verfassung im Mittelalter. Band II.* Stuttgart: Verlag W. Kohlhammer.

Sen, A. (1970) *Collective Choice and Social Welfare.* San Francisco: Holden–Day, Inc.

Sen, A. (1992) *Inequality Reexamined.* Oxford: Clarendon Press.

Sen, A. and Williams, B. (eds.) (1982) *Utilitarianism and Beyond.* New York: Cambridge University Press.

Seneca (1969) *Letters from a Stoic*. Harmondsworth: Penguin.

Shepsle, K.A. (1979) 'Institutional arrangements and equilibrium in multidimensional voting models', *American Journal of Political Science*, Vol. 23: 27–59.

Shepsle, K.A. (1986) 'Institutional equilibrium and equilibrium institutions' in H.F. Weisberg (ed.) *Political Science: The Science of Politics*. New York: Agathon Press.

Shepsle, K.A. (1989) 'Studying Institutions: some lessons from the rational choice approach', *Journal of Theoretical Politics*, Vil. 1: 131–47.

Shubik, M. (1987) *Game Theory in the Social Sciences*. Cambridge, MA: The MIT Press.

Shugart, M.S. and Carey, J. M. (1992) *Presidents and Assemblies*. New York: Cambridge University Press.

Simmonds, N.E. (1986) *Central Issues in Jurisprudence: justice, law and rights*. London: Sweet and Maxwell.

Skinner, Q. (1993) *The Foundations of Modern Political Thought. Vol. 2: The Age of Reformation*. New York: Cambridge University Press.

Skinner, Q. (1994) *The Foundations of Modern Political Thought. Vol. 1: The Renaissance*. New York: Cambridge University Press.

Smart, J.J.C. and Williams, B. (1973) *Utilitarianism. For and Against*. New York: Cambridge University Press.

Smith, S. de and Brazier, R. (1990) *Constitutional and Administrative Law*. London: Penguin Books.

Sommerville, J. P. (1991) 'Absolutism and royalism' in Burns and Goldie, *The Cambridge History of Political Thought*, pp. 347–73.

Stankiewicz, W.J. (1980) *Approaches to Democracy*. London: Edward Arnold.

Stein, P. G. (1991) 'Roman law' in Burns, *The Cambridge History of Medieval Political Thought*, pp. 37–50.

Stephan, A. and Skach, C. (1993) 'Constitutional frameworks and democratic consolidation: parliamentarianism versus presidentialism', *World Politics*, Vol. 46: 1–21.

Steunenberg, B. (1994) 'Regulatory policymaking in a parliamentary setting', *Jahrbuch für Neue Politische Ökonomie*, Vol. 13, 36–57.

Stevens, Anne (1992) *The Government and Politics of France*. London: Macmillan.

Stoner, J. R. jr. (1992) *Commom Law and Liberal Theory. Coke, Hobbes and the Origins of American Constitutionalism*. Kansas: University Press of Kansas.

Streek, W. (1992) *Social Institutions and Economic Performance*. London: Sage.

Sundhaussen, U. (1989) 'Indonesia: past and present encounters with democracy' in Diamond, Linz and Lipset, Vol. 3, *Democracy in Developing*

Countries, pp. 423–74.

Tacitus (1989) *The Annals of Imperial Rome*. Harmondsworth: Penguin.

Tate, C.N. and Vallinder, T. (1995) *The Global Expansion of Judicial Power*. New York: New York University Press.

Tawney, R.H. (1964) *Equality*. London: Unwin Books.

Taylor, C. (1990) *Sources of the Self*. Cambridge: Cambridge University Press.

Taylor, M. (1987) *The Possibility of Cooperation*. New York: Cambridge University Press.

Thompson, M.R. (1993) 'The limits of democratisation in ASEAN', *Third World Quarterly*, Vol.14, No.3.

Tierney, B. (1979) *Church Law and Constitutional Thought in the Middle Ages*. London: Variorum Reprints.

Tierney, B. (1982) *Religion, Law, and the Growth of Constitutional Thought 1150–1650*. Cambridge: Cambridge University Press.

Tocqueville, A. de (1951) *Oevres complètes. Tome I: De la Dèmocratie en Amèrique*. Paris.

Todd, E. (1983) *La Troisième Planète: structures familiales et systèmes idéologiques*. Paris: Seuil.

Törnquist, O. (1993) 'Democratic "empowerment" and democratisation of politics: radical popular movements and the May 1992 Philippine elections', *Third World Quarterly*, Vol.14, No.3.

Tsebelis, G. (1990) *Nested Games*. Berkeley: University of California Press.

Tsebelis, G. (1995) 'Decision–making in political systems: Veto players in presidentialism, parliamentarianism, multicameralism, and multipartyism', *British Journal of Political Science* Vol. 25, pp. 289–325.

Tuck, R. (1993a) *Natural Rights Theories. Their Origin and Development*. New York: Cambridge University Press.

Tuck, R. (1993b) *Philosophy and Government 1572–1651*. New York: Cambridge University Press.

Tully, J. (1991) 'Locke' in Burns and Goldie, *The Cambridge History of Political Thought*, pp. 616–52.

Uhlin, A. (1993) 'Transnational democratic diffusion and Indonesian democracy discourses', *Third World Quarterly*, Vol.14, No.3.

Ullmann, W. (1966) *Principles of Government and Politics in the Middle Ages*. London:Methuen.

Ullmann, W. (1975) *Law and Politics in the Middle Ages: an introduction to the sources of medieval political ideas*. London: Sources of History Ltd.

Ullmann, W. (1980) *Jurisprudence in the Middle Ages*. London: Variorum Reprints.

Ullmann, W. (1988) *Law and Jurisdiction in the Middle Ages*. London: Variorum Reprints.

UNDP: *Human Development Report 1993, 1994*. New York: United Nations

Development Programme.

Urmson, J. O. (1968) *The Emotive Theory of Ethics*. London: Hutchinson and Co.

Valenzuela, A. (1989) 'Chile: Origins, consolidation, and breakdown of a democratic regime' in Diamond, Linz and Lipset, Vol.4, *Democracy in Developing Countries*, pp. 159–206.

Vallinder, T. (ed.) (1994) 'The judicialization of politics', *International Political Science Review*, Vol. 15 (special issue).

Vile, M.J.C. (1967) *Constitutionalism and the Separation of Powers*. Oxford: Oxford University Press.

Villiers, de B. (ed.) (1994) *Evaluating Federal Systems*. Dordrecht: Martinus Niehoff.

Vincent, A. (1987) *Theories of the State*. Oxford: Basil Blackwell.

Viroli, M. (1991) *From Politics to Reason of State. The acquisition and transformation of the language of politics 1250–1600*. Cambridge: Cambridge University Press.

Vlastos, G. (1985) 'Justice and Equality', in *Waldron* (1985) (ed.), pp. 41–76.

Volcansek, M.L. (ed.) (1992) 'Judicial politics and policy-making in Western Europe', *West European Politics*, Vol. 15 (special issue)

Waisman, C. H. (1989) 'Argentina: Autarkic industrialization and illegitimacy' in Diamond, Linz and Lipset, Vol.4, *Democracy in Developing Countries*, pp. 59–110.

Waldron, J. (1985) *Theories of Rights*. New York: Oxford University Press.

Waluchow, W.J. (1994) *Inclusive Legal Positivism*. Oxford: Clarendon Press.

Walzer, M. (1983) *Spheres of Justice*. New York: Basic Books.

Watt, J. A. (1991) 'Spiritual and temporal powers' in Burns, *The Cambridge History of Medieval Political Thought*, pp. 367–423.

Weaver, R.K. and Rockman, B.A. (eds.) (1993) *Do Institutions Matter? Government capabilities in the United States and abroad*. Washington, DC: Brookings Institution.

Weston, C. C. (1991) 'England: ancient constitution and common law' in Burns and Goldie, *The Cambridge History of Political Thought*, pp. 374–411.

Wheare, K. (1966) *Modern Constitutions*. New York: Oxford University Press.

Wheeler, H. (1975) 'Constitutionalism' in Greenstein, F.I. and Polsby, N.W. (eds.) *Handbook of Political Science*, Vol. 5: *Governmental Institutions and Processes*. Reading, MA: Addison-Wesley, 1–90.

Wicksell, K. (1967) 'A new principle of just taxation', in Musgrave, R.A. and Peacock, A.T. (eds.) *Classics in the Theory of Public Finance*. New York: St Martin's Press.

Williams, B. (1962) 'The Idea of Equality', in Laslett, P. and Runciman, W.G. (eds.) *Philosophy, Politics and Society*. Oxford: Basil Blackwell.

Williams, H. (1983) *Kant's Political Philosophy*. Oxford: Basil Blackwell.

Williamson, O.E. (1985) *The Economic Institutions of Capitalism*. New York: Free Press.

Williamson, O.E. (1986) *Economic Organization. Firms, Markets and Policy Control*. New York: Harvester Wheatsheaf.

Williamson, O.E. (ed.) (1990) *Organization Theory. From Chester Barnard to the Present and Beyond*. New York: Oxford University Press.

Wiseman, J.A. (1993) 'Democracy and the new political pluralism in Africa: causes, consequences and significance', *Third World Quarterly*, Vol.14, No.3.

Wittfogel, K. (1957) *Oriental Despotism*. New Haven: Yale University Press.

Wolin, S.S. (1960) *Politics and Vision*. Boston: Little Brown.

Wolin, S.S. (1990) *The Presence of the Past. Essays on the State and the Constitution*. Baltimore: Johns Hopkins University Press.

Wootton, D. (ed.) (1986) *Divine Right and Democracy. An Anthology of Political Writing in Stuart England*. London: Penguin Books.

Wootton, D. (1991) 'Leveller democracy and the Puritan revolution' in Burns and Goldie, *The Cambridge History of Political Thought*, pp. 412–42.

World Bank: *World Development Report, 1994*. New York: Oxford University Press.

Worden, B. (1985) 'The Commonwealth Kidney of Algernon Sidney', *Journal of British Studies*, Vol. 24: 1–40.

Worden, B. (1991) 'English republicanism' in Burns and Goldie, *The Cambridge History of Political Thought*, pp. 443–78.

Wormuth, F.D. (1949) *The Origins of Modern Constitutionalism*. New York: Harper.

Wright, L.M. (1982) 'A comparative survey of economic freedoms', in Gastil, R.D. (ed.) *Freedom in the World: political rights and civil liberties*. Westport: Greenwood Press, pp. 51–90.

Yardley, D.C.M. (1986) *Principles of Administrative Law*. London: Butterworth.

Zimmermann, J. F. (1992) *Contemporary American Federalism. The Growth of National Power*. Leicester and London: Leicester University Press.

Zurcher, A.J. (ed.) (1951) *Constitutions and Constitutional Trends since World War II*. New York: New York University Press.

Index